QUALITATIVE RESEARCH:
Applications in Organizational Communication

SCA Applied Communication Publication Program

Gary L. Kreps, Editor
Northern Illinois University

The SCA Program in Applied Communication supports the Speech Communication Association mission of promoting the study, criticism, research, teaching, and application of artistic, humanistic, and scientific principles of communication. Specifically, the goal of this publication program is to develop an innovative, theoretically informed, and socially relevant body of scholarly works that examine a wide range of applied communication topics. Each publication clearly demonstrates the value of human communication in addressing serious social issues and challenges.

QUALITATIVE RESEARCH:
Applications in Organizational Communication

Editors:

Sandra L. Herndon
Ithaca College

Gary L. Kreps
Northern Illinois University

HD
30.3
. Q35
1993
West

Hampton Press, Inc.
Cresskill, New Jersey

Speech Communication Association
Annandale, Virginia

Printed in the United States of America

Library of Congress Cataloging-in-Publication Data

Qualitative research: applications in organizational communication/
    edited by Sandra L. Herndon and Gary L. Kreps
        p. cm. — (SCA applied communication publication program)
    Includes bibliographic references and indexes.
    ISBN 1-881303-38-1 (cloth). — ISBN 1-881303-39-X (paper)
    1. Herndon, Sandra L.   II. Kreps, Gary L.   III. Series: Speech
    Communication Association/Hampton Press applied communication
    program
    HD30.3.Q35   1993   92-38373
    302.3'5—dc20   CIP

Hampton Press, Inc.
23 Broadway
Cresskill, NJ 07626

Contents

About the Authors

PAT ARNESON (Ph.D., Ohio University) is Assistant Professor of Speech Communication at the University of Northern Colorado. Her main areas of interest are philosophy of communication, qualitative research methods, communication theory, interpersonal communication, and communication ethics. She has presented her ideas in numerous conference papers, journal articles, and book chapters.

CHARLES R. BANTZ (Ph.D., Ohio State University) is Professor and Chair of the Communication Department at Arizona State University. His research centers on communication processes in organizations, television news, television news organizations, and research methods. He recently completed *Understanding Organizations: Interpreting Organizational Communication Cultures.* Co-author of *Social Conflict and Television News* and co-editor of *Foundations of Organizational Communication: A Reader,* he has published articles in *American Behavioral Scientist, Communication Monographs, Journalism Quarterly, Journal of Broadcasting and Electronic Media, Quarterly Journal of Speech, Western Journal of Speech Communication,* and *Communication.* He is editor of *Communication Monographs.*

MARY HELEN BROWN (Ph.D., University of Texas at Austin) is Associate Professor and Graduate Program Officer in the Department of Communication at Auburn University. Author of numerous journal articles and convention papers, she is currently interested in examining narratives in a variety of settings, especially in psychological rehabilitation and tabloid journalism.

JENNIFER DREYER (B.A., San Diego State University) is a graduate student in the Speech Communication Department at San Diego State University. Her research interests include organizational structure and ideology and communication in health care delivery. She has presented her work at ICA and SCA and has published an article in a special issue of the *Western Journal of Communication* (1993).

LYNETTE SECCOMBE EASTLAND (Ph.D. University of Utah) is Assistant Professor in the Communication Department at Lewis and Clark College. Her ethnographic research interests include the organization of human experience, organizational contradictions and dilemmas, and interaction strategies. Her work includes a chapter on contradiction and change in *Women Communicating*.

PATRICIA GEIST (Ph.D., Purdue University) is an Assistant Professor in the Speech Communication Department at San Diego State University. Her research interests include organizational change, ideology, decision making, and control. Her work is published in *Communication Monographs, Southern Communication Journal, Health Communication, Advances in Medical Sociology, Studies in Symbolic Interaction, Management Communication Quarterly,* and *Case Studies in Health Communication.* Her book *Negotiating the Crisis: DRGs and the Transformations of Hospitals* is the culmination of a longitudinal study of negotiating policy changes in the hospital organization.

SANDRA L. (FISH) HERNDON (Ph.D., Southern Illinois University) is Associate Professor and former Chair of the Department of Corporate Communication, Ithaca College. Past President of the Eastern Communication Association, she is co-editor and author of a chapter in *Talking to Strangers: Mediated Therapeutic Communication.* She is also author of a chapter on gender and communication in the forthcoming anthology *Bridging Both Worlds: The Communication Consultant in Corporate America,* edited by Rebecca Ray, as well as an essay on listening in *The Bureaucratic Experience,* 2nd ed. by R. P. Hummel. Her work is published in *Journal of Applied Communication Research, The Howard Journal of Communications,* and *Public Administration Quarterly.* Her research interests include gender and communication, workplace diversity, the impact of communication technology on organizations, therapeutic communication, and qualitative methods. She is currently on the editorial board of *World Communication* and *Communication Quarterly.*

MARK HICKSON III (Ph.D., Southern Illinois University) is Professor and Chair of the Department of Communication Studies at the University of Alabama at Birmingham and Vice President of Communication Management Resources. Founding editor and publisher of the *Journal of Applied Communication Research,* he has published a number of books and articles on such subjects as nonverbal communication, communication theory, administrative communication, social types, and qualitative research methods. Currently, he is editor of *World Communication.*

RUSSELL JENNINGS (Ph.D., Southern Illinois University) is a founding Principal, Communication Management Resources, Phoenix, AZ, a consortium of professionals in business, industry, government, and institutions. Formerly on the faculty of Southern Illinois University and currently adjunct faculty at Scottsdale Community College, he is the author of a number of publications on communication, employee selection, urban conflict, and gerontology. Prior to establishing his counseling and consulting practice, he was a human resources executive in the nuclear industry, a conference management consultant, and a marketing manager in the property management industry.

GARY L. KREPS (Ph.D., University of Southern California) is Professor of Communication Studies and a member of the Gerontology Faculty (Social Science Research Institute) at Northern Illinois University. He has published fifteen books and more than 100 articles and chapters examining the role of communication in organizational life, health promotion, and education.

SUSAN A. MASON (M.A., SUNY-Albany; M.S., Ithaca College) is Principal, Vital Visions, in Eaton, NY, a consulting group addressing personal, public, and organizational communication. On the faculty of Hamilton College, she has presented a number of conference papers and is a member of the Eastern Communication Association, New York State Speech Communication Association, and the American Society for Training and Development.

PAULA MICHAL-JOHNSON (Ph.D., University of Denver) is Assistant Professor at Villanova University. Her health communication research with Sheryl Perlmutter Bowen has been supported by grants from the American Foundation for AIDS Research. Author of a critical incident study of managerial termination, she has published in a number of communication and health-related journals. She serves as chair of the Commission on Health Communication for the Speech Communication Association and also of the Institutional Review Board for Human Subjects at Villanova University.

JAN MUTO (Ph.D., University of Utah) is Assistant Professor of Corporate Communication at Ithaca College. The author of several journal articles and convention papers, she pursues research in such areas as differences between blue- and white-collar worklives, the relationship between work and home life roles, the interplay of interpersonal and organizational roles, prescribed and emergent roles in the workplace, organizational culture, and feminist issues. She is a member of the Human Subjects Review Committee at Ithaca College.

JIM L. QUERY, JR. (Ph.D., Ohio University) is Assistant Professor of
Communication at the University of Tulsa and President of the
Alzheimer's Association of Tulsa. His research focuses on the communication of social support across life crises and transitions, communica-
tion in health care, and organizational communication. He received a
teaching award and two outstanding graduate student awards from the
School of Interpersonal Communication, Ohio University. In addition
to receiving a Student Research Fellowship with the National Cancer
Institute, he has written and received numerous other grants. His publications are found in the *Journal of Health Communication,*
Interdisciplinary Casebook in Geriatric Communication, Speech
Communication: Essays to Commemorate the 75th Anniversary of SCA, and
the *Journal of Applied Communication Research.* He holds or has held sev-
eral offices in the Speech Communication Association and the
International Communication Association.

■ 1

Introduction: The Power of Qualitative Research to Address Organizational Issues

Gary L. Kreps
Northern Illinois University
Dekalb, IL

Sandra L. Herndon
Ithaca College
Ithaca, NY

Pat Arneson
University of Northern Colorado
Greeley, CO

Qualitative research in the field of communication has emerged since the 1970s as a legitimate and widely recognized phenomenon in two ways: It has produced a growing body of literature, and it has developed a significant group of methods by which to study the process of communication. The application of qualitative methods to the study of organizations has proven to be one of the most fertile areas of research in this field.

This book's purpose is to identify and examine qualitative research methods—a term which, for our purposes, encompasses a variety of methods variously referred to as interpretive, naturalistic, phenomenological, or ethnographic—and to demonstrate their application in organizational settings. This introductory chapter situates the study of organizational communication in the following ways: (a) it provides a brief overview of general areas of research and specific topics of organizational inquiry since 1985; (b) it identifies the role of communication research, in general, in understanding organizational change and adaptation; (c) it identifies the pragmatic value of using qualitative methods in particular to

1

address these and other organizational issues; (d) it describes the relationship between interpretive methods and organizational reflexivity; and (e) it introduces the chapters to follow which describe and examine specific applications of various forms of qualitative research in organizations.

ORGANIZATIONAL COMMUNICATION RESEARCH SINCE 1985

Organizational communication research has included many topics since it emerged in the 1940s. Diversity and plurality typify inquiry in this area. Putnam and Cheney (1985) expressed an expectation that the field "will eventually move toward a clearer image of itself, a coherent identity embracing preferred concepts, theories, methods, and interventions" (p. 156). This section overviews the development of general areas of research and specific topics of organizational inquiry since 1985.

Collectively, individual works and edited volumes document six broad areas of organizational communication research. First, scholars clarified the history of organizational communication (Putnam & Cheney, 1985; Redding, 1985). Second, researchers discussed theoretical perspectives and conceptual advances (Farace & MacDonald, 1974; Goldhaber & Barnett, 1988; Jablin, Putnam, Roberts, & Porter, 1987; McPhee & Tompkins, 1985). Third, methodologists reviewed various approaches to examining organizational communication (Dennis, Goldhaber, & Yates, 1978; Goldhaber & Barnett, 1988; Putnam, 1982a, 1982b; Putnam & Cheney, 1983; Redding, 1979). Fourth, scholars examined organizational communication environments or contexts (Jablin, et al., 1987; Putnam & Cheney, 1985). Fifth, researchers documented organizational relationships which determine organizational structure (Farace & MacDonald, 1974; Jablin et al., 1987; Monge, 1982; Putnam & Cheney, 1985). Sixth, individuals discussed message and message-exchange processes (Farace & MacDonald, 1974; Jablin, et al., 1987; Putnam & Cheney, 1985). These works provide the background for contemporary organizational research.

Contemporary organizational literature (1985-1991) reveals two research goals: an increased understanding of employee behavior and an expanded knowledge regarding various aspects of the organization. Scholars explore a plurality of issues in both of these areas. The following overview identifies lines of contemporary organizational research.

The Individual in the Organization

Research examining the role of the individual in organizations is plentiful. A review of recent organizational literature identified seven topics in this area currently being pursued by researchers. Each of these topics present numerous opportunities for applied organizational research.

The process of employee adaptation to the organization is noteworthy. An increasing number of studies examine the role of employee socialization/acculturation, especially in relation to job satisfaction and organizational commitment (Chatman, 1989, 1991; O'Reilly, Chatman, & Caldwell, 1991). The way newcomers to the organization seek information in the initial socialization process helps us understand how they reformulate their interpretive schemes and adapt to the organization (Miller & Jablin, 1991; Reichers, 1987). An organization's patterns of socialization affect employee adjustment to the organizational culture (Jones, 1986). During an individual's socialization and identification with an organization, 15 types of turning points have been identified (Bullis & Bach, 1989). Organizational members use stories to express their knowledge, understanding, and commitment to an organization. As employees move through the socialization process, stories more closely relate to organizational values and culture (Brown, 1985). Socially desirable responding behavior (Zerbe & Paulhus, 1987) plays an important role in understanding employee acculturation. Further, Nahavandi and Malekzadeh (1988) discussed acculturation stress in organizational mergers. Employee socialization processes strongly influence the commitment an employee feels toward the organization.

Another area of study addresses an individual's commitment to the organization. Sass and Canary (1991) identified organizational commitment as an outcome of the process of organizational identification. Scholars identified the development of organizational commitment (Fichman & Levinthal, 1991) and predictors of employee commitment (Glisson & Durick, 1988). In addition, researchers investigated issues of freedom of speech (Gordon & Infante, 1991) and employee responses to organizational dissatisfaction (Withey & Cooper, 1989). Employee commitment closely relates to worker motivation.

Understanding how to enhance an individual's motivation to meet organizational goals is of interest to organizational decision makers. Thomas and Velthouse (1990) first developed a cognitive model linking employee motivation to worker empowerment. Klein (1990) identified a curvilinear relationship between feasibility (resources available to perform a task) and employee motivation. In addition, Sullivan (1988) suggested expanding current motivation theory to include the impact of speech acts on worker motivation. Completing assigned goals involves making choices; Tubbs and Ekeberg (1991) reconceptualized goals and intentions to represent cognitively both means and ends, clarifying the process of worker motivation.

Superior-subordinate communication greatly influences the manner with which individuals approach tasks. Achieving organizational goals depends on effective superior-subordinate communication. Tsui and O'Reilly (1989) found superior-subordinate demographics affect performance ratings, liking, role ambiguity, and conflict. Lamude, Daniels, and Graham (1988) related biological sex of the superior-subordinate pair, coorientation, and job satisfaction. Waldron (1991) identified the upward communication maintenance tactics used by subordinates. The superior-subordinate relationship affects the behavior of organizational members.

Supervision involves aspects of leadership. Penley and Hawkins (1985) urged researchers to focus attention on leaders' communication. Thomas (1988) refuted earlier leadership studies and reinforced that leaders do make a difference in organizational performance. Biological sex of leaders was not shown to significantly influence leadership style; male and female leaders exhibit equal amounts of initiating structure and consideration and have equally satisfied subordinates (Dobbins & Platz, 1986). The role of external leaders of self-managing work teams differs from traditional and participative leadership roles (Manz & Sims, 1987). Manz (1986) developed an expanded view of "self-leadership," a central control mechanism within organizations. More recently, Meindl (1989) examined managerial leadership in resolving resource allocation problems.

An individual's ethical behavior may determine his or her leadership potential. Research in the area of ethics includes examinations of individual and corporate ethical principles. Kahn (1990) encouraged scholars to approach the study of business ethics research by creating dialectical, historical, imaginative, and communal connections. In this way, "knowing how" to apply ethical codes becomes an important extension to traditional ethical theory (Brady, 1986). Jansen and Von Glinow (1985) considered individuals' ethical ambivalence in the organization. In contrast, Dozier and Miceli (1985) identified specific personality and situational variables that predict the occurrence of whistle-blowing behavior. Trevino (1986) proposed an interactionist model of ethical decision making in organizations that combine individual and situational variables to explain the ethical decision-making behaviors of individuals in organizations. Victor and Cullen (1988) emphasized the organization rather than the individual, outlining five major dimensions of an organizational climate that enable ethical behavior. Jones (1991) suggested placing emphasis on the ethical issue itself and offered an issue-contingent model of individual ethical decision making containing a new set of variables called moral intensity.

The last area of organizational research currently underway concerns the implementation of new technology in the workplace. Organizational leaders are interested in employee responses to increasing technological opportunities. Rice and Aydin (1991) examined the impact of social information on an individual's view of technology. Papa and Papa (1990) identified a significant relationship between new technology and perceptual and communicative factors. Huber (1990) examined the impact of technology on organizational decision making and found the quality of an organizational decision is largely a result of both the quality of the organizational intelligence and the decision-making process. Technical communication within an organization (Zanger & Lawrence, 1989) will become increasingly important with the expanded use of advanced technology in organizations.

This section of the overview has identified recent studies of the individual's organizational communication behavior. In addition to research in the area of employee behavior, scholars offer research pertaining to the organizational entity. The literature revealed four topics for consideration: organizational culture, interorganizational linkages, multiculturalism in the organizational environment, and organizational "death."

Examining the Organization

Qualitative researchers closely attend to cultural issues. Sackmann (1990) offered three different conceptions of organizational culture—as variable, metaphor, and dynamic construct. Further, three classes of industry variables create an organizational culture: competitive environment, customer requirements, and societal expectations (Gordon, 1991). Wilkins and Dyer (1988) identified some organizational cultures to be more resistant to change than others and identified patterns of cultural change. Goodall (1990) noted that organizational changes affect its cultural identity. Organizational memory plays a significant role in organizational culture (Walsh & Ungson, 1991).

An organization's culture may not be limited to specific boundaries. The relationship between interorganizational linkages and organizational survival has become a significant area of study (Baum & Oliver, 1991). Fombrun (1986) recast the concept of organizational structure to recognize corresponding infra-, socio-, and superstructures joined through technological, political, and social exchanges in and around organizations. Oliver (1990) noted critical, efficiency, and reciprocity contingencies which shape the decision to initiate an interorganizational relationship. Levinthal and Fichman (1988) examined the development and duration dependence of interorganizational relationships. The increasing occurrence of international joint ventures affords increased attention to personnel issues associated with these mergers (Shenkar & Zeira, 1987).

An emergent area of inquiry involves multicultural organizational communication. Limaye and Victor (1991) addressed limitations of the Western, linear paradigm on multicultural business communication. Foeman and Pressley (1987) considered how differing interpersonal styles can add to the organizational environment. Fish (1991) identified strategies taken by a Fortune 500 company in its efforts to "value" diversity in its managerial ranks. Fine (1991) developed a framework for understanding multicultural communication in organizations based on the assumption of cultural difference, rather than cultural similarity.

Despite efforts toward adaptation and productivity, conditions may force an organization toward decline and death. Sutton (1987) identified characteristics of dying organizations and offered a sequential model of the death of an organization. Refining this research, Weitzel and Johnson (1989) offered a dynamic framework which identifies decline in its early stages. D'Aveni (1989) related patterns of decline to the timing or consequences of decline, including managerial imbalance, actions concerned with efficiency, centralization effects, and strategic paralysis. Organizational decline may also be associated with organizational age (Levinthal, 1991). In conjunction with organizational mortality, Harris and Sutton (1986) indicated parting ceremonies serve an important function for members displaced by organizational deaths.

This section of the overview has examined recent inquiry in the field of organizational communication research, including emphases on the individual and the organization. This foundation offers insight for qualitative researchers in framing research questions or confirming category emergence. Following the construction of research questions directed toward solving practical problems, investigators must select and apply the most appropriate research method(s). In the following sections of this chapter we examine several ways that qualitative data can be used in modern organizational life.

COMMUNICATION RESEARCH AND ORGANIZATIONAL CHANGE

According to the second law of thermodynamics in general systems theory, every living system inevitably decays, becomes disorganized, and moves towards entropy unless concerted efforts are taken to resist this natural degradation, to reenergize and rebuild the system so it can achieve negative entropy (Berrien, 1976; Bertalanffy, 1968). Based on this principle, it follows that for organizations to survive and prosper they must actively resist the inevitable threat of entropy by continually adapting, improving, and ultimately enhancing effectiveness of organizational processes (Kreps, 1990a; Mitroff & Kilmann, 1975; Schein, 1969, 1985, 1987).

Communication researchers are particularly well situated to help promote organizational adaptation and change because the success of organizing activities is largely dependent on how well organization members are able to communicate and use important information (Axley, 1980; Kreps, 1985, 1990a; Pace, 1983). Organization members depend on their use of internal communication channels to elicit cooperation from others to coordinate the accomplishment of organizational activities, promoting order, stability, and predictability in organizing. Organizational actors also depend on their use of external communication channels to adapt to and influence their organization's environment, identifying external constraints and opportunities and directing organizational innovation (Kreps, 1985, 1990a). The coordinated use of internal and external channels of communication enables members to create and maintain an ongoing state of organization, balancing the interdependent, yet often contradictory, organizational needs for stability and innovation (Kreps, 1990a, 1990b).

The need for adaptation is in striking contrast to the related need for order in organizations. Although organizational change occurs naturally, such change is not necessarily in the best interests of organization since it is haphazard and undirected (Cohen, March, & Olsen, 1972; Kreps, 1990a; Weick, 1979, 1987). Innovation is a special type of change that is planned and directed to address specific problems and improve organizational life. Due to emergent internal and external constraints and challenges to the accomplishment of organizational goals, there is a constant need for innovative ideas to direct the responses of organization members in addressing these challenges (Berrien, 1976; Kreps, 1990a). Researchers can increase organizational effectiveness by gathering data to examine internal and external organizational communication. Such data can be used to identify relevant issues, opportunities, and constraints on effective communication and to fuel organizational adaptation and development (Kreps, 1989b, 1990c).

Organizational communication research has great potential for generating data that can provide feedback which can help people identify pressing problems and facilitate development of problem-solving interventions. An effective research and development strategy for the researcher is to help members resolve organizational problems by facilitating discovery and examination of the underlying symbolic structures, constraints, and opportunities of organizational life (Kreps, 1989b; Schein, 1969, 1987). Qualitative methods are best used to address questions focusing on meaning and symbolic structures.

THE PRAGMATIC VALUE OF
INTERPRETIVE ORGANIZATIONAL RESEARCH

The interpretive approach to organizational communication research is a qualitative research strategy that can be used to gather data about organizational actors' experiences and insights into organizational life.

Interpretive methods are a significant departure from more traditional quantitative, close-ended, survey-based approaches to conducting organizational communication research (Deetz, 1982; Putnam, 1982b). Interpretive research is ethnographic, designed to describe more fully the symbolic structures members create about their organization and the communication behavior they perform to develop and maintain these collective symbolic structures. Interpretive research is phenomenologically based, in that it strives to understand the organization from the perspective of the organization member (Fish, 1990; Fish & Dorris, 1975). The qualitative, ethnographic nature of interpretive research provides richly textured "thick descriptions" of organizational phenomena that enable the researcher to describe many of the complexities of organizations issues (Geertz, 1973; Pacanowsky, 1988; Weick & Browning, 1986; Wilkins, 1984, 1983).

A strength of qualitative research is the depth of the data generated and the complexity of organizational issues described by interpretive methods (Pacanowsky, 1988). Nondirective, ethnographic forms of data gathering, in which researchers are concerned about observing actual communication behaviors, examining texts and artifacts, and encouraging full accounts of members' perspectives on organizational performance (rather than constraining subjects' responses to limited-response, close-ended measurement scales) can provide very relevant and revealing data (Deetz, 1982; Koch & Deetz, 1981; Manning, 1979; Martin & Powers, 1983; Pettigrew, 1979; Putnam & Pacanowsky, 1983).

Interpretive data can help researchers decipher, understand, and even anticipate the significant issues, symbols, and communication rituals that comprise organizational life. Such data can be used to evaluate the current status and health of the organization from the perspective of its members and representatives of the environment. The interpretive researcher probes members' and environmental representatives' interpretations of organizational life by observing their communicative behaviors and rituals, by conducting open-ended, unstructured, in-depth interviews, and by analyzing key communication texts and artifacts (stories, metaphors, symbols, documents) to identify issues confronting the organization.

INTERPRETIVE RESEARCH
AND ORGANIZATIONAL REFLEXIVITY

The process of identifying and analyzing the underlying symbolic logic in organizations can have potentially powerful benefits for the organization and its members because it enables them to review and assess organizational activities and performance (Kreps, 1989b; Schein, 1987). The introspective data gathered by interpretive research can provide insight into organizational phenomena and be used to direct organizational activities to better accomplish individual and organizational goals. The ability to gather information about the critical reactions others have about organizational behaviors enables members to evaluate the relative effectiveness of messages sent. Interpretive organizational communication research generates data that can inform members about how the organization is being perceived by others (both internal and external to the organization), offering a clearer picture of the reactions key audiences have to organizational communication (Kreps, 1989b).

Interpretive research with organization members and environmental representatives is a way to provide data to help organization decision makers clearly see the internal state of the organization from the point of view of its membership, as well as understand the perspectives of members of the environment, thereby promoting increased organizational reflexivity (Kreps, 1989a). Organization members need feedback about organizational activities to direct successful innovation (Nadler, 1977; Rowe & Boise, 1973). Interpretive research should provide salient information about both environmental changes and constraints and internal organizational conditions to guide innovation. According to Greenbaum (1974), organizations need to conduct regular communication "audits" to identify and diagnose potential difficulties; interpretive methods offer an excellent avenue to accomplish those goals.

Increased reflexivity enables organization members to recognize important performance gaps (Kreps, 1990a, 1989b). "Performance gaps are discrepancies between an organization's expectations and its actual performance" (Rogers & Agarwala-Rogers, 1976, p. 70). Performance gaps occur in all situations in which organizational goals are not fully accomplished. Interpretive research methods may be used to gather information about the nature and seriousness of such gaps, the recognition of which is a crucial element in organizational renewal and development because it enables the researcher to diagnose specific organizational problems and design adaptive strategies for innovation (French & Bell, 1973; French, Bell, & Zawacki, 1978; Pavlock, 1982). By examining important performance gaps, the researcher helps the organization chart directions for organizational innovation.

Interpretive research can also help organizations become increasingly proactive. In proactive organizations members direct innovative activities to meet upcoming problems before they occur, staying at least one step ahead of performance gaps. To become proactive, members need information from key sources—which interpretive research can provide—to stay on top of changing environmental and internal organizational conditions.

In addition to examining performance gaps, interpretive research can also assist organizations as they "learn to learn." Morgan (1986) defines "double-loop learning" as the self-questioning ability "to detect and correct errors in operating norms and thus influence the standards that guide their detailed operation" (p. 87). This doubly reflexive process, requiring that an organization "review and challenge basic norms, policies, and operating procedures in relation to changes occuring in their environment" (p. 89), could be aided through the use of interpretive techniques such as interviews and focus groups. Insights thus generated are important in "reframing knowledge and giving choices that previously were hidden by the accepted knowledge, standard practices, and existing concepts" (Deetz, 1982, p. 138).

Additionally, interpretive research can be used to formulate a critique leading to fundamental organizational changes. In uncovering previously obscured understandings, interpretive research may reveal "systematically distorted communication" which has led to "false consensus" (Deetz, 1982, p. 140). A final outcome for interpretive research may be the reformulation of organizational processes and practices to allow greater openness and participation.

CONCLUSION AND OVERVIEW

Interpretive research provides data that go beyond the outward manifestations of organizational problems (which generally provide little insight into resolving complex organizational issues), providing more in-depth information than can generally be gathered with traditional survey methods. Interventions that focus on the symptoms of problems without addressing the underlying concerns not only fail to solve problems but often actually exacerbate the difficulties.

Qualitative research can provide researchers with data for diagnosing and designing strategies to address organizational difficulties. Interpretive methods can be used to generate in-depth insights into the many complexities of organizational life. One of the benefits of such research is its ability to identify performance gaps in organizational activities. Such information can promote reflexivity among organization members, helping them recognize and solve problems and make needed fundamental changes. The use of such research to generate information about organizational activities can help organizations become increasingly proactive, enabling decision makers to design strategies for avoiding potential problems before they become serious difficulties.

In order to provide an examination of qualitative research in organizational communication, the editors invited 12 other authors to join in exploring a variety of methods. The result is an original anthology which, although not exhaustive in scope, examines 10 qualitative methods, describes their applications in numerous organizational settings, and explores various theoretical, pragmatic, practical, political, and ethical issues inherent in this kind of research.

In Chapter 2, Jan Muto examines some of the political and pragmatic problems that arise in conducting qualitative organizational communication research. In Chapter 3 Susan Mason describes communication strategies for conducting qualitative interviews in organizational contexts. Sandra Herndon describes the uses of focus group interviews in organizational research in Chapter 4. Mary Helen Brown and Gary Kreps in Chapter 5 describe the use of narrative analysis to direct organizational development. In Chapter 6, Jim Query and Gary Kreps describe the use of the critical incident technique to promote organizational effectiveness. Patricia Geist and Jennifer Dreyer describe the uses of account analysis to study organizational behavior in Chapter 7. In Chapter 8 Charles Bantz suggests a research procedure for ethnographic analysis of organizational culture. Lynette Eastland in chapter 9 examines some of the intricacies of conducting ethnographic research in organizations. In Chapter 10 Mark Hickson and Russell Jennings describe and illustrate triangulation of methods in applied research. Pat Arneson in Chapter 11 suggests three additional methods for applied research in organizations: historical documentation techniques, the case study method, and the critical approach to organizational analysis. Examining the criteria used in defining qualitative research, in Chapter 12 Paula Michal-Johnson identifies some of the social and ethical issues inherent in the use of qualitative methods, focusing on their impact on organizational ecology.

Our hope is that this volume will provide some guidance to organizational researchers in their selection of method, perhaps stimulating new ways of viewing organizational communication, as well as generating new and provocative lines of thought about the human experience of organizing.

REFERENCES

Axley, S. R. (1980, May). *Communication's role in organizational change: A review of the literature.* Paper presented to the International Communication Association conference, Acapulco, Mexico.

Baum, J. A. C., & Oliver, C. (1991). Institutional linkages and organizational mortality. *Administrative Science Quarterly, 36,* 187-218.

Berrien, F. K. (1976). A general systems approach to organizations. In M. Dunnette (Ed.), *Handbook of industrial and organizational psychology* (pp. 41-62). Chicago: Rand McNally.

Bertalanffy, L. (1968). *General systems theory.* New York: Braziller.

Brady, F. N. (1986). Aesthetic components of management ethics. *Academy of Management Review, 11,* 337-344.

Brown, M. H. (1985). That reminds me of a story: Speech action in organizational socialization. *Western Journal of Speech Communication, 49,* 27-42.

Bullis, C., & Bach, B. W. (1989). Socialization turning points: An examination of change in organizational identification. *Western Journal of Speech Communication, 53,* 273-293.

Chatman, J. (1989). Improving interactional organization research: A model of person-organization fit. *Academy of Management Review, 14,* 333-349.

Chatman, J. S. (1991). Matching people and organizations: Selection and socialization in public accounting firms. *Administrative Science Quarterly, 36,* 459-484.

Cohen, M.D., March, J.G., & Olson, J.P., (1972) A garbage can model of organizational choice. *Administrative Science Quarterly, 17,* 1-25.

D'Aveni, R. A. (1989). The aftermath of organizationa decline: A longitudinal study of the strategic and managerial characteristics of declining firms. *Academy of Management Journal, 32,* 577-605.

Deetz, S. A. (1982). Critical interpretive research in organizational communication. *Western Journal of Speech Communication, 46,* 131-149.

Dennis, H. S., Goldhaber, G. M., & Yates, M. P. (1978). Organizational communication theory and research: An overview of research methods. In B. D. Ruben (Ed.), *Communication yearbook 2.* New Brunswick, NJ: Transaction Books.

Dobbins, G. H., & Platz, S. J. (1986). Sex differences in leadership: How real are they? *Academy of Management Review, 11,* 118-127.

Dozier, J. B., & Miceli, M. P. (1985). Potential predictors of whistle-blowing: A prosocial behavior perspective. *Academy of Management Review, 10,* 823-886.

Farace, R. V., & MacDonald, D. (1974). New directions in the study of organizational communication. *Personnel Psychology, 27,* 1-15.

Fichman, M., & Levinthal, D. A. (1991). Honeymoons and the liability of adolescence: A new perspective on duration dependence in social and organizational relationships. *Academy of Management Review, 16,* 442-468.

Fine, M. G. (1991). New voices in the workplace: Research directions in multicultural communication. *Journal of Business Communication, 28,* 259-275.

Fish, S. L. (1990). Interpretive research: A new way of viewing organizational communication. *Public Administration Quarterly, 14,* 66-74.

Fish, S. L. (1991). Preparation for the year 2000: One corporation's attempt to address the issues of gender and race. *The Howard Journal of Communications, 3*, 61-72.

Fish, S. L., & Dorris, J. M. (1975). Phenomenology and communication research. *Journal of Applied Communication Research, 3*, 9-26.

Foeman, A. K., & Pressley, G. (1987). Ethnic culture and corporate culture: Using black styles in organizations. *Communication Quarterly, 35*, 293-307.

Fombrun, C. J. (1986). Structural dynamics within and between organizations. *Administrative Science Quarterly, 31*, 403-421.

French, W., & Bell, C. (Eds.). (1973). *Organization development: Behavioral science interventions for organization improvement.* Englewood Cliffs, NJ: Prentice-Hall.

French, W., Bell, C., & Zawacki, R. (Eds.). (1978). *Organization development: Theory, practice, and research.* Dallas: Business Publications.

Geertz, C. (1973). *The interpretation of cultures.* New York: Basic Books.

Glisson, C., & Durick, M. (1988). Predictors of job satisfaction and organizational commitment in human service organizations. *Administrative Science Quarterly, 33*, 61-81.

Goldhaber, G. M., & Barnett, G. A. (Eds.). (1988). *Handbook of organizational communication.* Norwood, NJ: Ablex.

Goodall, H. L., Jr. (1990). A theatre of motives and the 'meaningful orders of persons and things.' In J. A. Anderson (Ed.), *Communication yearbook 13* (pp. 69-94). Newbury Park: Sage.

Gordon, G. G. (1991). Industry determinants of organizational culture. *Academy of Management Review, 16*, 396-415.

Gordon, W. I., & Infante, D. A. (1991). Test of a communication model of organizational commitment. *Communication Quarterly, 39*, 144-155.

Greenbaum, H. H. (1974). The audit of organizational communication. *Academy of Management Journal, 17*, 750-752.

Harris, S. G., & Sutton, R. I. (1986). Functions of parting ceremonies in dying organizations. *Academy of Management Journal, 29*, 5-30.

Huber, G. P. (1990). A theory of effects of advanced information technologies on organizational design, intelligence, and decision making. *Academy of Management Review, 15*, 47-71.

Jablin, F. M., Putnam, L. L., Roberts, K. H., & Porter, L. W. (1987). *Handbook of organizational communication: An interdisciplinary perspective.* Newbury Park: Sage.

Jansen, E., & Von Glinow, M. A. (1985). Ethical ambivalence and organizational reward systems. *Academy of Management Review, 10*, 814-822.

Jones, G. R. (1986). Socialization tactics, self-efficacy, and newcomers' adjustments to organizations. *Academy of Management Journal, 29*, 262-279.

Jones, T. M. (1991). Ethical decision making by individuals in organizations: An issue-contingent model. *Academy of Management Review, 16*, 366-395.

Kahn, W. A. (1990). Toward an agenda for business ethics research. *Academy of Management Review, 15,* 311-328.

Klein, J. I. (1990). Feasibility theory: A resource-munificence model of work motivation and behavior. *Academy of Management Review, 15,* 646-665.

Koch, S., & Deetz, S. (1981). Metaphor analysis of social reality in organization. *Journal of Applied Communication Research, 9,* 1-15.

Kreps, G. L. (1985). Organizational communication and organizational effectiveness. *World Communication, 15,* 55-70.

Kreps, G. L. (1989a). Reflexivity and internal public relations: The role of information in directing organizational development. In C. Botan & V. Hazleton (Eds.), *Public relations theory* (pp. 265-279). Hillsdale, NJ: Erlbaum.

Kreps, G. L. (1989b). A therapeutic model of organizational communication consultation: Application of interpretive field methods. *Southern Communication Journal, 54,* 1-21.

Kreps, G. L. (1990a). *Organizational communication: Theory and practice* (2nd ed). White Plains, NY: Longman.

Kreps, G. L. (1990b). Narrative research and organizationa development: Stories as repositories of organizational intelligence. In J. Anderson (Ed.), *Communication yearbook 13* (pp. 191-202). Newbury Park, CA: Sage.

Kreps, G. L. (1990c). Organizational communication research and organizational development. In D. O'Hair & G. Kreps (Eds.), *Applied communication theory and research* (pp. 103-121). Hillsdale, NJ: Erlbaum.

Lamude, K. G., Daniels, T. D., & Graham, E. E. (1988). The paradoxical influence of sex on communication rules coorientation and communication satisfaction in superior-subordinate relationships. *Western Journal of Speech Communication, 52,* 122-134.

Levinthal, D. (1991). Random walks and organizational mortality. *Administrative Science Quaterly, 36,* 397-420.

Levinthal, D. A., & Fichman, M. (1988). Dynamics of interorganizational attachments: Auditor-client relationships. *Administrative Science Quarterly, 33,* 345-369.

Limaye, M. R., & Victor, D. A. (1991). Cross-cultural business communication research: State of the art and hypotheses for the 1990s. *Journal of Business Communication, 28,* 277-299.

Manning, P. K. (1979). Metaphors of the field: Varieties of organizational discourse. *Administrative Science Quarterly, 84,* 796-810.

Manz, C. C. (1986). Self-leadership: Toward an expanded theory of self-influence processes in organizations. *Academy of Management Review, 11,* 585-600.

Manz, C. C., & Sims, H. R., Jr. (1987). Leading workers to lead themselves: The external leadership of self-managing work teams.

Administrative Science Quarterly, 32, 106-129.

Martin, J., & Powers, M. (1983). Organizational stories: More vivid and persuasive than quantitative data. In B. M. Staw (Ed.), *Psychological foundations of organizational behavior* (pp. 161-168). Glenview, IL: Scott, Foresman.

McPhee, R. E., & Tompkins, P. K. (1985). *Organizational communication: Traditional themes and new directions.* Beverly Hills: Sage.

Meindl, J. R. (1989). Managing to be fair: An exploration of values, motives, and leadership. *Administrative Science Quarterly, 34,* 252-276.

Miller, V. D., & Jablin, F. M. (1991). Information seeking during organizational entry: Influences, tactics, and a model of the process. *Academy of Management Review, 16,* 92-120.

Mitroff, I., & Kilmann, R. (1975). Stories managers tell: A new tool for organizational problem solving. *Management Review, 64,* 19-20.

Monge, P. R. (1982). Systems theory and research in the study of organizational communication: The correspondence problem. *Human Communication Research, 8,* 245-261.

Morgan, G. (1986). *Images of organization.* Beverly Hills, CA: Sage.

Nadler, D. R. (1977). *Feedback and organization development: Using data based methods.* Reading, MA: Addison-Wesley.

Nahavandi, A., & Malekzadeh, A. R. (1988). Acculturation in mergers and acquisitions. *Academy of Management Review, 13,* 79-90.

Oliver, C. (1990). Determinants of interorganizational relationships: Integration and future directions. *Academy of Management Review, 15,* 241-265.

O'Reilly, C. A., III, Chatman, J., & Caldwell, D. F. (1991). People and organizational culture: A profile comparison approach to assessing person-organization fit. *Academy of Management Journal, 34,* 487-516.

Pacanowsky, M. (1988). Slouching towards Chicago. *Quarterly Journal of Speech, 74,* 453-467.

Pace, R. W. (1983). *Organizational communication: Foundations for human resource development.* Englewood Cliffs, NJ: Prentice-Hall.

Papa, M. J., & Papa, W. H. (1990). Perceptual and communicative indices of employee performance with new technology. *Western Journal of Speech Communication, 54,* 21-41.

Pavlock, E. J. (Ed.). (1982). *Organization development: Managing transitions.* Washington, DC: American Society for Training and Development.

Penley, L. E., & Hawkins, B. (1985). Studying interpersonal communication in organizations: A leadership application. *Academy of Management Journal, 28,* 309-326.

Pettigrew, A. M. (1979). On studying organizational culture. *Administrative Science Quarterly, 24,* 570-581.

Putnam, L. L. (1982a). The interpretive perspective: An alternative to functionalism. In L. L. Putnam & M. E. Pacanowsky (Eds.),

Communication and organizations: An interpretive approach (pp. 31-54). Beverly Hills, CA: Sage.

Putnam, L. L. (1982b). Paradigms for organizational communication research: An overview and synthesis. *Western Journal of Speech Communication, 46,* 192-206.

Putnam, L. L., & Cheney, G. (1983). A critical review of research traditions in organizational communication. In M. Mander (Ed.), *Communications in transition: Issues and debates in current research* (pp. 206-224). New York: Praeger.

Putnam, L. L., & Cheney, G. (1985). Organizational communication: Historical development and future directions. In T. Benson (Ed.), *Speech communication in the twentieth century* (pp. 130-156). Carbondale: Southern Illinois University Press.

Putnam, L., & Pacanowsky, M. (Eds.). (1983). *Communication and organizations: An interpretive approach.* Beverly Hills, CA: Sage.

Redding, W. C. (1979). Organizational communication theory and ideology: An overview. In D. Nimmo (Ed.), *Communication yearbook 3* (pp. 309-341). New Brunswick, NJ: ICA/ Transaction Books.

Redding, W. C. (1985). Stumbling toward identity: The emergence of organizational communication as a field of study. In R. D. McPhee & P. K. Tompkins (Eds.), *Organizational communication: Traditional themes and new directions* (pp. 15-54). Beverly Hills: Sage.

Reichers, A. E. (1987). An interactionist perspective on newcomer socialization rules. *Academy of Management Review, 12,* 278-287.

Rice, R. E., & Aydin, C. (1991). Attitudes toward new organizational technology: Network proximity as a mechanism for social information processing. *Administrative Science Quarterly, 36,* 219-244.

Rogers, E., & Agarwala-Rogers, R. (1976). *Communication in organizations.* New York: The Free Press.

Rowe, L., & Boise, W. (Eds.). (1973). *Organizational and managerial innovation.* Pacific Palisades, CA: Goodyear Publishing.

Sackmann, S. A. (1990). Managing organizational culture: Dreams and possibilities. In J. A. Anderson (Ed.), *Communication yearbook 13* (pp. 114-148). Newbury Park, CA: Sage.

Sass, J. S., & Canary, D. J. (1991). Organizational commitment and identification: An examination of conceptual and operational convergence. *Western Journal of Speech Communication, 55,* 275-293.

Schein, E. H. (1969). *Process consultation: Its role in organization development.* Reading, MA: Addison-Wesley.

Schein, E. H. (1985). *Organizational culture and leadership.* San Francisco: Jossey-Bass.

Schein, E. H. (1987). *The clinical perspective in fieldwork.* Newbury Park, CA: Sage.

Shenkar, O., & Zeira, Y. (1987). Human resources management in international joint ventures: Directions for research. *Academy of Management Review, 12,* 546-557.

Sullivan, J. J. (1988). Three roles of language in motivation theory. *Academy of Management Review, 13,* 104-115.

Sutton, R. I. (1987). The process of organizational death: Disbanding and reconnecting. *Administrative Science Quarterly, 32,* 542-569.

Thomas, A. B. (1988). Does leadership make a difference to organizational performance? *Administrative Science Quarterly, 33,* 388-400.

Thomas, K. W., & Velthouse, B. A. (1990). Cognitive elements of empowerment: An 'interpretive' model of intrinsic task motivation. *Academy of Management Review, 15,* 666-681.

Trevino, L. K. (1986). Ethical decision-making in organizations: A person-situation interaction model. *Academy of Management Review, 11,* 601-617.

Tsui, A. S., & O'Reilly, C. A., III. (1989). Beyond simple demographic effects: The importance of relational demography in superior-subordinate dyads. *Academy of Management Journal, 32,* 402-423.

Tubbs, M. E., & Ekeberg, S. E. (1991). The role of intentions in work motivation: Implications for goal-setting theory and research. *Academy of Management Review, 16,* 180-199.

Victor, B., & Cullen, J. B. (1988). The organizational bases of ethical work climates. Administrative Science Quarterly, 33, 101-125.

Waldron, V. (1991). Achieving communication goals in superior-subordinate relationships: The multi-functionality of upward maintenance tactics. Communication Monographs, 58, 289-306.

Walsh, J. P., & Ungson, G. R. (1991). Organizational memory. Academy of Management Review, 16, 57-91.

Weick, K. E. (1987). Theorizing about organizational communication. In F. Jablin, L. Putnam, K. H. Roberts, & L. Porter (Eds.), *Handbook of organizational communication* (pp. 97-122). Newbury Park, CA: Sage.

Weick, K. E. (1979). *The social psychology of organizing* (2nd ed). Reading, MA: Addison-Wesley.

Weick, K. E., & Browning, L. D. (1986). Argument and narration in organizational communication. *Journal of Management, 12,* 243-259.

Weitzel, W., & Johnson, E. (1989). Decline in organizations: A literature integration and extension. *Administrative Science Quarterly, 34,* 91-109.

Wilkins, A. L. (1983). The cultures audit: A tool for understanding organizations. *Organizational Dynamics, 12,* 24-38.

Wilkins, A. L. (1984). The creation of cultures: The role of stories and human resource systems. *Human Resource Management, 23,* 41-60.

Wilkins, A. L., & Dyer, W. G., Jr. (1988). Toward culturally sensitive theories of cultural change. *Academy of Management Review, 13,* 522-533.

Withey, M., & Cooper, W. H. (1989). Predicting exit, voice, loyalty, and neglect. *Administrative Science Quarterly, 34,* 521-539.

Zanger, T. R., & Lawrence, B. S. (1989). Organizational demography: The differential effects of age and tenure distributions on technical communication. *Academy of Management Journal, 32,* 353-376.

Zerbe, W. J., & Paulhus, D. L. (1987). Socially desirable responding in organizational behavior: A reconception. *Academy of Management Review, 12,* 250-264.

◼ 2

"Who's That in My Bed?": The Strange Bedfellows Made by the Politics of Applied Qualitative Organizational Research

Jan Muto

Ithaca College
Ithaca, NY

◼ *Jan Muto emphasizes the essentially political nature of qualitative organizational research. Problems of access, confidentiality, multiple constituencies, role definitions and boundaries, and the consequences of research findings are some of the thorny issues Muto addresses through an extended example of her own work.*

The use of qualitative data within the field of organizational communication has become more popular as a result of the development of interpretive approaches in the late 1970s and early 1980s. While the results of qualitative studies are noteworthy in and of themselves, the purpose of this piece is to address the political considerations faced by field researchers. The potential pitfalls, cliffs, and fine lines to be tread by those whose research domain lies beyond the library are well documented in research methodology texts. Unfortunately, the very real confrontation of researcher with business reality is often overlooked by theoretical writings. In this chapter, I turn to those points of conflict between the applied qualitative organizational communication researcher and the membership of the research site.

Throughout the research process, the organizational communication specialist must make decisions which take into account several constituencies: the Human Subjects Review Board, organization decision mak-

An earlier version of this chapter was presented at the Eastern Communication Association convention in Philadelphia, PA, April 1990.

ers, organization membership, the community of scholars for whom the researcher writes, and the research goal (although not human in form, it is powerful in influence). The competition among these critical members of the project can leave the inexperienced analyst daydreaming about a new profession, ingesting massive quantities of antacid or, at best, merely losing sleep. In the following pages, the political tensions faced by one researcher in an applied organizational research setting are offered in the hopes of preserving the sanity of those whose paths take a similar turn.

GETTING IN THE DOOR

As any field researcher knows, gaining access to the research site can be an enormous problem. For the organizational communication researcher, that problem has particular characteristics. Many organizations are leery of admitting researchers because of the potential harm they may induce. For example, some managers believe that an outsider may not understand their unique organizational processes, or that an outsider may "stir up" feelings of antagonism or resentment among the workers, or that the researcher may simply just take too much of the work time and thus negatively impact productivity. These are very serious concerns not to be trivialized by the researcher. Researchers often forget or overlook these concerns, not maliciously, but because the everyday work of academics has such a different complexion from that of the business world. Before attempting to gain access to an organization, these issues must be honestly considered by the researcher.

On the more positive side, many managers are appreciative of the potential benefits an organizational analysis can yield. For example, the research can be used to gain a more holistic understanding of the company, can facilitate communication between management and staff, or can lend a fresh perspective on the happenings within the organization. These "plusses" are the ones on which most field researchers rely in arguing for access. Another effective "foot in the door" is to find out what problem the prospective organization may be facing that the researcher can aid in solving.

Through chance, as many potential sites are discovered, I was able to find an organization which needed me as much as I needed them. I met Sam at a cocktail party. Between chomps on hors d'oeuvres we introduced ourselves and engaged in fairly standard small talk. When I told him about my interest in communication in organizations, he replied in the way almost everyone I meet does: "Boy, you should see the communication where I work! We could really use someone like you!" And so, the door presented itself with a nameplate.

This is still far too early for the researcher to get excited. My introduction to Sam was followed by meeting for drinks after work at a local restaurant to get more details about the company. Then Sam approached his supervisor, Harley (a member of the organization's management team), to see if he could act as my advocate with the president of the firm. After a brief phone conversation, Harley invited me to the plant for a meeting and tour. Although he liked the idea, I still had to meet with the president. Even the president's approval wasn't the last hurdle: He wanted the management team to approve the project. The reader should note that almost six months had passed from my first meeting with Sam to final approval for my access.

These six months were spent not sitting by the telephone but performing tasks which are suggested to most first-time job applicants in professional fields. I tried to gain as much information as possible about the company through these meetings and as a result tailored my argument for access to their concerns as closely as possible. I discovered that the benefits of the analysis for the organization were two-fold. First, the management had completed an in-house survey consisting of open- and closed-ended questions approximately two months prior to my meeting with the president. One of the problems management faced was how to make sense out of the comments made by members on the open-ended portion of the survey. Since no one on the staff was familiar with analyzing qualitative data, management was at a bit of a loss as to how the responses should be interpreted. Because they were all so close to the work setting, they had a difficult time stepping back and looking for major themes. Second, because the survey revealed some very serious concerns, management suspected that something needed to be done but was unsure of exactly what the next move should be. The proposal I made to management focused on how bringing in an outsider would help to alleviate these problems. As a nonmember, a researcher can more easily "see the forest for the trees" since he or she is not personally invested in any one particular issue. Additionally, because I had previous consulting experience with managers in the industrial sector, I could bring that knowledge and expertise to the organization. This was particularly important for the organization, since all of their managers were promoted to management as a result of their expertise in areas of manufacturing specialities—none was trained to be managers in a formal sense; they each had been trained as engineers or laborers, for example. Finally, the president recognized that allowing members to be interviewed individually might serve as a reward device or demonstrate managerial openness (a la the Hawthorne effect). Because of these characteristics of the researcher and research process, using an outsider appeared to be a viable option for the organization.

Lest the reader assume that the process of gaining access (convincing the organization's decision makers that you should be allowed to come in, take time from productivity, perhaps rile the emotions of the membership) is a linear progression, realize that while all of this is going on the researcher has to weigh research method options. We would like to believe that organizations are our labs, but they are not; businesses exist to make profits, not publishable research results. The field researcher must be willing to adapt to the constraints posited by the organization of choice. The research method must be one which the organization can tolerate. You may enter the setting with a very sincere desire to perfect your skills at participant observation, only to discover that the decision maker finds that method unacceptable.

Here, too, the research goals come into play. Are you willing to modify your research question (since the choice of method is driven by the statement of the problem) in order to get field data? If the answer is "no," then you may find yourself in a constant search for the obliging organization. Of course, you also must consider your research skills. By now the reader should realize that I have just presented at least five balls to juggle while one is trying to get his or her foot in the door:

1. the research question or goal
2. the research method
3. the researcher's data collection skills
4. gaining access
5. unique organizational properties

Don't trip yet, it gets worse: each of these is defined from two distinct perspectives—the researcher's and the organization's. Collecting the data, analyzing the results, and reporting back to management must seem like a breezy revolving door. But just wait, it now gets really interesting.

THE "DOCTOR" IS IN

Have you ever experienced running into a student at the supermarket or laundromat and noticed how stunned he or she is that you have to buy groceries or wash clothes? As professors, we sometimes face the unenviable position of being labeled as unidimensional intellectuals. The problem can be magnified when a researcher travels the terrain of the 9-to-5 worker. You may be accustomed to talking with people who have PhDs; most folks aren't. Some are intimidated, some are full of disdain, some think that you are a slightly lesser version of an MD, and some quite frankly don't give your academic credentials a second thought. Once inside an organization, the researcher is often confronted with diverse interpretations of who he or she is and the purpose of her or his presence. How you conduct yourself throughout the research process can feed negative stereotypes or dispel them.

Because the organization consisted of employees whose educational backgrounds ranged from high school diplomas through master's degrees in engineering, I needed a method which would afford some flexibility in obtaining information. Open-ended, loosely structured interviews answered the need. This approach provided the necessary conceptual flexibility, drew upon my research strengths, and made sense to the management. Importantly, the conversational nature of the interviews allowed me to explore a range of issues from the members' points of view, while balancing management's interests with the research goal. Furthermore, the "guided conversation" nature of interviews helped keep the interaction within the comfort range of the participants (Loflund, 1971, p. 84).

Prior to conducting the interviews, I met with the president to review the interview protocol. This may sound unpalatable to the research purist, but consider at least two reasons for complying with such a request. First, the president, a former laborer within the company, was an excellent "test case" for the appropriateness of the interview guide language. Second, while the president's motive may not have been entirely philanthropic (he may not have wanted to see the interview guide merely for the purpose of helping me, he may have wanted to know specifically what his people were going to talk to me about), that is not an unreasonable position. He was giving me many hours of company time free of charge, and allowing him to review the interview questions was a risk I was willing to take. Although already in the door, it is important for the applied researcher at this point to maintain a cooperative relationship with decision makers. The researcher is still only at the beginning of negotiating role boundaries, but he or she should also view this process as part of data collection. Any interaction with organization members becomes part of the definition of the research scene. In this case, the president made useful suggestions for language changes that were easily accommodated.

The president and I agreed that I should be introduced to the entire membership at a regularly scheduled quarterly meeting. We both wanted some input into the ways in which members would interpret my presence, objective, and technique. We realized that many members would be skeptical, thinking that I was a tool of management to get inside information on productivity levels. This fear was reinforced by the fact that the research interviews with employees coincided with annual performance reviews. After scrutinizing my interpersonal communication skills during our several meetings, the president was convinced that I could gain the cooperation of members if I was allowed to present myself and my project to them as a group.

These considerations stemmed from my meetings with the contact person, Sam, his supervisor, and the president. I would like to take credit for all of these ideas, but that would be dishonest. The organization members with whom I had initial contact helped a great deal in assuring the successful completion of the study. They were, quite literally, my allies. Seeing yourself as the all-knowing expert is a dangerous portrait to paint; you might easily find yourself with a very limited palette. By enlisting the contact members of the organization as "content experts"—the ones who best know the site—the researcher can avoid violating cultural norms, begin to learn the language of the group, and use their insights to facilitate acceptance of the researcher by the membership.

If you believe that reality is socially constructed (Berger & Luckmann, 1967), and if you choose to adopt that perspective in your research, then don't contradict those beliefs with your actions. As a qualitative researcher, believe that your role is communicatively constructed by all participants in the research (see Anderson, 1987; Bogdan & Taylor, 1975; Mishler, 1986). You do not own the definition of yourself as "interested outsider" or the research process. All of the groundwork laid to the point of collecting data is not made of stone. Through interactions with organization members, who you are and what your purpose is and why you are talking to them all become decisions appropriated by the participants in the study. In short, you are jumping into their world; understand that where you land is determined as much by the members and their unique circumstances as it is by your thorough intellectual preparation.

I entered the interview setting with the tools of our trade in hand: multiple copies of the interview guide, additional copies of the release form for permission to audiotape the interview, a copy of the organizational chart, tape recorder with AC power (and batteries), lots of audiotapes, pens, paper, and my wristwatch. After the first few days I added one more thing: my coffee mug. Since all the members had their own coffee cups and many brought them into the interviews, I decided that I would look more like I belonged there if I also had one. While this may sound trivial, remember that once on site the researcher is closely observed by the members. Promoting an air of familiarity and comfort within the organization may facilitate interaction during the interviews.

Each interview was scheduled to take between 20 and 30 minutes. Surprisingly, they ranged in length from 10 minutes to over two hours although the majority were approximately 20 minutes long. All but one member of the organization agreed to be interviewed (no incentives or punishments were implemented) resulting in a total of 86 interviews. This very high completion rate and the excessive length of some interviews might be the result of several perceptual frames beyond the researcher's control.

First, since there was quite a bit of dismay expressed in the recent in-house survey, perhaps the members saw this research as a way to get management's attention. Second, since this research was being conducted by an outsider, perhaps members saw this as an opportunity to voice concerns they were hesitant to express to co-workers for fear of retribution (confidentiality was guaranteed). Third, once the interviews began and word spread among the membership about the seemingly innocuous nature of the questions, perhaps respondents were more inclined to talk. Finally, members may have viewed the interview as a means to get out of doing work. Regardless of the reason, a 99% completion rate for interviews is difficult to ignore.

One factor within the researcher's control is the tone of the open-ended or loosely structured interview. The intended conversational nature of the interviews produced interactions similar to those encountered in everyday life (Loflund, 1971). The interviews were not sterile or objective; their purpose was to explore with the participant the relationship among work and home roles. Many of the interviews took on the tone of casual conversation, some awkward first time meetings, and others intense intimate talk. The personal frustration of some members became a central topic. One man talked at length about his therapy sessions, another about the recent loss of a spouse, another about how unrewarding his life was. Quite a few talked about their displeasure with their supervisor, providing gory details of bad performance appraisal reviews, interpersonal conflict, salary discrepancies, and sexual discrimination. I was invited to cheer the company volleyball team and encouraged to join the happy hour group. I heard financial and marital woes. The level of openness and self-disclosure was shocking until I thought carefully about why some members viewed me as a confidant.

When entering an organization, the researcher must take into account the impact he or she may have on the lives of the participants as well as the impact respondents may have on the researcher. Neither party is free from influence in the professional and personal realm. Listening, day in and day out, face to face, to persons recant the traumas and joys of their lives is hard work. I've heard colleagues liken my form of work to reading a novel or watching a soap opera, but it's much harder. A book I can put down. A television I can turn off. While reading or watching television I can laugh or cry without anyone knowing. During interviews, that luxury does not exist. Applied qualitative organizational communication research necessarily includes the clashing of lifeworlds, the expression of emotion, and the hopefully enduring impact of the world of work on research.

It is hard to predict the ways in which the researcher's role may be defined by the organization members. Close attention to site circumstances can yield insight into how the researcher's presence is socially constructed and thus into the contextualized meanings of participants.

DON'T SLAM THE DOOR ON YOUR WAY OUT

When discussing my research with a colleague, she said, "Wow, what you do really affects people's lives!" That, in a nutshell, characterizes the ethical implications of performing applied organizational research. The analyst is faced with how the project results will impact the lives of the organization members. Therefore, each suggestion for change submitted to management must be carefully weighed to determine its relevance and potential. While the easiest route is to rely on well-worn options or traditional solutions, grounding recommendations in qualitative data requires the capacity and willingness to listen to the participants. The ethical considerations can be discussed in three contexts: maintaining confidentiality, management's influence on the results, and reporting to the membership.

In order to obtain useful information from members regarding organizational change, the researcher must protect the identity of the informants. Granted, this is standard procedure for any research; however, when it comes time to report salient issues to management, there may be some pressure exerted to identify the source(s) of complaints or compliments. For example, when the president heard that only one member declined participation in the interview, he pressed hard for the person's identity; he even tried guessing. What appeared here as a quite natural curiosity is often taught to be taboo in the research community.

It is important for the researcher to report results in such a way as to mask any identifying characteristics without diluting the data. In this study, one unit's membership consistently expressed extreme discontent with their supervisor. Some of the members were so distraught that their interviews contained quite lengthy and explicit references to the ineffectual behavior of their boss. I struggled for weeks over how to relay the information to the president without violating the confidentiality of the respondents. The decision was complicated by the necessity to provide meaningful recommendations for change. I wanted to make suggestions that responded to the concerns of the membership, but was bound by an ethical responsibility to preserve the identity of respondents so that no retribution might occur. The president knew of this department's displeasure; he informed me of it prior to the interviews and showed me a memo he had received from the group stating their concerns. The issue of confidentiality centered more on the form of the final report. Members of the management team (which included the indicted supervisor) as well as any organizational member who requested a copy would see the report. So, not only was I concerned about preserving the confidentiality of the respondents, but I also had no desire to publicly humiliate the supervisor. There is no easy answer to this dilemma. In the written report, I chose the most inoffensive solution, saying that at least two units were dissatisfied (a truth); in my final meeting with the president I verbally reinforced his knowledge of the unit's discontent.

Related to the problem of making relevant or representative suggestions is the tendency to be influenced by management's interests. While any recommendation must be assessed for its feasibility (which includes the support of decision makers), the researcher must guard against ruling out possible suggestions merely on the basis of management's potential disapproval. Most of us know, as humans, the difficulty of being the bearer of bad news. The researcher who asks for free access (as opposed to being a paid consultant) is also familiar with fighting the tendency to reward the management for allowing that access. During my last meeting with the president, when I brought a copy of the report for his review, I found myself in a position of wanting to "tone down" the concerns of the members in order to preserve our relationship. This internal conflict was sharpened when the president looked up from the report, about half-way through, and asked how much I charge for consulting.

As a qualitative researcher, in particular, the analyst becomes familiar with the personnel and workings of the organization. That familiarity often sets the stage for future work with the company. Most managers will readily recognize the benefits of hiring a consultant who has already spent perhaps hundreds of hours free of charge getting to know the organization. The analyst faces an ethical dilemma of prioritizing at least three levels of interest: the membership's, management's, and one's own.

The competition of these interests becomes most apparent when the researcher reports back to the participants. If the researcher has effectively balanced the interests of all concerned, then the response of the members to the report should not be one of shock or surprise, but rather one of comprehension or insight. When assuming the naturalist stance, the researcher needs this feedback as a check on interpretive expertise. Thus, with applied qualitative research we come full circle: The effectiveness of the report is judged by the collective from whom it was derived.

Pragmatically, this circle, perhaps appearing vicious to some, is the cornerstone of applied qualitative organizational communication research. The researcher must rely on knowledge of the organization gained through the membership—not solely through management, not solely through books, not solely through tradition. In that way the research outcome is decidedly unique, rich, and lively. The results should be meaningful to the participants, the researcher, and the research community. The parties involved in the field research process may find themselves at odds or aligned with one another, depending on the issues at hand. Predicting those points of contention or peace is difficult whenever lifeworlds collide, whenever a door presents itself for your use.

REFERENCES

Anderson, J. A. (1987). *Communication research: Issues and methods.* New York: McGraw-Hill.

Berger, P. L., & Luckmann, T. (1967). *The social construction of reality.* New York: Doubleday.

Bogdan, R., & Taylor, S. (1975). *Introduction to qualitative research methods: A phenomenological approach to the social sciences.* New York: Wiley-Interscience.

Loflund, J. (1971). *Analyzing social settings: A guide to qualitative observation and analysis.* Belmont, CA: Wadsworth.

Mishler, E. G. (1986). *Research interviewing: Context and narrative.* Cambridge, MA: Harvard University Press.

■ 3

Communication Processes in the Field Research Interview Setting

Susan A. Mason
Hamilton College
Clinton, NY

■ *The nondirective interview is universally recognized as a qualitative research tool. Susan Mason describes and positions its use in a statewide project involving multiple methods, identifying the necessary preparation as well as pragmatic problems to be addressed.*

For those of us who are involved in research of any type, gathering information that will be complete, relevant, and untainted is the ultimate goal. This is especially true in the social sciences where looking at human interaction and social systems usually means getting close to the data through qualitative field research. Within this realm, one of the most rewarding and perhaps most difficult methods of gathering data is the field research interview. In order to utilize this method, the researcher must not only be knowledgeable of the theoretical background of the study, but must also be well versed and practiced in a wide variety of communication skills. The field research interview is not, as some researchers observe, merely a stimulus/response event. As Mishler (1986) notes, "the interview is a form of discourse . . . shaped and organized by asking and answering questions" (p.vii). Within this structured talk, the researcher can find rich data after resolving assumptions about the relationship between discourse and meaning.

This work was done in association with Smithers Institute for Alcohol and Workplace Studies, School of Industrial and Labor Relations, Cornell University, Ithaca, NY. I would like to acknowledge the contributions of Barbara L. Hathaway, Assistant Professor William J. Sonnenstuhl, ILR/Cornell University, and Professor Harrison M. Trice, ILR/Cornell University. An earlier version of this chapter was presented at the Eastern Communication Association convention in Philadelphia, PA, April 1990.

The field research interview is a dynamic, nonlinear process which uses active listening and empathetic interpersonal skills to generate grounded theory. This chapter will discusses the execution of a research project utilizing the interview method in the field. The first section discusses research interviewing methods and approaches. Next there is a description of the research project and its methodological rationale. Last, there will be a summary of how the research team (of which I was a member) prepared for and enacted research interviews in the field.

THE RESEARCH INTERVIEW

Conducting structured research in an unstructured setting is a real challenge to the field researcher. The uniformity of nature is a reasonable assumption in the world of physical objects and their characteristics, but in the area of social behavior such assumptions are not warranted. Human nature is much more complex than the sum of its many discrete elements (Best & Kahn, 1986). To further compound this situation, communication acts—like other acts—do not have single consequences. They have multiple consequences. Each can have, at one and the same time, both intended and unintended, manifest and latent, practical and expressive, and functional and dysfunctional consequences (Trice & Beyer, 1984). Also, from a cultural perspective all actions, whether intentionally communicative or not, have the potential for expressing meaning, that is, for communicating (Beyer & Trice, 1988).

Amazingly, out of this apparent chaos develops the richness and "thick description" (Geertz, 1973) of the research interview method. If it is viewed as a form of discourse in which (a) research interviews are speech events, (b) the discourse of interviews is constructed jointly by interviewers and respondents, (c) analysis and interpretation are based on a theory of discourse and meaning, and (d) the meanings of questions and answers are contextually grounded (Glaser & Strauss, 1967; Mishler, 1986), then the power of the data collected in the interview setting will be significant.

The research interview method offers several useful approaches, such as clinical, ethnographic, survey, and life history. The survey research method is the most well-developed and widely used interview method. It is directive in nature, and because it features a standard format of interview schedules and an emphasis on fixed-response categories combined with systematic methods, it is regarded as a close approximation to the dominant model of scientific research (Mishler, 1986). The clinical, ethnographic, and life-history research interview approaches are more nondirective, featuring a structure that is not fixed by predetermined questions, but designed to provide the informant with freedom to introduce materials that are not anticipated by the interviewer (Whyte, 1960). Clearly, use of the research interview method in the field requires a bit of ingenuity, flexibility, and persistence (Hathaway, Mason, & Sonnenstuhl, 1989), but the richness of the data gathered justifies the effort required.

The following chronicles the processes that the five members of this research team used to collect data from the field via the nondirective research interview approach.

THE PROJECT AND METHOD

Describing the Project

Employee assistance programs (EAPs) are a major vehicle for the prevention and treatment of alcohol, drug and other emotional health problems within the workplace. Since 1970, thousands of people with a wide range of occupational and educational experiences have become involved in employee assistance work. Because it is considered an emergent occupation, there is not yet common consensus on what tasks actually constitute EAP work. Therefore, in 1985, Cornell University's Program on Alcoholism and Occupational Health together with the New York State Division of Alcoholism and Alcohol Abuse launched a program called the Employee Assistance Education and Research Program (EAERP). The goal of the program was twofold: (a) to bring quality and consistent education to the EAP workers of New York State by teaching the core tasks of EAP work and the crucial balance between the workplace and the treatment place; and (b) to study the socialization processes associated with the emergent occupation of EAPs. The research program looked to four specific EAP populations: EAERP graduates (n=113), EAERP drop-outs (n=32), EAERP inquiries (n=59), and a sample of New York State Employee Assistance Professional Association members (n=74).

Methodological Rationale

Research methods lie along a continuum. At one end are the qualitative methods such as participant observation and in-depth interviewing; at the other are the quantitative ones such as surveys and experiments (Best & Kahn, 1986; Sonnenstuhl & Trice, 1985). Each has its strengths and weaknesses.

Qualitative methods are strong for understanding the meanings people attach to their behavior, discovering new things about a phenomenon, and generating hypotheses; however, they are weak methods for testing hypotheses. On the other hand, quantitative methods are strong for testing hypotheses and generating new ones, but weak for understanding peoples' interpretations and discovering new insights. Research that uses a sequence of qualitative techniques to illuminate the phenomenon and the quantitative ones to test the generated hypotheses often offer the most supportable results. Research then is a process in which hypotheses are continuously tested, modified, and clarified (Sonnenstuhl & Trice, 1985).

In the process of selecting the appropriate research methodology for this study, we as researchers continually asked two questions. Which method(s) will (a) increase the validity, reliability, and generalizability of data generated, and (b) maximize the amount of useful data generated on the question? As a response to these questions, some researchers advocate combining methods. This idea is called triangulation (Denzin, 1978; Webb, Campbell, Schwartz, & Sechrest, 1966) and is similar to navigators taking several different citings in order to determine where they are. In so doing, researchers attempt to balance the inherent weaknesses and strengths of methods.

To address these points in the EAERP project we used several qualitative methods, including program histories, participant observations, and research interviews. This triangulation of methods insured that our emergent concepts and hypotheses would be valid. Later, these concepts were converted into a survey instrument in order to test the hypotheses statistically. This process of moving from qualitative field observations to instrument building and administration helped insure that the final data were both valid and reliable.

Throughout the project we used three investigators to collect and analyze the data. Such investigator triangulation insures that the data are reliable, because multiple researchers (i.e., similar instruments) listen to and observe the same phenomenon. This reduces potential biases that may be introduced inadvertently by an individual investigator.

Finally, as described earlier, we used data triangulation by collecting the data from four different EAP populations. The differences in these populations can be used to test the validity and reliability of the data. For example, validity could be tested by comparing the data obtained under similar circumstances, and reliability could be tested by comparing data obtained under different circumstances (Sonnenstuhl & Trice, 1985).

The constant comparative method (Glaser & Strauss, 1967) is used to analyze the data. This method is designed to develop rich descriptions of a social phenomenon, to make new discoveries about it, to generate hypotheses and theory about it, and to provisionally test those hypotheses and theory. The constant comparative method produces theory that practitioners can apply to their work prior to further rigorous testing. At the same time, survey researchers can easily adapt the theory for more rigorous testing (Sonnenstuhl & Trice, 1985).

USING THE FIELD RESEARCH INTERVIEW

Preparing to Enter the Field

Before we embarked on this study, it was first necessary that *we* became sufficiently socialized to the role of field researcher. This process was primarily accomplished during weekly meetings devoted to the development of research methodology, during which we discussed various details of the field research interview experience.

Several of our weekly research meetings were used as "dress rehearsals" for the field experience. Under the merciless scrutiny of the more seasoned members of our research team and, worse yet, a painfully honest video camera, team members took turns role playing the interview guidelines. In order to emulate a real-life interview within this artificial environment, it was emphatically stressed that no participating actor was to break role under any circumstances. If we broke role we were "just wasting time." So fully armed with tape recorder and interview guidelines, each researcher would alternately conduct an interview, act the part of the interviewee, and constructively observe and discuss the efforts of fellow team members.

The interview instrument itself was not a simple, structured survey; rather, it consisted of a series of open-ended guidelines designed to encourage research participants to elaborate on their ideas and experiences relative to EAPs. When administered, it could last from 30 minutes to 1-1/2 hours or longer, depending on the duration of the interviewee's EAP experience. The researcher's major role during the interview was to present the guidelines and—most importantly—to listen. The progression of the interview depended heavily on the content of the participant's responses. Often the nature of the interview was such that the guidelines were more logically explored out of sequence. As the interviewee addressed a guideline, it was the researcher's responsibility to probe for more information. It was also left to the researcher's discretion to decide when a guideline was fully exhausted and, subsequently, to introduce another guideline.

If the participant strayed from the pertinent areas of interest—as was often the case—the researcher had to learn to politely interrupt and refocus the conversation. However, since the purpose of this study was discovery, it was sometimes difficult to discern whether an interviewee was off the subject entirely or disclosing fresh insights. To manage this dilemma, researchers had to continually resolve the question, "What guideline am I on?" Unless the answer was "none," or time was running short, there was usually no need to interfere with the dialogue.

Through these repeated attempts at role playing, we as researchers were granted the opportunity to experience a variety of situations that could actually arise in the field and to develop strategies for handling these uncertainties. Without question, role playing proved to be an effective training exercise, as well as a tremendous confidence builder. When the time arrived to meet the "real-life" subject, the interview process was comfortable and familiar.

Finding the Sample

It was then time to find the sample and, once again, our communication skills came into play as we utilized the telephone. After using an elaborate process to select and track down the sample, we would then, we hoped, get our research subject on the phone. In our efforts to persuade our sample to participate, we employed persuasive strategies focusing on ethos, pathos, and logos. For example, after we introduced ourselves— emphasizing our affiliation with Cornell University and the New York State Division of Alcoholism and Alcohol Abuse (trust and credibility for this audience)—we'd generally explain the research program, its potential impact on the EAP field (logic), and how critically important their experiences and ideas relating to EAP were for the success of the study and the occupation (emotional appeal). The overall process of scheduling these interviews could also be compared in some respects to telesales. We were asking people to "buy" our interview: the cost was roughly one hour of their time. For some persons in our sample this was equivalent to over $100.00. Our job was to demonstrate that the benefits of our "product" were worth their investment. Beyond our Cornell business card and a thank you letter, there was little to offer the participant, so we appealed to their sense of compassion and dedication to the EAP field: "Your unique viewpoints and experiences are vitally important to furthering EAP education and research." That statement was worth its weight in gold.

A vital strategy for closing sales is to learn to anticipate objections. Though these objections did vary, we found several responses that were most effective in swaying the research subject to participate. "Your present occupation may not be directly related to EAP work, but some of our most valuable and innovative insights have come from people like you who are not directly in EAP work." It had the right appeal!

In order to accommodate the frenzied schedules and time shortages characteristic of many EAPers, flexibility was invaluable. Additionally, like good salespersons, we had to learn to "speak the many languages" of the broad range of occupational and professional groups we encountered. Though we avoided stereotyping any one particular group or occupation, we did need to quickly "read" the signals we were receiving from the setting and the interviewee and adjust our communication strategies appropriately. This influenced what we'd say and how we'd say it so that we could maximize our chances of gaining the participant's cooperation.

We also knew that one important way to gain cooperation from this particular sample was to show our respect for and application of confidentiality throughout the entire research process. Because we were taping the exchange, we had to deal with this question and concern immediately or we would (a) not get the interview, or (b) not get much out of the interview. In reality this must be a major issue for any researcher. In this case, elaborate measures were taken to secure these materials and maintain the anonymity of the interviewee.

Of course, letters of confirmation were sent to all interviewees reiterating all of the main points discussed thus far.

The Research Setting

As already noted, EAP workers and enthusiasts lurk in a wide variety of habitats. Needless to say, the setting not only tells a great amount about the organization and the circumstances of the EAP within the organization, but also decides how the interview will be conducted. Battered metal trailers in a Buffalo tire factory to plushly carpeted Madison Avenue suites offered unique challenges. But not all interviews were conducted at the interviewee's worksite. Sometimes "neutral locations" were selected such as hotel lobbies, a restaurant, or the participant's home. Generally, interviews conducted outside of a worksite took on a less formal, more relaxed air, and thus participants seemed to share more detailed and personal feelings. On the other hand, when interviews were conducted at the worksite, the "professional" work roles inserted themselves into the interview. Though neither type of setting necessarily gave us "better" information than the other, it did give us interesting insights into how people view their work, organization, and themselves within the worksite.

Administering and Adapting the Research Interview

After arriving at the interview site, checking the tape recorder, and sharing a handshake, the researcher once again needed to mentally consider what he or she knew about the interviewee and what "language" should be spoken. We began with a review of all the points presented during the phone interaction with a special emphasis on their importance to the project— their uniqueness. One of the most unpredictable portions of the interview process was this introductory phase—the time prior to the introduction of the first guideline. This was when tactfully gaining control of the conversation and establishing a working rapport with the participant was important. Depending on the participant, different strategies were applied to secure the researcher's role during the interview. Usually by the time codes and confidentiality were discussed and the tape recorder was tested, the interviewee was "all ears" and ready to cooperate. It was almost as though all this research jargon symbolized that they were engaged in "real" research—something unique and special. In fact, some became solemn, eager, and intent: They had been given a mission!

As noted, the tactical role adopted at each interview varied depending on the nature of the interviewee. Our core identity was always that of the scientific researcher. Yet, sometimes it was useful to become more of a student, especially with knowledgeable, talkative subjects who had a great deal to contribute. Naive, quiet, or insecure individuals required more guidance and direction on our part and responded better to an interviewer who acted more like an "EAP authority." There were those who had rather strong-willed and domineering personalities. They required a lot of guidance during the course of the discussion because they tended to stray in order to share their own pet theories or knowledge. A fairly effective strategy used with these subjects was to appear rather naive and ask a lot of simplistic questions in an effort to make sure they kept to their story and their ideas were focused.

Fortunately, these 278 interviews were conducted over a 3-year period of time by three researchers, because burn-out in this setting is rampant. The energy needed during the actual interview to listen, to choose the right role and "language" to guide the participant, to probe for more information as appropriate, to deal with the environment presented by the setting, and to maximize the time spent together to gather as much information as possible is enormous.

Analysis

During 1990-91, analysis of the data collected in EAERP was performed with the assistance of the mainframe qualitative research program, QUALOG. QUALOG was created under the basic assumption that the virtual memory and storage capacity of a mainframe computer can process many more megabytes of information than the memory of virtually any human being. The programs basic function is to efficiently organize, search, and sort coded data and memos generated during researcher analysis. Once researchers are relieved of these mechanical burdens, they are able to focus more clearly on conceptual tasks, which are the heart of qualitative research.

Based on initial results, several grounded theories developed. To test these theories a 20-page quantitative instrument was developed.

Subsequently shortened to 11 pages, this instrument was mailed to all of the EAERP research sample. Six weeks after the initial mailing, participants who had not yet returned their questionnaires were contacted by phone and mail to solicit participation. To date the response rate is running ahead of initial expectations. The research team believes that this level of participation is based on the interpersonal relationships established with the interviewers during the field research interview process. (Additional research on the validity of this belief might prove productive in the area of research methodology.)

SUMMARY

As one reviews the uses and benefits of the field research interview method, there are several additional points that should be considered.

First is the sociocultural framework in which (a) interviewers frame and ask questions, (b) respondents attempt to understand not only the questions but also their own experiences, (c) respondents attempt to structure coherent answers, and (d) researchers interpret the responses (verbal and nonverbal). As our awareness, appreciation, and sensitivity to issues of human diversity expands, questions of reliability and validity may need to be reviewed and research methodology and data analysis adapted to give enlightened insights into human interaction.

Second is empowerment of the respondent through the interview process. Because all communication has consequences, the field research interview by form and content is not "neutral." The interview is a powerful tool by which the researcher can view humanity and create opportunities for growth and change in the interviewee. Yet, we as researchers have done little to make the research event an opportunity for interviewees to move beyond their story to useful action (Mishler, 1986). To enact this kind of change, the research setting must be viewed as one in which the interviewer and interviewee are equals and where each can be changed through meaningful discourse.

As more researchers enact qualitative research and utilize the field research interview approach, methods for assessing and evaluating the adequacy of particular studies will be developed. Questions about the objectivity, reliability, validity, and replicability of findings—the standard issues of scientific research—will continue to be asked, but answers will take a form appropriate to the methods applied to the research question versus the mainstream model (Mishler, 1986). It will be in this environment that analysis and theory generation will become reflective of the human discourse on which it is built.

REFERENCES

Best, J. W., & Kahn, J. V. (1986). *Research in education.* Englewood Cliffs, NJ: Prentice-Hall.

Beyer, J. M., & Trice, H. M. (1988). The communication of power relations in organizations through cultural rites. In M. Jones, M. Moore, & R. Snyder (Eds.), *Inside organization: Understanding the human dimension* (pp. 141-157). Beverly Hills, CA: Sage Publications

Denzin, K. (1978). *The research act.* Chicago, IL: Aldine Publishing Company.

Geertz, C. (1973). *The interpretation of cultures.* New York: Basic Books.

Glaser, B. G., & Strauss, A. L. (1967). *The discovery of grounded theory strategies for qualitative research.* Chicago, IL: Aldine Publishing Company.

Hathaway, B. L., Mason, S. A., & Sonnenstuhl, W. J. (1989). Inside EAPs: View from the New York State Thruway. *Journal of Drug Issues, 19*(4), 473-487.

Mishler, E. G. (1986). *Research interviewing: Context and narrative.* Cambridge, MA: Harvard University Press.

Sonnenstuhl, W. J., & Trice, H. M. (1985). What is EAP? The place of qualitative and quantitative research in understanding programs. *EAP Annual Review, 2,* 93-109.

Trice, H. M., & Beyer, J. M. (1984). Work related outcomes of the constructive confrontation strategy in a job-based alcoholism program. *Journal of Studies on Alcoholism, 45,* 393-404.

Webb, E. T., Campbell, R. D., & Schwartz, L. S., Sechrest, L. (1966). *Unobtrusive measures.* Chicago, IL: Rand McNally and Co.

Whyte, W. F. (1960). Interviewing in field research. In R. N. Adams & J. J. Preiss (Eds.), *Human organization research, field relations and techniques.* Homewood, IL: The Dorsey Press.

■ 4

Using Focus Group Interviews for Preliminary Investigation

Sandra L. Herndon
Ithaca College
Ithaca, NY

■ *Identifying their strengths and limitations, Sandra Herndon defines and describes focus group interviews, a qualitative research method only recently utilized in organizational communication research. She then illustrates their utility as a tool for preliminary investigation in an organizational research project, followed by practical considerations for their use.*

INTRODUCTION

Focus group interviews have derived their current popularity from marketing research where they are used to obtain information regarding attitudes or behaviors toward concepts, products, or services (Greenbaum, 1988). Although there has been considerable description of their use in marketing research, relatively little has been written about focus groups as a tool for qualitative research in the social sciences.

The purposes of this chapter are (a) to define and describe focus group interviews, identifying and assessing their strengths and limitations as a research tool in organizational communication; (b) to illustrate the use of focus group interviews in an organizational research project; and (c) to suggest some practical considerations when using focus group interviews in organizational research.

DEFINITION AND DESCRIPTION

Because focus groups are often described as group interviews (Morgan,

An earlier version of this chapter was presented at the annual convention of the Eastern Communication Association, Philadelphia, PA, April 1990

1988), they must be distinguished both from a traditional interview format and from group interaction in general. Greenbaum (1988) identifies four distinguishing characteristics of focus groups: multiple respondents performing together, interaction of participants, presence of a moderator, and a discussion outline. Typically, a focus group interview consists of five to ten people who, with a moderator (who may also be the researcher), discuss a series of topics or questions prepared by the researcher for no more than two hours in order to provide information and insights useful to the researcher. Thus, focus groups rely primarily on member interaction rather than on the question-and-answer format usually associated with an interview; they are, however, more "focused" than a casual or spontaneous group interaction; hence, the name. In identifying focus group interviewing as a specific technique within the category of group interviewing, Morgan (1988) argues that the "hallmark of focus groups is *the explicit use of the group interaction to produce data and insights that would be less accessible without the interaction found in a group"* (p. 12, emphasis in original).

Fern (1982) identified three dimensions along which focus groups vary: size of group, moderated vs. unmoderated, and strangers vs. acquaintances as participants. In comparing and evaluating focus groups along these dimensions, he found that the quantity of the produced ideas did not double nor did their quality become superior when the group size increased from four to eight. Further, while it can be argued that moderated groups are preferable to unmoderated and groups of strangers preferable to groups of acquaintances, the differences were not significant. Flexibility thus seems to be an attractive characteristic of focus groups.

Calder (1977) classified focus groups according to the type of information or knowledge being researched. Exploratory groups are used to generate hypotheses; clinical groups offer insights into the unconscious motivations of participants; and phenomenological groups provide access to the participants' perceptions and experiences. Therefore, focus group interviews can be categorized on the basis of researcher intent and purpose which determines both the way the group is conducted as well as the way the data are interpreted.

In organizational communication research, focus group interviews may provide useful information in and of themselves and may also be used in triangulation with other methods of research, both quantitative and qualitative.

Because focus group interviews provide access to more subjective data when used in conjunction with quantitative methods (conducted either before or after) such as surveys or experiments, it is evident that focus groups add validity to such research. However, conventional wisdom assumes that the findings of focus group research must be reinforced by quantitative research in order to be valid. Calder (1977) argues, to the contrary, that focus group research is not necessarily provisional and indeed can stand alone.

Focus group interviews used in triangulation with another qualitative method, such as individual interviews or participant observation, may provide information otherwise inaccessible. Relying on verbal self-reports, focus group interviews, like individual interviews, are better suited to topics of attitudes and cognitions (Morgan, 1988). More structured and less spontaneous than participant observation, focus groups are less structured and more spontaneous than individual interviews. Consequently, the researcher maintains more control than in participant observation, but less than in individual interviews.

Additionally, focus group interviews offer a synergistic output, rather than a sum of individual interviews, which might never emerge in the one-to-one setting (Lederman, 1990). Circumstances may suggest the desirability of a particular technique. For example, if access to an organization is rather tightly controlled, participation observation may not be an available choice for the researcher. Although noted for their flexibility, focus group interviews are not well suited for highly controversial topics nor for studies of roles and organizations per se (Morgan, 1988).

Finally, as a research tool, focus group interviews require less time, and therefore potentially less cost, than either participant observation or extended interviews. Focus groups have the advantage of allowing the opportunity for participation among individuals in the safety of a group (McCracken, 1988) and thus permit the researcher to observe a great deal of group interaction in a limited time period.

One important use of focus group interviews is in preliminary investigation to provide the basis for extended individual interviews, allowing the researcher the opportunity to devise an interview schedule grounded in participant understanding of the topic (Morgan & Spanish, 1984). Such a use is described below.

FOCUS GROUP INTERVIEWS: AN ILLUSTRATION

With the help of a research assistant, I investigated a Fortune 500 company ("SCIENCETECH") in upstate New York that was attempting to diversify its managerial ranks in response to demographic changes and predictions, with its initial efforts limited to "women and blacks" (Fish, 1991). The goals of the study were (a) to examine the communication strategies and tactics utilized by SCIENCETECH in developing and implementing its diversity process; (b) to describe organizational members' responses to the process during implementation; and (c) to suggest some relationships between organizational culture and leadership, based on the findings of this research.

There were three primary avenues for gathering information. First, and throughout the study, I reviewed relevant documented material to become as fully acquainted as possible with the publicly stated purposes and plans regarding the diversity effort in order to guide my question formation.

Second, a series of five 2-hour confidential focus group interviews were conducted (and audio-recorded for researchers' use only) to gather a wide range of perceptions on the diversity effort held by members of management levels of SCIENCETECH.

Third, a series of 32 extended, confidential, individual interviews were conducted (and audio-recorded for researchers' use only) with individuals ranging from middle management through the CEO, chosen from various divisions of the company.

A principal use of focus group interviews in this research project was to serve as preliminary investigation on which to base the extended interview questions. The five focus groups varied in size from six to nine individuals from various parts of the company. In order to encourage open discussion, they were segregated by race and gender in the following manner: one group of blacks (male and female), two groups of white females, and two groups of white males, totaling 37 people. Because of the sensitive nature of the topic—workplace diversity aimed at women and blacks—we felt that the groups should be separated first by race, then by gender. The group of blacks had seven males and one female; only one group of blacks was used primarily because of the very low numbers of blacks in the company at managerial levels. The remaining four groups were all white and segregated by gender. On the basis of Fern's (1982) dimensions, these groups varied slightly in size, were composed of potential acquaintances, and were led by a moderator.

Based on a review of the documented material, I provided a skeleton framework of open-ended questions for the groups to discuss. After being introduced by the Director of Human Resource Planning and Development who had made arrangements for the groups (and who then left the room), I served as moderator for each group. Assuring the group of the confidentiality of the proceedings and securing permission to audiotape the session, I then guided the group through a 2-hour loosely structured discussion of the diversity process as currently being implemented by SCIENCETECH. While my presence as visibly white and female could have been a potential hindrance to discussion, the fact that I was identified as an outsider with considerable interest but no personal stake in the process could have counteracted this drawback. Vigorous, sustained discussion ensued in all groups.

The focus group interviews provided two outcomes which aided in the construction and refinement of the questions for the extended interviews. First, they offered an extensive overview of the issues surrounding the diversity process at SCIENCETECH. The fullness of the discussions and the richness of detail as stimulated by the interaction of those closest to the process could not have been achieved as well in another format. Second, the discussions provided considerable specificity of information regarding matters unique to SCIENCETECH and its diversity issues and problems that significantly aided in the interview process. On the basis of Calder's (1977) classification, these groups would be categorized as phenomenological, providing access to participants' perspectives and experiences.

Overall, the focus group and individual interviews yielded approximately 55 hours of confidential audio-recording that served as primary data. I listened carefully and thoroughly to each recorded interview and took extensive notes, retaining the recording for reference. The focus group interviews were organized around a series of open-ended questions, the responses to which were categorized to identify themes. Each of the five groups initiated virtually identical theme issues in response to the questions with illustrations varying by group. These theme issues then served as a guide for the construction of the probe questions in the individual interviews (which followed the same basic outline as the focus group interviews). The individual interviews were analyzed and thematized in the same manner as the focus group interviews. The result was a series of summary statements which attempted to capture the sense of the interviewees' meanings regarding the diversity effort at SCIENCETECH. Research of the type undertaken here does not produce quantitative outcomes, but rather results in "thick," intensive data that illuminate the meanings the participants ascribe to their own experience.

Ideally, focus group interviews should be conducted early in the research project in order to guide construction of the interview questions. Morgan (1988) argues that this process is most useful when the subject or the population to be researched has not been significantly studied, a condition operating in this research project, which was focused on the current implementation of an organizational plan for increased diversification of the workplace. The use of focus group interviews for preliminary investigation at SCIENCETECH to aid in the construction and refinement of the extended interview questions proved highly valuable.

PRACTICAL CONSIDERATIONS

There are a number of practical considerations when using focus group interviews in organizational research. The first decision, of course, is whether to use them at all. If the subject under discussion is of such a nature that participants do not feel comfortable disclosing their views in a group, then focus groups should be avoided (Morgan, 1988). Further, ample time must be available for both the researcher (to prepare for, conduct, and analyze the groups) and the participants (to schedule and participate in the group interaction) in order for focus groups to be of value. For example, it took several weeks of logistical arrangements to organize the focus groups at SCIENCETECH, even after all initial permissions and approvals had been granted. Following the conduct of the focus groups, time had to be allowed for analysis of the interaction in order to construct the interview schedule and to arrange the interviews.

A further determining factor may be cost. In organizational terms, time is money; consequently, not only is there a potential cost for the researcher for such items as travel, space, and equipment, but also the "lost time" of participants may be a cost for management.

The source of participants is a major consideration. If a study is conducted within an organization, it is inevitable that some participants will know one another, and possibly the moderator(s) as well, raising questions of confidentiality as discussed below. Other factors, which will depend on the nature of the research topic, include participants' gender, race, rank, area of expertise, manner of selection, and so on. Segregation by these or other factors may be advisable if it will promote open interaction. For example, I successfully segregated by race and gender in order to reduce inhibitions in a discussion of workplace diversity.

Choice of moderator is important. Ideally, a focus group moderator is an individual who can identify with the participants and gently guide a group in discussing a topic. Group process skill and experience is essential. While Fern (1982) suggests that it is possible to conduct a focus group with no moderator, the resulting lack of structure is likely to reduce its usefulness for research purposes.

Number and size of groups must be determined in advance. While there are no definitive parameters, more than one group is virtually always warranted; Calder (1977) suggests that groups, usually three or four, should be continued until the moderator can predict or anticipate what will be said. Size of group can vary, typically from 5 to 12 members, with ease of interaction the primary criterion. A specific commitment from each participant in advance will ensure the likelihood of having a functional group.

Finally, the potential problem of confidentiality in focus group interviews deserves consideration. Especially in a research project on a sensitive topic involving individuals who work in proximity to one another, confidentiality must be emphasized if genuinely open interaction is to be achieved. Ensuring confidentiality in such situations relies not merely on the ethical stance of the researcher, but also on the behaviors of other participants who are not under the researcher's control. There is, however, generally less inhibition in group interaction than in individual interviews because of the presumed protection of numbers.

The issue of confidentiality is highlighted by the virtual necessity of tape recording the proceedings. Emphasis by the moderator of the significance of confidentiality, combined with a written statement by the researcher outlining the specific uses of the data gathered, is helpful in alleviating the problem of researcher confidentiality.

Overall, focus group interviews provide no more practical or logistical problems than many other research techniques. However, it is important that these issues be identified and addressed before the research takes place.

CONCLUSION

Despite its history in marketing research, the focus group interview is a qualitative research technique with relatively little use or examination but considerable potential utility in organizational communication research. Whether conducted in triangulation with other methods (quantitative or qualitative) or as an independent research project, focus group interviews offer a unique vantage point from which to study the perspectives and experiences of organizational members via their interaction.

REFERENCES

Calder, B. J. (1977). Focus groups and the nature of qualitative marketing research. *Journal of Marketing Research, 14,* 353-364.

Fern, E. F. (1982). The use of focus groups for idea generation: The effects of group size, acquaintanceship, and moderator on response quantity and quality. *Journal of Marketing Research, 19,* 1-13.

Fish, S. L. (1991). Preparation for the year 2000: One corporation's attempt to address the issues of gender and race. *The Howard Journal of Communications, 3,* 61-72.

Greenbaum, T. L. (1988). *The practical handbook and guide to focus group research.* Lexington, MA: Lexington Books.

Lederman, L. C. (1990, April). Assessing educational effectiveness: The focus group interview as a technique for data collection. *Communication Education, 39*(2), 117-127.

McCracken, G. (1988). *The long interview* (Qualitative Research Methods Series 13). Newbury Park, CA: Sage.

Morgan, D. L. (1988). *Focus groups as qualitative research* (Qualitative Research Methods Series 16). Newbury Park, CA: Sage.

Morgan D. L., & Spanish, M. T. (1984). Focus groups: A new tool for qualitative research. *Qualitative Sociology, 7,* 253-270.

■ 5

Narrative Analysis and Organizational Development

Mary Helen Brown
Auburn University
Auburn, AL

Gary L. Kreps
Northern Illinois University
DeKalb, IL

■ *Using the narrative paradigm, Mary Helen Brown and Gary Kreps apply the use of organizational stories to organizational development efforts. They then describe creative narratives which present factual content through fiction-writing techniques. Methods of collecting stories and a model for their use provide the basis for narrative analysis in OD consultation.*

Organizational development(OD) is a renewal and change effort planned (usually organization-wide and managed from the top of the organization) to increase effectiveness through the implementation of interventions in organizational activities directed from insights provided by rigorously gathered data (Beckhard, 1969). An OD effort involves a systematic diagnosis of the specific problems and constraints facing an organization, the development of strategic plans for helping the organization effectively address the problems diagnosed, the mobilization of resources to carry out the intervention strategies, as well as evaluation of the short and long-term influence of interventions on organizational performance. In this chapter we describe how narrative analysis can guide OD efforts by facilitating the discovery and examination of relevant information (organizational intelligence) held by key organizational actors (members, stakeholders, consumers, and representatives of relevant organizational environments) to identify impending organizational constraints and opportunities. Organizational development specialists can also use specific stories to develop creative narratives to examine organizations. In this way, creative narratives can act as evidence establishing the need for change, as a training device, and as a tool for measuring change.

STORIES, REFLEXIVITY, AND ORGANIZATIONAL DEVELOPMENT

The interpretation of organizational stories is a particularly effective data-gathering strategy for promoting organizational development (Kreps, 1989). Weick (1979) describes the organizing process as adaptation to equivocal situations. Stories reduce the equivocality (complexity, ambiguity, unpredictability) of organizational life, helping organizational actors interpret and respond to equivocal situations by providing organizational intelligence (Brown, 1990; Kreps, 1990a; Weick, 1979). Organizational intelligence develops from retention of key information about how the organization has responded in the past (Kreps, 1990a; Weick, 1979). Every time members cope with a unique situation they learn something new about how to organize. Rather than responding to every situation as though it were unique, in effect "reinventing the wheel," members can utilize information gained from past organizational experiences and stored in organizational intelligence (Kreps, 1990c). Stories about organizational triumphs and failures give members insight into how problems have been dealt with in the past, providing information about how they can effectively respond to present situations.

OD efforts depend on relevant information about changing environmental constraints on activities and products to develop adaptive intervention strategies (Nadler, 1977). Story analysis can be used to gather organizational intelligence from members and relevant others about the nature and seriousness of organizational performance gaps (Kreps, 1990a). By providing decision makers with information about organizational difficulties generated from narrative analysis, OD specialists can enhance organizational reflexivity (the ability of key members to see clearly the current state of the organization) and guide successful organizational interventions (Kreps, 1990b; Rowe & Boise, 1973). Increased reflexivity helps organization leaders assess the adequacy of organizing processes, detect the need for innovating organizational activities, and direct the development and implementation of innovation strategies for promoting ongoing organizational development (Kreps, 1989).

THE POWER OF STORIES

Stories hold great promise as a tool in the organizational development process. Stories enable practitioners to identify points of concern, points of stagnation, and points of promise. Stories act as a vehicle through which members can offer definitions and explanations of their worklife. Stories serve as a communicative format that is, at once, concrete, memorable, and persuasive. Stories can also be adapted to show how differing outcomes could result from changes in organizational policy, behavior, or structure (Kreps, 1990a).

Stories are a powerful communication form. In a series of essays, Fisher (1984, 1985a, 1985b, 1987, 1989) advances the narrative as a paradigm for communication. Individuals act as story-generating and story-interpreting creatures. People organize and recreate their experiences through stories. In this view, organizational members are characters, and events are elements in a plot. Fisher (1989) argues that the narrative paradigm presents "an approach to interpretation and assessment of human communication—assuming that all forms of human communication can be seen fundamentally as stories, as interpretations of aspects of the world occurring in time and shaped by history, culture, and character" (p. 57).

Stories act as a metacode transmitting shared meanings (White, 1981). The meanings and values present in a particular situation can be apprehended and presented through stories (Scholes, 1981). In this way, stories establish definitional boundaries through which members judge and understand the situation at hand. These boundaries are most effective and efficient when exhibiting narrative fidelity, the sense that the story rings true, and narrative probability, the coherence of the story (Fisher, 1984). Also, boundaries are most influential when a story directs the audience toward understanding of a specific issue (Lucaites & Condit, 1985).

Stories are particularly important communication devices in organizations. Martin (1982) points out that all members hear and tell stories, while Brown (1990) argues that organizational stories function to reduce uncertainty, manage meaning, and promote bonding and identification among members. From this perspective, organizational stories have meanings beyond the words exchanged around the water cooler, in the break room, along the line, and in the board room.

Of course, stories transmit meaning. But stories also persuade, reinforce, define, and educate (Georges, 1987). Further, stories grow from and present different organizational value sets, steering members and decision makers toward a particular view of the organization (Kreps, 1983). Thus, the same sequence of events may serve as the foundation of a variety of stories reflecting the differing value sets present in the organization (Scholes, 1981).

Stories are subject to developmental changes and changes in interpretation resulting from differences in participants and perspectives (Farrell, 1985). Thus, a certain story about a series of events may become "the truth" for one group, while a second, different story about the same set of circumstances may reflect that group's reality.

For example, consider the following stories about the same event. The first story relates the incident from the management's perspective. The second presents the episode from the worker's perspective.

Story A

All of them [employees] can be trouble sometimes, but there's this one, Carol [all names changed] who makes me nuts. In the first place, we made an exception in just hiring her for the position. She worked in another department, and when this job came open she went in and sweet talked the big boss, and now my department is stuck with her even though none of us wanted her.

Anyway, she came into my office the other day wanting us to let her work overtime the next month so she could have an extra two weeks of vacation. I told her that it wouldn't be possible. In our department [communications] we aren't hourly workers anyway, so there's no such thing as overtime. We work overtime almost every day.

So she started telling me that Pat, a supervisor in her old department, said that I could write a letter to personnel and payroll explaining that Carol was going to be working extra hours to extend her vacation. I pointed out that Pat's department was paid on an hourly basis and that ours wasn't and that our policies weren't the same. Then Carol started in again that I could write that letter. I kept saying "no," and she kept telling me I could write the letter.

I finally figured out that she thought I thought I couldn't write a letter. So I told her I could write a letter, I just wasn't going to write the letter. Somewhere in the midst of all of this it came out that she wanted the extra two weeks because she was—get this—getting married and going on a month-long honeymoon. She hadn't even been in the department. I guess she thought that me being a woman would make me more open to a romantic excuse.

Anyhow, she kept on talking until I got fed up and got ugly. I finally said, "Carol, which part of my answer did you not understand? The N or the O?" She stuck out her lip and stomped off toward my boss's office. I'll probably hear about it later, but I swear some of our people are completely clueless, and you just have to get tough with them.

Story B

Our upper-level managers are really not very flexible. We had this one girl, Carol, who needed some time off for personal reasons. It was really important to her. She went in to talk to Sue, her supervisor, about making arrangements to work extra time in exchange for a few days of extra vacation.

Carol said that Pat used to let them do that all the time, but Pat's cool because she came up from the bottom and Sue has always been in management. Carol said she tried and tried to explain that it was important and that all the other departments would make an exception but that Sue wouldn't listen to reason.

She said Sue finally got real snotty with her and gave her a smartass answer trying to make Carol feel stupid. Carol said she thought about taking it to the grievance office, but that usually doesn't work because all of them back each other up.

SAME CIRCUMSTANCES, DIFFERENT INTERPRETATIONS

From management's perspective, a questionable employee is making an unreasonable demand that violates standard operating procedure. The employee was seen as not understanding her role in her department and as not understanding the reasons she was given for the denial of this privilege. The manager indicated that because normal explanations were not working in this case, it was necessary to resort to blunt tactics.

On the other hand, the worker in Story B presents the same episode in a them vs. us format. Carol is seen as making a reasonable request for a justifiable exception to standard policies. Sue is seen as being unresponsive and inflexible to the point of being rude. The story concludes with the notion that fighting the system is, for all practical purposes, impossible because a sort of managerial conspiracy exists to keep workers in their place.

COLLECTING THE ORGANIZATIONAL STORIES

The first step in this process is to gather the specific stories used as the basis for OD efforts. Stories should be collected from all levels of the focal organization. Stories should not be confined to those told by managers. All members of the organization use stories to present their values and inter-pretations of their life at work (Deal & Kennedy, 1983; Myrsiadis, 1987), and story use is widespread throughout the organization (Morgan, 1986).

Observations of contradictory storylines such as those expressed in Stories A and B above are just as valuable, if not more so, as observations of consistent storylines to the organizational development specialist (Reimann & Wiener, 1988; Riley, 1983). These conflicting storylines are likely spots to examine in searching for overall differences in value sets among organizational members.

Stories can be captured in two ways. First, focus interviews can be conducted with members of the organization. These interviews should concentrate on problem areas identified by the organization's leadership and areas which have traditionally been seen as likely sources of conflict. Likely areas for examination include: conflict, job satisfaction, organiza-tional assets (equipment, salary, working conditions, etc.), and superior/subordinate relationships, to name a few.

An alternative method involves participant/observation tech-niques. Here, the researcher becomes involved in the workplace, and rather than relying on interview techniques, gathers stories that arise in the course of everyday conversation on the job. For example, the researcher might spend time with workers in their break room or with management in meetings to assess the stories they tell.

Since individuals are surrounded by stories most of their lives, recognizing stories in the workplace is a relatively simple, almost natural task. Stories are discrete, narrative episodes relating a sequence of events (McLaughlin, 1984). In the workplace, these episodes provide examples and evidence of organizational functioning. The actual structure of a story consists of three major elements.

First, the preface serves as a transition between the story and the talk immediately preceding it (Jefferson, 1978). The preface indicates the significance of the story and its relevance. The second section, the recounting, is usually the longest part of the story. In it, the setting, back-ground information, the sequence of events, and the outcome of those events are presented (Goodwin, 1984; McLaughlin, 1984). In the closing some indication is made that the story has been completed and/or the relevance or moral of the story is established.

For example, in Story A above, the preface connects between the topic—troublesome employees—and the episode. The recounting sequence presents background information—Carol's employment histo-ry, normal vacation policy, and so on—and the sequence of events that took place. The closing presents the end of the story and an overall con-clusion—"some workers only respond to blunt directives" and a moral—"at times, managers have to be tough."

OD AND THE THERAPEUTIC MODEL OF CONSULTATION

Kreps (1989) describes a therapeutic model of organizational communication consultation that can be used to direct OD efforts. This model has six successive cyclic phases:

1. *Collaboration*, in which the OD specialist/researcher and representatives of the organization develop a cooperative plan to examine and solve troublesome organizational problems (Kreps, 1989; Schein, 1969, 1987). By building a cooperative relationship with organization members, the researcher can limit resistance and gain support for OD efforts.
2. *Data-Gathering*, in which narrative research is conducted to gather relevant organizational stories from individuals representing different areas and levels of the organization, as well as from members of organizations' relevant environments. These stories enable the researcher to identify and examine different problems confronting the organization.
3. *Feedback and Diagnosis*, in which the narratives gathered are described to representatives of the organization and jointly interpreted by the researcher and organization members. The stories gathered should provide organization members with salient information about environmental changes and constraints, as well as information about internal organizational conditions to guide organizational innovation, increasing organizational reflexivity (Kreps, 1990b).
4. *Intervention Planning*, in which the researcher and organizational representatives jointly plan strategies for resolving organizational problems by applying data generated through narrative analysis to the development of interventions. By cooperatively evaluating strategies to address the underlying issues causing difficulties, the researcher and organizational decision makers can develop realistic plans for organizational intervention. The organizational representatives know what has been used in the past and what kinds of interventions are likely to work well in their particular organization.
5. *Intervention Implementation*, in which the intervention strategies that were planned are put into action within the organization. The researcher works closely with the organization in bringing intervention plans to life, helping to direct implementation of the intervention strategies. Care must be taken to inform and involve all members of the organization in implementing any innovations to reduce the natural resistance many organization

members may have to changing their job rituals.

6. *Intervention Evaluation*, in which evaluation data are gathered about the impact of the intervention on the organization to identify the effectiveness of the innovations implemented. Data should be gathered about the short-and long-term effectiveness of organizational interventions so that interventions can be refined. Since the intervention evaluation phase often facilitates recognition of new and potential performance gaps, it can bring the researcher and the organization back full cycle to the first phase of the therapeutic model—collaboration—by introducing new issues for examination.

This model of OD should be interpreted as if it were a flow chart, with each phase leading successively to the next phase. The last of the six phases—intervention evaluation—eventually leads back to the first phase. The cyclic nature of the model illustrates the perpetual need for innovation in organizational life. (See Figure 1 for a depiction of the Therapeutic Model of Consultation.)

1.	Collaboration
2.	Data Gathering
3.	Feedback and Diagnosis
4.	Intervention Planning
5.	Intervention Implementation
6.	Intervention Evaluation

Figure 1. The Therapeutic Model of Consultation.

THE CREATIVE NARRATIVE AS ORGANIZATIONAL EXEMPLAR

Elements of the specific organizational stories gathered form the basis of creative organizational narratives. A creative narrative blends the actual dialogue told in specific stories to form a composite, interpretive narrative that relates an impressionistic account of the concept under investigation (Brown & McMillan, 1991). Creative narratives can be used in several ways in OD efforts.

Van Maanen (1988) points out that this sort of interactionist/impressionist story presents facts and speculations in a nonanalytic narrative, allowing readers to analyze a particular situation. To accomplish this task, Van Maanen (1990) proposes that techniques associated with

fiction writing can be used to create nonfiction "texts" representing a culture or its component parts. In this way, as Gergen and Gergen (1986) note,
the reader or the audience determine a narrative's meaning.

The use of a narrative of this sort enables members to see or hear
different interpretations of the same set of circumstances. For example,
managers might be presented with a form of the line workers' interpretation of the incident above. The possibility exists that the organization's
leadership might not "see" the other side of the story. The contrary may
also be true. Staff members might not realize the position the manager
felt she was forced to use.

The use of interpretive narrative to report events has its roots in
journalism and literature. This type of writing acknowledges that capturing the essence of events as perceived by participants was impossible using
the techniques of traditional journalism. In much the same way, standard
forms of research have been found lacking in capturing the depth of cultural systems. The evidence, or data, is simply too rich for standard, for-
mulaic methods that are traditionally employed in these settings (Boylan,
1984; Weber, 1974).

Thus, an interpretive narrative acts as an effective method of
relating the "essence of living better than analysis, or reporting" (Kramer,
1981, p. 331). Templeton and Groce (1990) point out that interpretive
narrative more accurately reflects the way in which inhabitants understand their world than do traditional techniques which Hellmann (1981)
claims make a setting and its subjects seem strange or unreal. For example, it seems likely that organizational members would see the stories
above as more compelling evidence of the presence of contradictory values than the results of a survey on superior-subordinate communication.

In this way, stories bring evidence to life. After all, as Martin and
Powers (1983) point out, stories have more impact than statistics; further,
organizational members perceive policy statements as being more credi-
ble when supported by stories. This notion is echoed by Agar (1990) who
states that the "friction caused by the blend of documentary report and
fiction exposed a nerve—credibility" (p. 75).

CHARACTERISTICS OF THE CREATIVE NARRATIVE

In general, a creative narrative communicates factual content through techniques associated with fiction writing. Agar (1990) claims that four major
elements are necessary for the creation of an effective creative narrative.

First, the narrative must relate the story's scenic frame. The writer
reports events in a manner which allows readers to sense the emotions of
the setting and its physical characteristics—its smells, sights, sounds, and

so on. These contextual elements form the foundation of the story. This foundation frames the narrative and relates to readers the sort of story being told and how it should be interpreted (Babcock, 1977). Thus, the presentation of a creative narrative about an organization requires that the organizational development should reveal elements from the life world of the members.

Second, the use of plotting devices is a critical aspect of the creative narrative. Among the devices available for use are asides, flashbacks, and foreshadowing. The writer should be concerned with building dramatic tension to attract and hold the audience's attention.

In developing the narrative's plot, the writer must be aware that real time need not necessarily match "story" time. As Chatman (1981) concludes, "all narratives, in whatever medium, combine the time sequence of plot events, the time of the historic ('story-time') with the time of the presentation of those events in the text" (p. 118). As such, elements from the individual stories are sorted and assigned to characters according to their dramatic or sense-making potential and their potential to reveal organizational reality rather than according to their strict historical occurrence.

A third characteristic is character development. The narrative is presented through the actions and words of a few "rounded" characters, with other characters entering and exiting the focal character's world. "Internal monologues" representing a character's thought processes may also be used as a scripting device.

Thus, a few characters "speak" the words of many. Elements from individual stories form the basis of the dialogues presented in the narrative. No discussion of hierarchy is necessary when a character reports on a situation from his, or her own organizational level. On the other hand, when a character reports on an issue raised by a respondent at another level, the statement should be attributed to another character not directly in the narrative occupying the accurate hierarchical level.

For example, in constructing characters and dialogue from the stories above (and other stories about the same incident), a manager might report the feelings expressed by a staff member at another level, "I was talking with Sally the other day. She used to work with Carol, and she said that Carol was always looking for a break." Thus, the manager reports what a staff member says by attributing the information to a former co-worker.

Fourth, the authorial presence is housed in a creative narrative; the author is part of the story. As Agar (1990) notes, "he or she is . . . the force that makes coherent meaning through skillful rendering of the details, a coherent meaning" (p. 78). This position acknowledges that absolute objectivity is neither expected nor required in this process (Hersey, 1990).

Weber (1974) could just as easily be addressing researchers as well as reporters when writing, "to deny the shaping presence of the reporter because of the theoretical demands of detachment and objectivity is to be fundamentally dishonest with the reader as well as oneself" (p. 18). Therefore in composing a creative narrative to be used as a tool in organizational development, the specialist recognizes that his or her presence shapes the text and also hopes that this presence clarifies, rather than distorts, the experiences of the organization's members.

This philosophy is not without precedent in conducting organizational studies. For example, Goodall (1989) presents detective stories to examine clues underlying organizational cultures. Also, Pacanowsky (1988) uses fiction-writing techniques to present the culture he encounters. These sorts of narratives act as "realistic fiction" through which the author strives "to commit equally to artistic and empirical truth" (Agar, 1990, p. 77).

Sims (1984) adds to Agar's characteristics by pointing out that the development of creative narrative also requires accuracy, the truthful reporting of events, responsibility, and consideration of the effect of the narrative on others. In the approach outlined here, the correct reporting of elements from members' specific stories should preserve the accuracy of their comments and feelings. In this way, their reality is given a fair presentation. Further, by combining elements from the stories told by a variety of members into the "voices" of a few fictitious characters, the rights of subjects are protected by masking their identities.

Further, once the narrative is complete, it should be checked for the accuracy of the dialogue obtained through examinations of the specific stories. Also, the story should be examined by selected organizational members to make sure that it "rings true"; that is, the story should make sense in the organizational context. The utility of the story as an organizational development tool depends on the extent to which it matches members' perceptions of their workplace (Weick & Browning, 1986). If these actions are taken, the value of the creative narrative is enhanced. These creative narratives offer an effective way to present organizational information through a method that is meaningful to the membership and outside observers.

USING NARRATIVE ANALYSIS TO GUIDE OD

An OD study was conducted to gather information about public perceptions and attitudes toward an under-utilized, residential, adolescent, substance-abuse rehabilitation program in a large midwestern city, as well as to identify strategies for increasing public acceptance and support for the program (Kreps, 1988). Three groups of parents participated in this research program: (a) parents with children who had already completed treatment at the program; (b) parents with children who were currently in treatment at the program; and (c) representative parents with children who were within the *potential* age range and geographic region served by the program. Focus group discussions were held with each of these three groups of parents to gather stories about their key experiences, ideas, and concerns about the specific programs and services offered by the program, and to describe the parents' more general beliefs and values about adolescent substance-abuse, substance abuse treatment, and sources of information about treatment and support.

In the focus group discussions, parents were encouraged to discuss as openly as possible their ideas and experiences concerning adolescent substance abuse and treatment. Each of the three focus group discussions was audiotaped to preserve the stories generated for in-depth analysis. The audiotapes were transcribed and content-analyzed. Through content analysis the data were arranged into primary content themes concerning parents' specific impressions of and experiences with the program and their general experiences and ideas about adolescent substance abuse and treatment. Parents often told stories about their experiences. The stories were used to identify specific strengths and weaknesses within the program and to direct future marketing, education, and public relations efforts.

The data gathered in this research program increased organizational reflexivity by helping program administrators understand the experiences, ideas, and concerns of their customers. The parents were able to provide the program administrators with organizational intelligence about which elements of the program worked most effectively and which worked least effectively. These data led to the development of several strategic interventions and revisions within the organization and to new marketing and public education strategies. Evaluation data indicated that the organizational interventions have helped the program to address many of the concerns the parents expressed, to provide parents with relevant information about substance abuse, and to increase the effectiveness of public relations efforts (Kreps, 1988).

For example, a story recounted by a parent in the potential treatment group demonstrating concern about identifying substance-abuse behavioral warning signals illustrates the parent's indecision about interpreting the child's behavior and identifies an area in which the organization was not meeting the needs of the parents in their relevant environment by providing them with relevant diagnostic information and support.

Story C

I might mention one situation myself. My son is just uh finishing up sixth grade and uh I'd say between fifth and sixth grade I started seeing some changes in his behavior. But, what I said was, and I think it's probably true, um, that it's a stage, ya know. It's like a change because sometimes it's hard to differentiate if it might be a problem or if they're just kind of changing because of their age or ya know. I was aware there was a change and even knowing exactly and you don't want to think the worst. But, you're aware of some of the behavior changes. And right away I just kind of talked with other parents. And oh they'll go through with what they'll go through that so I just said okay it's a stage. I wasn't really liking it in terms of the behavior and the attitude problem and kind of thing.

The information gathered from this and other stories provided a wealth of information about public perceptions and attitudes toward the program and adolescent substance-abuse treatment and specific suggestions for increasing public acceptance and support for the program. The themes expressed in the stories clearly indicated directions for promoting the program and answering the concerns of parents. Public support for the program appeared to be high among the completed and current treatment groups, but more neutral in the potential group, indicating a need for reaching the potential group with positive information about the programs.

In fact, vignettes from the stories generated (creative narratives) were used in developing advertising media to reach the potential parents in the target community, providing the public with some of the organizational intelligence acquired by the parents who had experience with the program. Parents were found to be concerned about adolescent substance abuse and clearly indicated a need for more information about risks, symptoms, and services. Based on these data the organization developed public relations programs to attract community support and developed and implemented information dissemination promotional programs to meet the information needs identified by parents in the study.

CONCLUSION

Narrative analysis can generate powerful data for fueling OD efforts. Since stories are repositories for organizational intelligence, and are important equivocality-reducing communication mechanisms for organizational actors, they have the potential to provide OD specialists and organizational decision makers with insights into critical issues in organizational life, promoting organizational reflexivity. Narrative analysis can generate information for diagnosing organizational difficulties and developing organizational interventions, enabling researchers to use organizational intelligence to guide ongoing organizational development. The therapeutic model of consultation provides a clear structure for applying narrative analysis to OD. Creative narratives are dramatic composites of stories gathered from organizational actors that can be used to illustrate key interpretations of organizational life, to educate organizational actors about the experiences of others, and to increase organizational effectiveness.

REFERENCES

Agar, M. (1990). Text and fieldwork: Exploring the excluded middle. *Journal of Contemporary Ethnography, 19*, 73-88.

Babcock, B. A. (1977). The story in the story: Metanarration in folk narrative. In R. Bauman (Ed.), *Verbal arts as performance* (pp. 61-79). Prospect Heights, IL: Waveland.

Beckhard, R. (1969). *Organizational development: Strategies and models.* Reading, MA: Addison-Wesley.

Boylan, J. (1984). Publicity of the great depression: Newspaper default and literary reportage. In C. L. Covert & J. D. Stevens (Eds.), *Mass media between the wars* (pp. 156-178). Syracuse, NY: Syracuse University Press.

Brown, M. H. (1990). Defining stories in organizations: Characteristics and functions. In J. A. Anderson (Ed.), *Communication Yearbook 13* (pp. 162-190). Newbury Park, CA: Sage.

Brown, M. H., & McMillan, J. J. (1991). Culture as text: The development of an organizational narrative. *Southern Communication Journal, 57*, 49-60.

Chatman, S. (1981). What novels can do that films can't (and vice versa). In W. J. T. Mitchell (Ed.), *On narrative* (pp. 117-136). Chicago: University of Chicago Press.

Deal, T. E., & Kennedy, A. A. (1983). Culture: A new look through old lenses. *Journal of Applied Behavioral Science, 19*, 498-505.

Farrell, T. B. (1985). Narrative in natural discourse: On conversation and rhetoric. *Journal of Communication, 35*, 109-127.

Fisher, W. R. (1984). Narration as human communication paradigm. *Communication Monographs, 51*, 1-22.

Fisher, W. R. (1985a). The narrative paradigm: An elaboration. *Communication Monographs, 52*, 347-367.

Fisher, W. R. (1985b). The narrative paradigm: In the beginning. *Journal of Communication, 35*, 74-89.

Fisher, W. R. (1987). *Human communication as narration: Toward a philosophy of reason, value, and action.* Columbia, SC: University of South Carolina Press.

Fisher, W. R. (1989). Clarifying the narrative paradigm. *Communication*

Monographs, 56, 55-58.

Georges, R. A. (1987). Timeliness and appropriateness in personal experience narrating. *Western Folklore, 46,* 115-120.

Gergen, K. J., & Gergen, M. M. (1986). Narrative form and the construction of psychological science. In T. R. Sarbin (Ed.), *Narrative psychology: The storied nature of human conduct.* New York: Praeger.

Goodall, H. L. (1989). *Casing a promised land.* Carbondale, IL: Southern University Press.

Goodwin, C. (1984). Notes on story structure and the organization of participation. In J. M. Atkinson & J. Heritage (Eds.), *Studies of social action: Studies in conversation analysis* (pp. 225-246). Cambridge: Cambridge University Press.

Hellmann, J. (1981). *Fables of fact: The new journalism as new fiction.* Urbana: University of Illinois Press.

Hersey, J. (1980). The legend on the license. *Yale Review, 70,* 1-25.

Jefferson, G. (1978). Sequential aspects of storytelling in conversation. In J. Schenkein (Ed.), *Studies in the organization of conversational interaction* (pp. 219-248). New York: Academic Press.

Kramer, V. A. (1981). Agee's skepticism about art and audience. *Southern Review, 17,* 320-331.

Kreps, G. L. (1983). The use of interpretive research to develop a socialization program at RCA. In L. L. Putnam & M. E. Pacanowsky (Eds.), *Communication and organizations: An interpretive approach* (pp. 243-256). Beverly Hills: Sage.

Kreps, G. L. (1988). *Rosecrance Center market research program executive summary.* Research report prepared for Rosecrance Center Adolescent Substance Abuse Rehabilitation Center, Rockford, IL.

Kreps, G. L. (1989). A therapeutic model of organizational communication consultation: Application of interpretive field methods. *Southern Communication Journal, 55,* 1-21.

Kreps, G. L. (1990a). Stories as repositories of organizational intelligence: Implications for organizational development. In J. A. Anderson (Ed.), *Communication yearbook 13* (pp. 191-202). Newbury Park, CA: Sage.

Kreps, G. L. (1990b). Organizational communication research and organizational development. In D. O'Hair & G. L. Kreps (Eds.), *Applied communication theory and research* (pp. 271-296). Hillsdale, NJ: Erlbaum.

Kreps, G. L. (1990c). *Organizational communication: Theory and practice.* White Plains, NY: Longman.

Lucaites, J. L., & Condit, C. M. (1985). Re-constructing narrative theory: A functionalist perspective. *Journal of Communication, 35,* 90-108.

Martin, J. (1982). Stories and scripts in organizational settings. In H. A. Hasdorf & A. M. Isen (Eds.), *Cognitive social psychology* (pp. 255-305).

Martin, J., & Powers, M. E. (1983). Organizational stories: More vivid and persuasive than quantitative data. In B. M. Staw (Ed.), *Psychological foundations of organizational behavior* (pp. 161-168). Glenview, IL: Scott, Foresman.

McLaughlin, M. L. (1984). *Conversation: How talk is organized.* Beverly Hills, CA: Sage.

Morgan, G. (1986). *Images of organizations.* Beverly Hills: Sage.

Myrsiadis, L. S. (1987). Corporate stories as cultural communications in the organizational setting. *Management Communication Quarterly, 1,* 84-120.

Nadler, D. R. (1977). *Feedback and organizational development: Using data based methods.* Reading, MA: Addison-Wesley.

Pacanowsky, M. E. (1988). Slouching towards Chicago. *Quarterly Journal of Speech, 74,* 453-467.

Reimann, B. C., & Wiener, Y. (1988). Corporate culture: Avoiding the elitist trap. *Business Horizons, 31,* 36-44.

Riley, P. (1983). A structuralist account of political culture. *Administrative Science Quarterly, 28,* 414-437.

Rowe, L., & Boise, W. (Eds.). (1973). *Organizational and managerial innovation.* Pacific Palisades, CA: Goodyear Publishing.

Schein, E. H. (1969). *Process consultation: Its role in organization development.* Reading, MA: Addison-Wesley.

Schein, E. H. (1987). *The clinical perspective in fieldwork.* Newbury Park, CA: Sage.

Scholes, R. (1981). Language, narrative, and anti-narrative. In W. J. T. Mitchell (Ed.), *On narrative* (pp. 200-208). Chicago: University of Chicago Press.

Sims, N. (1984). *The literary journalists.* New York: Ballentine Books.

Templeton, A., & Groce, S. B. (1990). Sociology and literature. *Sociological Inquiry, 60,* 34-46.

Van Maanen, J. (1988). *Tales of the field: On writing ethnography.* Chicago: University of Chicago Press.

Van Maanen, J. (1990). Great moments in ethnography: An editor's introduction. *Journal of Contemporary Ethnography, 19,* 3-7.

Weber, R. (1974). *The reporter as artist: A look at the new journalism controversy.* New York: Hastings House.

Weick, K. E. (1979). *The social psychology of organizing.* Reading, MA: Addison-Wesley.

Weick, K. E., & Browning, L. D. (1986). Argument and narration in organizational communication. *Journal of Management, 12,* 243-259.

White, H. (1981). The value of narrativity in the representation of reality. In W. J. T. Mitchell (Ed.), *On narrative* (pp. 1-23). Chicago: University of Chicago Press.

■ 6

Using the Critical Incident Method to Evaluate and Enhance Organizational Effectiveness

Jim L. Query, Jr.
University of Tulsa
Tulsa, OK

Gary L. Kreps
Northern Illinois University
DeKalb, IL

■ *Elaborating the procedures used in the critical incident technique (CIT), Jim Query and Gary Kreps ground this method theoretically in the narrative paradigm. They then illustrate the utility of CIT in promoting organizational development in a nursing home, followed by its application in service organizations.*

INTRODUCTION

The Critical Incident Technique (CIT) is an innovative research strategy which is rarely used by communication investigators, but has the potential to generate valid and reliable communication data which can be easily used to address theoretical and practical issues. The method involves gathering self-reported data (using interviews or questionnaires) about

Special acknowledgments go to: Rich Baer, former Administrator of the DeKalb County Nursing Home and the residents and staff at the nursing home for allowing access to the data in this report; students in Dr. Kreps' COMS 407 Health Communication class, Spring 1989, for establishing relationships with nursing home residents and gathering the data presented in this report; to Dr. Art Doederlein, for coding a sample of the transcripts to test the reliability of the coding scheme; to secretary, Debbie Wootton, who helped type the transcripts; and to Linda R. Query, who helped with the typing of manuscript revisions.

subjects' most memorable positive and negative experiences within a specific, social context. It is a straightforward, powerful, systematic, tightly controlled, yet adaptive, qualitative research strategy. This technique is especially effective at gathering narrative data from individuals to assess the quality of organizational practices and life.

KEY FEATURES OF THE
CRITICAL INCIDENT TECHNIQUE (CIT)

The CIT, initially developed by Flanagan (1954), involves asking probing questions to elicit detailed accounts of subjects' experiences of effective and ineffective behavior within a specific context, thereby providing data to evaluate that situation (Nyquist, Bitner, & Booms, 1985). In CIT, a schedule of open-ended questions is asked of subjects to elicit critical incident information. The particular interviewing strategy used in CIT elicits both richness in detail and depth of personal experience from participants. Ample research has demonstrated that CIT data are both valid and reliable, and the results can also be applied as a formative evaluation to develop operational policy for organizational development (Andersson & Nilsson, 1964; Patton, 1980; Ronan & Latham, 1974; Stein, 1981; White & Locke, 1981).

To enhance the technique's validity and reliability levels, five sequential steps must be closely followed (Flanagan, 1954). The first step is to establish the general aim of the activity to be studied. CIT research should be guided by clear goals about the nature of the activities under examination.

The second step is to develop explicit standards for data collection and inclusion. CIT research should be guided by a clear understanding of the nature of the data to be gathered through the interviews conducted. In particular, all reported incidents must meet the minimal criteria of consisting of actual behaviors, having been directly observed by the subject, providing all relevant factors surrounding the incident, and including a clear evaluative judgment by the observer as to why the incident is important.

The third step is data collection. CIT requires a carefully structured process of data collection. The interviews are designed to elicit specific, candid, open-ended responses which describe behaviors that have been observed to result in success or failure in accomplishing specific goals.

The fourth step centers on analysis and classification of data. The CIT classification system is a structured three-part process which involves repeated, careful examinations of the data and sorting of the critical incidents into categories and subcategories according to similarities in the reported experiences. The three parts of the CIT classification system include: identification of a general framework which will account for all incidents; inductive development of major area and subarea categories that will be useful in sorting the incidents; and selection of the most appropriate level of specificity for reporting the data (Flanagan, 1954).

The fifth step is data interpretation. The critical incident categories identified in the CIT classification system should provide descriptive information concerning the ways subjects think about the key constraints which influence their activities. Inherent in the critical incidents gathered should be specific examples of what ought to be done, as well as what ought not to be done, in the context under investigation.

THE THEORETICAL JUSTIFICATION FOR CIT

The narrative paradigm suggests that the telling of stories is a fundamental and universal human activity (Fisher, 1984, 1985, 1987; Lucaites & Condit, 1985). People tell stories to recount and account for their experiences, using narratives to constitute social reality (Fisher, 1984). As Smith (1987) suggests, "It is through the telling of stories about ourselves and the events around us that we define reality, explain who we are to one another, and set the stage for future action" (p. 17). The reality-making function and persuasive potential of stories is accomplished by shaping the "listeners' opinions, while also reinforcing the tellers' own beliefs and attitudes" (Jones, Moore, & Snyder, 1988, p. 43). Several other scholars support the important role of stories in sense making and as behavior catalysts (Chafe, 1990; Freimuth, 1985; Kreps, 1991; Piore, 1983; Schrag & Rosenfeld, 1987; Smith, 1992; White, 1980; Wilkins, 1984).

The merit of the narrative paradigm is further evident when one considers its descriptive, explanatory, and predictive qualities. According to Fisher (1987, p. 87), "if one's character can be determined and if one's story in regard to a particular issue can be ascertained, it is possible to predict a person's probable actions." The narrative paradigm offers three additional advantages relative to other possible theoretical foundations. First, this perspective subsumes and expands upon many existing theories such as attribution, symbolic interactionism, constructivism, and social convergence (see Fisher, 1987, pp. 86-98). Second, the approach provides a "new" logic for analyzing human discourse through the concept of narrative rationality (Fisher, 1987, p. 87). The main premise undergirding the rationality construct is that some degree of relationship exists among the narrative account, personal values, reality, and subsequent behaviors. Smith (1987) concurs, "as we listen to the stories others tell us we learn what is important to them, what they believe is memorable, who in their stories is what kind of person, and what kinds of values justify decisions and actions" (p. 17). The third benefit of the narrative paradigm is that it directly captures the "lived experience" of subjects by detailing their causal and interpretive stories (Bochner & Ellis, 1992, p. 167); in contrast, traditional social science approaches have emphasized causal explanations and an objective reality.

Bochner and Ellis (1992) highlight the preceding advantage by noting, "the goal of understanding and coping with lived experience should be valued as highly as predicting and controlling it" (p. 167).

Armed with the rationality construct, social science investigators can weigh the utility of narratives according to their probability and fidelity. An example of this approach's usefulness is demonstrated by Kleinman (1988) through his analysis of illness and disease narratives. By reporting and evaluating patient narratives, Kleinman cogently advances the claim that a symbolic bridge exists connecting biological processes, meanings, and relationships, so that one's external environment is inextricably linked to his or her inner experiences (Kleinman, 1988, p. xiii).

Another example of narrative research is provided by Vanderford, Smith, and Harris (1991). Employing a longitudinal design, pre- and postintervention measures, and in-depth interviews, the investigators assessed the impact of ethics training on physician residents who regularly interacted with HIV-positive clients. The findings revealed that physicians identified three key values that shaped their interactions: preventing the spread of AIDS; perpetuating the "puritan lifestyle" of monogamy and responsibility; and curing the disease. HIV-positive clients reported seven key values that influenced their interaction with the physician residents including timely and in-depth information, control, confidentiality, equal treatment, respect for individuality, acknowledgment of special needs, and quality of life. Interpreting the results, Vanderford et al. (1991) concluded that the postintervention stories of the physician, residents, and clients changed significantly to reflect less-conflicting values than those reported prior to the ethics intervention.

Taken together, the preceding studies demonstrate the potential of ethnographic methods firmly grounded in the narrative paradigm. In the remainder of this chapter, narrative studies that utilized another ethnographic method—the CIT—are explicated. These investigations were designed to collect and examine the stories which elderly individuals and service organization employees tell about their most satisfying and dissatisfying experiences across key organizational contexts. Analyses of these stories were conducted to identify the issues of greatest concern to the particular groups and to demonstrate the utility of the CIT method.

USING CIT TO PROMOTE ORGANIZATIONAL DEVELOPMENT IN A NURSING HOME

Kreps (1990a) suggests that organizational communication scholars can play a vital role in organizational development (OD) efforts. Broadly defined, OD encompasses a comprehensive and systematic plan to change or reframe human behavior to enhance organizational functioning and improve the quality of organizational life (Nadler, 1977, p. 6). As many nursing homes in the United States confront and grapple with deleterious problems, such as alarming staff turnover rates, spiraling numbers of persons with Alzheimer's disease and related disorders, stifling regulation, as well as pervasive negative images, an impetus is created for theoretical-grounded OD interventions. Recent investigations (Kreps, 1991, 1990b; Kreps & Query, 1992) reveal the potential of CIT as a powerful diagnostic tool for organizational communication scholars involved in OD.

The research design used in these studies combines survey and phenomenological research methods to examine the health care experiences of elderly individuals. While the research is designed to describe the perspective of a particular population (elderly health care consumers), it also attempts to provide a deeper understanding of the patterns of interaction and significant symbols that make up the health care culture for elderly health care consumers (Frey, Botan, Friedman, & Kreps, 1991). In-depth, open-ended critical incident interviews were conducted with the elderly in institutional (nursing home) and noninstitutional (home) contexts. The primary goal of the interviews was to elicit personal narratives from the participants who described satisfying and dissatisfying health care events they had experienced.

From January 1989 to May 1989, 29 undergraduate and graduate students, enrolled in a health communication course at a midwestern university, were paired with 29 elderly residents of a local nursing home. The residents were selected by the director of the nursing home based on their interest in receiving visitors, their ability to communicate, and their willingness to participate in this study. Students made weekly, friendly visits to the residents over the course of the semester to share information and establish relationships with the residents. At the end of the semester, each student conducted a critical incident technique interview with the resident with whom they had been meeting. (In four cases, students were unable to successfully complete the interviews with a nursing home resident because the residents were unable or unwilling to participate in the interview. The students then were allowed to interview other noninstitutionalized elderly.) The weekly visits helped foster rapport, respect, and understanding between students and residents and facilitated the collection of full and candid responses from the elderly in the critical incident interviews.

All interviews were tape-recorded, transcribed, and submitted to CIT classification system analysis. For this sample, three general content categories for critical incidents were identified: (a) satisfaction or dissatisfaction with communication, including positive or negative judgments of listening behaviors, caring, sensitivity, and information giving, as well as whether communication was rude, soothing, supportive, or irritating; (b) satisfaction or dissatisfaction with facility features, including positive or negative evaluations of cleanliness, food, equipment, expenses, staffing level, or any special activities (such as arts and crafts, or parties); and (c) satisfaction or dissatisfaction with treatment, including positive or negative judgments of the competence of health care providers, knowledge of personnel, the effectiveness of treatments, and whether health conditions of participants were getting better or worse.

A content analytic coding scheme was developed in which three general judgments, reflecting the incident categories, were to be made by coders:

1. Is this critical incident a predominantly positive or negative incident?
2. Does this critical incident pertain predominantly to characteristics of a health care facility, characteristics of health care treatment, or characteristics of communication?
3. Within each critical incident that was judged to pertain to communication, is each communication incident described primarily with or from health care staff, nursing home residents or health care consumers, family or friends, media (radio, television, etc.), or young children (including grandchildren)?

The transcripts of all 29 interviews were content-analyzed by the senior investigator. A random sample of the transcribed interviews was selected and submitted to analysis by a trained coder to test the reliability of the coding scheme. Interrater reliability between this coder and the senior investigator was very high, with the two coders agreeing on 24 out of 25 coding judgments, accounting for a .96 level of agreement.

Analysis of the 29 interviews generated 151 separate critical incidents. Of these 151 incidents, 77 were judged to be positive critical incidents (describing satisfying health care situations), and 74 were judged to be negative critical incidents (describing dissatisfying health care situations). Most of the critical incidents pertained to communication issues, as opposed to facility or treatment issues, with communication accounting for 71 of the 151 incidents (47%). Facility critical incidents accounted for 32% of all critical incidents, and treatment critical incidents accounted for 21% of all critical incidents.

Several of the critical incidents attest to the importance of effective communication between health care providers and elderly health care recipients in enhancing the quality of care the elderly receive. Due to the significantly higher presentation of communication themes in the initial study, a positive and negative communication critical incident is presented.

POSITIVE COMMUNICATION CRITICAL INCIDENT

A 69-year-old female, residing at home and in good health, recounted the following, positive ciitical incident. Her account illustrates how health care staff members provided her with relevant health information to explain and demystify potentially frightening health care procedures. The incident also reveals how the providers used comforting communication to reassure her that the medical procedure would not harm her.

> "Well, I've had some problems with my back and I went to the doctor, and he told me that I was going to have some tests taken on my back, and he informed me very well of everything that was going to have to be done, and when I got to the hospital, he was there and he talked to me, and the nurses talked to me, and it was a very difficult time. But they informed me of every test I would have to take and so I wasn't nearly so frightened when I had to go into the hospital. He explained everything, and he told me all the tests that I'd have to have, and about the x-rays, and the adjustments and everything on my back. They explained everything to me. And they were with me and they made me feel comfortable."

NEGATIVE COMMUNICATION CRITICAL INCIDENT

An 80-year-old male nursing home resident with heart problems and recovering from a stroke reported the following disturbing critical incident. The focus centered on an insensitive interaction in which the health care provider did not provide the client with relevant health information nor receive his informed consent for a very delicate and potentially uncomfortable treatment. The negative reaction this form of health communication engendered is made abundantly clear.

> "They're all ignorant. They just don't have no respect for nobody. A couple of days ago a little girl, a little lady named Dawn, she came into my room and said, 'Jeff, you're getting a suppository.' I'm laying in bed naked on my side and she shoved a suppository up my asshole. She didn't ask me if I wanted it or nothing. She didn't tell me anything and it makes me pissed off. I haven't shit yet either."

IMPLICATIONS

One of the most compelling findings of this line of research is that communication emerged as the greatest source of satisfaction and the greatest source of dissatisfaction for elderly health care consumers, accounting for 47% of both the positive and negative critical incidents reported. This finding is consistent with prior research, which has demonstrated that provider/consumer interactions in health care systems are a major source of satisfaction and dissatisfaction for health care consumers (Greenfield, Kaplan, & Ware, 1985; Lane, 1983, 1982; Street & Wiemann, 1987). Health care providers and consumers depend on communication to elicit cooperation from others within the health care system, to gather relevant information about health problems and health care treatments, as well as to provide relevant health information to key individuals within the health care system (Kreps, 1988).

The importance of communication within health care organizations is particularly relevant to the provision of health care to the elderly, since they are the dominant population of health care consumers in the modern health care system. A large body of literature concerning communication and aging also suggests that the elderly have unique communication needs which are frequently ignored or discounted by the modern health care system (Kreps, 1988; Kreps & Thornton, 1992; Nussbaum, 1983,1990; Nussbaum, Thompson, & Robinson, 1989; Query & James, 1989). The present line of inquiry supports the assumption that communication is an important process influencing health care for the elderly. The findings are also consistent with evidence which suggests that effective communication increases the quality of health care (Greenfield, et al., 1985; Lane, 1983; Salem & Williams, 1984).

To enhance the effectiveness of health care with the aged, the findings also suggest that a key strategy is to increase the effectiveness of communication between providers and the aged. Health care staff must be trained to communicate sensitively, caringly, and informatively with the elderly, developing supportive and friendly interpersonal relationships with elderly consumers (Nussbaum, 1990; Nussbaum et al., 1989). It is essential for health care providers to use communication as an effective tool, providing and gathering relevant health information, by respecting the elderly's perspectives, by involving them in treatment decisions, and by providing them with informed consent (Kreps, 1988; 1990c).

THE UTILITY OF CIT IN SERVICE ORGANIZATIONS

Similar to nursing homes, the relevant environment of other service organizations such as airlines, hotels, restaurants, and banks is marked by dynamic, fast-changing, and equivocal socioeconomic forces which threaten organizational viability and health. As the underlying tensions mount, the delicate balance between organizational stability and innovation often becomes precarious (Kreps, 1990d). Organizational communication scholars, engaged in OD, can help these organizations maintain the desired balance by evaluating the effectiveness of internal and external communication practices, by identifying communication difficulties, and by developing theoretically grounded intervention strategies to reduce these problems (Kreps, 1990a, p. 104). Within service organizations, OD specialists typically target the expectations, perceptions, and memories of customers and staff, since a tangible good or product is not being exchanged (Nyquist & West, 1991). The CIT is well suited to uncovering this type of data, and its utility is further revealed across key service organizations including airlines, hotels, and restaurants.

The research design of Nyquist and West (1991) employs CIT to assess employee-customer interaction quality and to discover communication difficulties. The resulting information can then be used to inform the development and implementation of communication training programs and/or organizational policy. This research is also designed to describe the orientation of a selected population (service organization employees) and it attempts to provide a richer understanding of the interaction patterns and key symbols that make up the culture of service organization employees (Frey et al., 1991).

Well-trained student interviewers conducted in-depth interviews with employees from airline, hotel, and restaurant organizations. Each critical incident was independent, included an employee-customer interaction, was viewed as difficult by the employee, and contained ample details (Nyquist & West, 1991, p. 8). This research design was unique, compared to the traditional use of CIT, since the investigators sought to identify troublesome interactions solely.

Every interview was recorded and 355 usable incidents were obtained in concert with the a priori criteria above. The data were categorized into two major classifications according to difficulty of interaction. The first category of difficult exchanges consisted of "customer expectations that exceed the capacity of the service delivery system to perform. These included unreasonable demands, demands against policies, unacceptable treatment of employees, drunkenness, breaking societal norms, and special-needs customers" (Nyquist & West, 1991, p. 9). The second category of troublesome exchanges was comprised of "firm or employee performance that does not match the capacity of the service delivery system. These included unavailable service/product, unacceptable slow performance, and unacceptable service/product" (Nyquist & West, 1991, p. 9). Examining the results further, Nyquist and West (1991) concluded that approximately 75% of the interaction difficulties were not related to the technical capabilities of the service organizations. Their findings thus suggest that the quality of employee-customer interaction significantly shapes customer satisfaction and problem resolution. Indeed, as Nyquist and West (1991) argue, terrible events such as a customer/client injury can even leave a favorable impression if the incident is handled in a timely, appropriate, and sensitive manner.

LIMITATIONS OF THE REVIEWED CIT RESEARCH

There are at least six limitations which hinder the descriptive power of the Kreps (1990b,1991) and Kreps and Query (1992) lines of research. The first two concerns center on the sample's characteristics. The size of the sample was 29 elderly health care consumers, and the sample selection was purposive rather than random. Although generalizability was decreased to some extent, the subsequent gains, in terms of depth and understanding of "information rich" incidents, outweigh the preceding, sample concerns (Patton, 1987, p. 52). A third issue addresses the seemingly one-shot nature of the data-collection process. Recall, however, that the student interviewers spent the semester making weekly visits designed to establish rapport with the elderly subjects. Thus, although the data were collected at only one point in time, we would argue that the incidents reflected a greater degree of detail than would be expected in a typical and rather impersonal, one-shot study. The fourth area that could be addressed by future research is the influence of the amount of time residents had spent in the nursing home. Unfortunately, this study did not assess this possible intervening factor. It could well be that there exists a relationship among the nursing home residents' length of time in the facility and the prevalence of satisfying and dissatisfying critical incidents.

The fifth area of concern focuses on the omission of ethnic identification among the residents. Since few investigations have included ethnic elderly (Mindel, 1983), it would have been helpful if subjects had identified their ethnic affiliation. The results might have then provided some insight into the "lived experience" of this relatively unexplored, demographic group. The sixth area encompasses the possible influence of prescribed medications on the memory of subjects. It could be that some degree of their recall was clouded. To guard against this possibility of data distortion, such information should be compiled in the future, assuming it could be obtained. In the present investigation, this issue was of less concern since the interviewers had developed a semester-long baseline for evaluating the quality of each subject's interaction.

Addressing the research of Nyquist and West (1991), at least four limitations curtail its descriptive power. An initial concern is the brisk discussion of data category derivation. For instance, few details are provided as to how the primary categories were deduced, and there is no reporting of interrater reliability levels in identifying the categories. The data classification scheme and interrater reliability levels, however, are reported in the larger version of the study (Nyquist et al., 1985). A second issue centers on the average length of the interviews and the strategies interviewers used to build rapport and trust prior to the interview process. It would have been helpful if some discussion had been provided within either report (Nyquist et al., 1985; Nyquist & West, 1991). A third area hinges on the one-shot nature of the data collection. Unlike the earlier research of Kreps (1990b) and Kreps and Query (1992), these interviewers apparently did not spend a lengthy amount of time interacting with the subjects prior to data collection. This concern should be tempered, however, as in most organizations, it is very difficult to obtain such interaction/access time over a 4-5 month time period. Moreover, the resulting knowledge gains, in terms of identifying actual communication difficulties and broad communication skill repertoires for service organization employees, outweigh the preceding data-collection concern (Nyquist & West, 1991, p. 13). The final concern is the lack of examples of the collected critical incidents. Although the investigators summarize the primary categories of difficult interaction, it would have been illustrative to report some actual incidents. Only brief summaries appear in both versions.

FUTURE USES OF CIT

A potentially rich and heuristic area of inquiry ready for exploration with CIT is the study of communication competence, social support, and health outcomes such as cognitive depression (see Query, Parry, & Flint, 1992). Query et al. argue that a formidable array of organizational stressors has the potential to erode personal efficacy by unduly taxing the coping abilities of individual members (p. 79). Communication specialists can help organizational members develop and refine coping skills through timely and sensitive communication with other individuals and an in-depth assessment of the context (see Kreps & Query, 1990).

CIT is especially well suited to this challenge since it can help individuals anticipate supportive and nonsupportive interactions, inform the development of communication skills for eliciting and providing social support, and foster the acquisition and refinement of "rules" for selecting appropriate responses. A similar argument is advanced by Nyquist and West (1991). The use of CIT could also be especially informative in terms of enhancing theory-building efforts across the many contexts in which social support is expressed. For instance, perplexing research questions, often resistant to traditional quantitative methods, could then be better examined. Some examples include: What types of messages characterize "supportive interaction" for providers and recipients of social support? What are the recurring themes in the interactions between depressed recipients and nondepressed providers? How do messages differ if providers are highly communicatively competent, and recipients are moderately communicatively competent? What themes appear in confrontative interaction in which positive behavior change occurs? A related question then surfaces, is this last situation properly classified as "social support?" (Flint, 1990, p. 3).

CIT appears to have the potential to provide additional insight into these pressing problems. The method can help policymakers, individuals, and communication scholars better understand the dynamics of social support by examining the "lived experience" of providers and recipients.

CONCLUSION

This chapter described the salient features of CIT, examined its theoretical base, and reviewed select studies which employed CIT, demonstrating that CIT can provide important information for enhancing organizational effectiveness. We encourage communication scholars to use CIT to assist organizations in adapting to environmental constraints and challenges. CIT can provide rich detail and insight into key organizational processes and organizational life that traditional quantitative methods, in isolation, rarely capture.

REFERENCES

Andersson, B., & Nilsson, S. (1964). Studies in the reliability and validity of the critical incident technique. *Journal of Applied Psychology, 48*(6), 398-403.

Bochner, A. P., & Ellis, C. (1992). Personal narrative as a social approach to interpersonal communication. *Communication Theory, 2*(2), 165-172.

Chafe, W. (1990). Some things that narratives tell us about the mind. In B.K. Britton & A. D. Pellegrini (Eds.), *Narrative thought and narrative language* (pp. 79-98). Hillsdale, NJ: Erlbaum.

Fisher, W. R. (1984). Narration as a human communication paradigm: The case of public moral argument. *Communication Monographs, 51*, 1-22.

Fisher, W.R. (1985). The narrative paradigm: An elaboration. *Communication Monographs, 52,* 347-367.

Fisher, W. R. (1987). *Human communication as narration: Toward a philosophy of reason, value and action.* Columbia, SC: University of South Carolina Press.

Flanagan, J. C. (1954). The critical incident technique. *Psychological Bulletin, 51,* 327-357.

Flint, L. J. (1990, November). *Potential mediators of employee substance abuse: The role of social support for alcoholics.* Paper presented at the annual meeting of the Speech Communication Association, Atlanta, GA.

Freimuth, V. (1985, May). *The story of the value dimension of health communication.* Paper presented at the annual meeting of the International Communication Association, Honolulu, HI.

Frey, L. R., Botan, C. H., Friedman, P. G., & Kreps, G. L. (1991). *Investigating communication: An introduction to research methods.* Englewood Cliffs, NJ: Prentice-Hall.

Greenfield, S., Kaplan, S., & Ware, J. (1985). Expanding patient involvement in care: Effects on patient outcomes. *Annals of Internal Medicine, 102,* 520-528.

Jones, M. O., Moore, M. D., Snyder, R. C. (Eds.). (1988). *Inside organizations: Understanding the human dimension.* Newbury Park, CA: Sage.

Kleinman, A. (1988). *The illness narratives.* New York: Basic Books.

Kreps, G. L. (1988). The pervasive role of information in health and health care: Implications of health communication policy. In J. Anderson (Ed.), *Communication yearbook 11* (pp. 238-276). Newbury Park, CA: Sage.

Kreps, G. L. (1990a). Organizational communication research and organizational development. In D. O'Hair & G. L. Kreps (Eds.), *Applied communication theory and research* (pp. 103-121). Hillsdale, NJ: Erlbaum.

Kreps, G. L. (1990b, June). *Key communication experiences of elderly health care consumers: A critical incidents analysis.* Paper presented at the annual meeting of the International Communication Association, Dublin, Ireland.

Kreps, G. L. (1990c). A systematic analysis of health communication with the aged. In H. Giles, N. Coupland, & J. M. Wiemann (Eds.), *Communication, health care, and the elderly* (pp. 135-154). Manchester, England: University of Manchester Press.

Kreps, G. L. (1990d). *Organizational communication* (2nd ed). New York: Longman.

Kreps, G. L. (1991, November). *Using the critical incident technique to study elderly health care consumers.* Paper presented at the annual meeting of the Speech Communication Association, Atlanta, GA.

Kreps, G. L., & Query, J. L., Jr. (1990). Health communication and interpersonal competence. In G. M. Phillips & J. T. Wood (Eds.), *Speech communication: Essays to commemorate the 75th Anniversary of the* Speech Communication Association (pp. 292-323). Carbondale, IL: Southern Illinois University Press.

Kreps, G. L., & Query, J.L., Jr. (1992, May). *Critical incidents and patient-centered health care for nursing home residents.* Paper presented at the annual meeting of the International Communication Association, Miami, FL.

Kreps, G. L. & Thornton, B. C. (1992). *Health communication: Theory and practice* (2nd ed). Prospect Heights, IL: Waveland Press.

Lane, S. (1982). Communication and patient compliance. In L. S. Pettegrew (Ed.), *Straight talk: Explorations in provider-patient interaction* (pp. 59-69). Louisville, KY: Humana.

Lane, S. (1983). Compliance, satisfaction, and physician-patient communication. In R. Bostrom (Ed.), *Communication yearbook 7* (pp. 772-799). Beverly Hills, CA: Sage.

Lucaites, J. L., & Condit, C. M. (1985). Reconstructing narrative theory: A functional perspective. *Journal of Communication, 35,* 90-108.

Mindel, C. H. (1983). The elderly in minority families. In T. H. Brubaker (Ed.), *Family relationships in later life* (pp. 193-208). Beverly Hills, CA: Sage.

Nadler, D. A. (1977). *Feedback and organization development: Using data-based methods.* Reading, MA: Addison-Wesley.

Nussbaum, J. F. (1983). Relational closeness of elderly interaction: Implications for life satisfaction. *Western Journal of Speech Communication, 47,* 229-243.

Nussbaum, J. F. (1990). Communication and the nursing home environment: Survivability as a function of resident-nursing staff affinity. In H. Giles, N. Coupland, & J. M. Wiemann (Eds.), *Communication, health care, and the elderly* (pp. 155-171). Manchester, England: University of Manchester Press.

Nussbaum, J. F., Thompson, T. L., & Robinson, J. D. (1989). *Communication and aging.* New York: Harper & Row.

Nyquist, J. D., Bitner, M. J., & Booms, B. H. (1985). Identifying communication difficulties in the service encounter: A critical incidents approach. In J. Czepiel, M. Solomon, & C. Surprenant (Eds.), *The service encounter: Managing employee-customer interaction in service businesses* (pp. 195-212). Lexington, MA: D. C. Heath and Company/Lexington Books.

Nyquist, J. D., & West, J. (1991, November). *Using the critical incident technique to study service industries.* Paper presented at the annual meeting of the Speech Communication Association, Atlanta, GA.

Patton, M. L. (1980). *Qualitative evaluation methods.* Beverly Hills, CA: Sage.

Patton, M. L. (1987). *How to use qualitative methods in evaluation.* Newbury Park, CA: Sage.

Piore, M. J. (1983). Qualitative research techniques in economics. In J. Van Maanen (Ed.), *Qualitative methodology* (pp. 71-85). Beverly Hills, CA: Sage.

Query, J. L., Jr., & James, A. C. (1989). The relationship between interpersonal communication competence and social support among elderly support groups in retirement communities. *Journal of Health Communication, 3,* 165-184.

Query, J. L., Parry, D., & Flint, L. J. (1992). The relationship among social support, communication competence, and cognitive depression for non-traditional students. *Journal of Applied Communication Research, 20*(1), 78-94.

Ronan, W. W., & Latham, G. P. (1974). The reliability and validity of the critical incidents technique: A closer look. *Studies in Personnel Psychology, 6,* 53-64.

Salem, P., & Williams, J. L. (1984). Uncertainty and satisfaction: The importance of information in hospital communication. *Journal of Applied Communication Research, 12,* 75-89.

Schrag, R., & Rosenfeld, L. (1987). Assessing the soap opera frame: Audience perceptions of value structures in soap opera and prime-time serial drama. *Southern Speech Communication Journal, 52,* 362-376.

Smith, D. H. (1987, February). *Stories, values, and patient care decisions.* Paper presented at the University of South Florida Communicating with Patients Conference, Tampa, FL.

Smith, D. H. (1992). Stories, values, and patient care decisions. In C. Conrad (Ed.), *The ethical nexus: Values in organizational decision making.* Norwood, NJ: Ablex.

Stein, D. S. (1981). Designing performance-oriented training programs. *Training and Development Journal, 35,* 12-16.

Street, R., & Wiemann, J. M. (1987). Patients' satisfaction with their physicians' interpersonal involvement, expressiveness, and dominance. In M. McLaughlin (Ed.), *Communication yearbook 10* (pp. 591-612). Newbury Park, CA: Sage.

Vanderford, M. L., Smith, D. H., & Harris, W. S. (1991, November). *Value identification in narrative discourse: Evaluation of an HIV education demonstration project.* Paper presented at the annual meeting of the Speech Communication Association, Atlanta, GA.

White, F. M., & Locke, E. A. (1981). Perceived determinants of high and low productivity in three occupational groups: A critical incidents study. *Journal of Management Studies, 18*(4), 375-387.

White, H. (1980). The value of narrativity in the representation of reality. *Critical Inquiry, 7,* 5-27.

Wilkins, A. (1984). The creation of company cultures: The role of stories and human resource systems. *Human Resource Management, 23,* 41-60.

■ 7

Juxtapositioning Accounts: Different Versions of Different Stories In the Health Care Context

Patricia Geist
San Diego State University
Jennifer Dreyer
San Diego State University
San Diego, CA

■ *Accounts reveal individuals' interpretations of their own and others' communication. Adapting the interview process to solicit accounts, Patricia Geist and Jennifer Dreyer investigate participatory health care. They juxtapose the accounts of hospitalized patients, their primary physicians, and the nurses primarily responsible for their care to gain greater insight into the process of understanding.*

In sickness and in health, we participate in health care delivery. For some, participation is limited to remedies and medical advice from friends or family without leaving home. But for others, participation occurs in the context of providers' offices and hospitals and ranges in frequency from annual visits for preventative care to daily interaction for treatment of serious or chronic illness. And, for still others, participation is defined as *providing* care to people, as a family member, a friend, or a health care professional.

When people talk about their experiences they account for their own and others' behavior in seeking, gaining, or providing health care. Accounting for their past, present, and future interactions in the health care context, patients and providers construct an interpretation of their own and others' reality (Berger & Luckmann, 1966), motives (Mills, 1940)

"Different versions of different, not the same, stories" is a phrase coined by Denzin (1992) in his article "Whose Cornerville Is It, Anyway?" He emphasizes, as we do, that there is no final telling to be told, just multiple, different accounts, each with as much validity as any other.

and identity (Goffman, 1959; Riessman, 1990; Shotter, 1984; Shotter & Gergen, 1990). By juxtapositioning the accounts of hospitalized patients, their primary physicians, and the nurses primarily responsible for their hospital care, this research grounds the accounting process in the larger health care context. Entering these individuals' health care worlds, we as researchers make sense out of the ways they view their interaction with each other by engaging them in dialogue. Their negotiated accounts explicate their similar and contradictory versions of reality and contribute to our understanding of patients' and providers' participation in health care.

In this chapter, we begin with a discussion of the perspective we take toward accounts as negotiated in context through dialogue. Then we take this perspective to the study of accounts in the context of health care delivery by analyzing the accounts of two patients and the providers who cared for them during their hospital stay. Finally, we offer additional suggestions for researching accounts in context.

ACCOUNTS IN CONTEXT

Accounts range from reflective efforts to understand to the recollection of events organized into narrative form. People can account for themselves in the sense of explaining or justifying their actions through simple statements without elaboration or through longer life stories (Burnett, 1991). Their accounts can be as short as a single-phrase statement or as long as a life story (Burnett, 1991). The accounting process, then, communicates something about the meanings people attach to their own and others' behaviors (Harre & Secord, 1972; Shotter, 1984). In this view of accounting, the focus is not on the structure or function of accounts in interaction, but instead the focus is on people's interpretations of what their behavior was, is, or might be (Buttny, 1985; Garfinkel, 1967; Harré & Secord, 1972; Shotter, 1984).

The goal in researching accounts from this perspective is not a search for general principles or rules that guide individuals' construction and use of accounts in interaction, but rather it is a search for individuals' interpretations of the actions and the setting involved, as well as the broader social context within which they take place (Semin & Manstead, 1983).

Accounts may reveal individuals' attempts to handle problematic situations such as unanticipated or untoward behavior (Scott & Lyman, 1968), intentional or unintentional breaches of social conventions or rules (Semin & Manstead, 1983), or major personal loss (Harvey, Weber, & Orbuch, 1990). At the same time, they may reveal individuals' interpretations of their own or others' handling of these situations, in the past, present, or future (Buttny, 1987; Geist & Chandler, 1984; Harré & Secord, 1972; Tompkins & Cheney, 1983).

Accounts reveal how individuals situate self and others in relation to the social order of a particular context. By situating themselves and others through accounts, individuals make an effort to restore alignment "under circumstances of stress, doubt, uncertainty, threatened identity, and the like" (Stokes & Hewitt, 1976, p. 845). We learn through their accounting process that "interaction is disrupted, identities are threatened, meanings are unclear, situations seem disorderly, people have intentions that run counter to others' wishes, [and] seemingly inexplicable events take place" (p. 845). Essentially, accounts reveal different versions of different stories about a context's social order—the way it is, the way it will be, or even the way it should be or could be.

By grounding the investigation of the accounting process in the larger context within which it occurs we learn how interaction is constrained or facilitated by features of a particular context. Accounts are not simply representations of the world, but are part of and shaped by the contexts in which they occur (Garfinkle, 1967; Gilbert & Abell, 1983; Hammersley & Atkinson, 1983; Sudnow, 1967; Wieder, 1974; Zimmerman, 1969). In this view, all accounts must be examined as social phenomena occurring in, and shaped by, particular contexts (Hammersley & Atkinson,1983).

One predominant feature of the health care context, in particular, is that it is filled with uncertainty, for patients and providers. The uncertainty providers face concerns not only the patients' physiological condition, but also their response to the care they are provided (Hardesty & Geist, 1990; Light, 1979; Strauss, Fagerhaugh, Suczek, & Wiener, 1985). The uncertainty patients face centers on limitations in their knowledge of their disease, concerns about others' responses to their illness, and turmoil about the complicated medical environment in which they receive care (Geist & Dreyer, in press).

In the midst of these diverse uncertainties, providers and patients communicate, more often than not, with a goal toward understanding. Dialogic theory offers a critique of the idealistic notion of communication in relationships, suggesting that the essence of dialogue is a simultaneous differentiation and fusion of the patients' and providers' ideology (Bakhtin, 1986; Baxter, 1991; Geist & Dreyer, in press). To communicate dialogically is to create an understanding that is more than a monologue of the patients' or providers' ideology—an understanding that acknowledges the social context within which communication occurs.

The dialogue, so essential to this understanding, is often constrained or obstructed by features of the context, provider or patient ideologies, or contradictory interpretations of communication (Geist & Dreyer, in press). If we embrace understanding as the essence of communication in the provider-patient relationship, then more research is needed to investigate the multiple selves that providers and patients reveal in their accounts of themselves and their relationships with one another. By grounding the accounting process in a specific context (Cody & McLaughlin, 1990), we can begin to develop a theory of understanding, both as it occurs in the provider-patient relationship and as it occurs in the relationship between interviewer and interviewee.

DIALOGIC INTERVIEWING

Interviews provide a valuable research method for initiating dialogue that produces accounts from individuals. The interview process informs us on questions of how individuals perceive, organize, give meaning to, and express their understandings of themselves, their experiences, and their worlds (Mishler, 1986b). During the process of soliciting accounts in interviews many unsolicited and unexpected accounts emerge as the interviewer and interviewee negotiate a shared understanding through discourse.

In our view, the standard research interview must be reconceptualized if respondents are to tell *their* entire stories. The interview process constitutes dialogue in which interviewees and interviewers jointly construct meaning (Mishler, 1986a). The interviewer often finds it necessary to reformulate, reframe, and rethink questions as respondents simultaneously frame their answers in terms of their reciprocal understanding as meanings emerge during the course of an interview (Mishler, 1986b). Hence, making sense of each others' questions and responses is achieved by engaging the other person in dialogue (Pacanowsky, 1989). The expectation is that interviewers and interviewees will achieve a mutually shared understanding (Mishler, 1986b).

Interviewers must not assume that they have all the answers and are simply looking for those answers (Kauffman, 1992). Indeed, the apparently misleading, irrelevant, or surprising data—that which is given in other terms than those for which it was asked—may be suggestive of the shared understanding and negotiated meaning between interviewer and interviewee (Webb & Webb, 1968; Wiersma, 1988). Hence, the variations in questions, responses, and meanings inevitable among interviewers and across interviews are not viewed as "errors", but as significant "data" for analysis (Mishler, 1986b).

By engaging others in dialogue in the interview process, interviewees may recreate their "world" through discourse organized around time and consequential events (Riesmann, 1990). Respondents are encouraged to find and speak in their own "voices" (Mishler, 1986b) and to become active participants, rather than passive objects of the ethnographic interview (Kauffman, 1992). When researching and analyzing data from this perspective, the person being interviewed tells us some sort of truth about him- or herself when he or she tells us anything at all—that is, "he or she gives us true data about *something* if we have but the wit to intepret it" (Dean & Whyte, 1958, as cited in Wiersma, 1988, p. 205).

Several authors (Geist & Dreyer, in press; Hammersley & Atkinson, 1983; Pacanowsky, 1989) have suggested the importance of and need for reflexivity in social research. We cannot, nor should we try to, escape the fact that we are part of the social world we study (Hammersley & Atkinson, 1983). It is our goal to explicate and understand the effects and responsibilities of the researcher in the interview process. The researchers' accounts of their experiences are provided to enhance understanding of the health care context.

Embracing this naturalistic, interpretive approach to the research process, our ethnographic report describes researchers' and participants' understandings as they are revealed in their accounts of communication and the health care context. The patient case reports begin with the researchers' accounts of their experiences and understandings of the particular health care context. The case narratives continue by presenting participants' accounts of their experiences and understandings.

INVESTIGATING PARTICIPATORY CARE IN THE
HEALTH CARE CONTEXT

The relationship between health care providers and patients is at the heart of quality health care (Ruben, 1990; Todd, 1989). Humane medicine, holistic medical knowledge, and participatory care are all terms used to refer to the need for health care providers and patients to understand each others' thoughts and feelings and to provide them with an "authentic voice" when conversing with each other about their illness (Silverman & Bloor, 1990). Dialogic interviews with patients and their providers generate accounts of their knowledge, concerns, emotions, and values. (See Appendix A and B for patient and provider interview guides.)

Our research of patients' and providers' accounting processes began after gaining approval from the Institutional Review Committee at Cofer General Hospital. Cofer General is a 415 bed hospital and staffs 1,300 physicians and approximately 500 nurses. Upon approval, we arranged a meeting with the Manager of Acute Care Nursing and the Clinical Coordinators of three different hospital units, two of which— Medical Surgery and Neuro Pulmonary—we focus on in this research.

After identifying eight patients in the hospital capable of being interviewed, we contacted their physicians and gained their participation both in allowing us to interview their patient and by arranging an interview with them at their office. Finally, an interview was scheduled with the nurse primarily responsible for caring for each of the eight patients. In essence, our research was designed to juxtaposition and analyze four accounts of these eight patient cases.

This chapter focuses on two cases, juxtapositioning the accounts of the researcher, patient, physician, and nurse. These particular cases were chosen for their contrasting contextual features: (a) private versus nonprivate room (b) short-term versus long-term condition, and (c) different units with distinctive features (e.g., physician specialties, degrees of predictability in patients' conditions).

JUXTAPOSITIONING ACCOUNTS OF UNDERSTANDING

Understanding in the Context of Caring for an AIDS Patient

As I walk down the long hall from the elevator to the Five South nurses' station, I search for Ellen's familiar face. Having met her the week before, I remember her as an easy-to-smile, helpful person. I feel a great sense of relief when I recognize her immediately. As I continue walking, I observe her talking with two other nurses behind the counter of the nurses' station located in the center of the circular unit.

> "Ellen, remember me, Emelia Conner?"
> "Yes, of course. How are you?"
> "Great, just fine. Anxious to begin this research."
> "How can I help?"

I explain that I need to familiarize myself with the unit and identify patients who are well enough to be interviewed. She identifies a number of patients, describes their illnesses, talks about the physicians who care for these patients, and then indicates that before we can begin the research we need approval from their physicians. Being her ever-helpful self, Ellen takes the time right then and there to get on the phone to call or page the two doctors who need to give their approval.

As it turns out this is not an easy task, and over the course of the next hour and a half, I wander around Five South, observing and talking as I wait to hear back from the doctors that Ellen has attempted to contact. I learn from Ellen and other nurses that Five South, Neuro Pulmonary, cares for patients with strokes, head and spinal injuries, pulmonary ailments, and AIDS. Patients on this unit are cared for in private rooms by nurses and doctors, including neurologists, internists, and infectious disease specialists. One of the nurses talks of the difficulty in working on this unit because they confront death on a regular basis. Also, because many of their patients are from diverse ethnic backgrounds, the nurses often witness quite unusual and bizarre death rituals, including chanting and food ceremonies.

I feel thankful for the time to browse, talk, and familiarize myself with the unit before I hear from Ellen that Dr. Gilbert has granted permission for the interview with his patient Tran. As I have wandered by Tran's room several times in my travels around the circular unit, I have noticed that his wife is present in the room. I can't decide if I should wait or interrupt, so I walk the circuit a few more times, trying to gain a better sense of what is happening in the room before I walk in. Earlier, in talking with his nurse, Lorie, I arranged an interview with her and learned that Tran had experienced a sleepless night and may or may not be up for an interview today. I'm prepared when he tells me:

> "No, please, not today. Tired, very tired."
> "Another day perhaps?"
> "Yes, another day."

I exit, disappointed, but encouraged about what I have learned about Five South and the people who work here.

A week later I return to the hospital, hoping to interview Tran. He is alone this time, sitting in a chair by the window, looking out, pensively. He remembers me, thank goodness. But again he refuses to be interviewed because, as he tells me, "it is hard to talk about his disease, his emotions". For him it is embarrassing. I tell him I am not here to make him feel uncomfortable, and that if I ask him a question he doesn't want to answer, that is not a problem. I emphasize that maybe by telling me what he is experiencing he can help others. He agrees to be interviewed, and this is where his account and his providers' accounts begin.

Tran is a 35-year-old Vietnamese American, diagnosed HIV positive. Experiencing the pain of an illness he has lived with for two years, he speaks of his hesitation to talk about his illness, his embarrassment. Tran narrates his account of his communication with his providers—Dr. Gilbert and nurse Lorie—and these two providers narrate their accounts of their communication with Tran. Dr. Gilbert is a 42-year-old Caucasian who has been practicing medicine for 14 years. His specialty is internal medicine, but in addition, he is a trained neurologist. Lorie is a 28-year-old Caucasian, who with a Bachelors degree in Nursing, has been active in nursing for seven years. In all three accounts we discover novel and similar versions of the circumstances surrounding the delivery of health care.

When I asked Tran if he feels comfortable talking about his feelings or emotions with his doctor, who has taken care of him throughout his illness, he tells me, "Some. Not all of them." Upon asking him which feelings he is comfortable telling him, he says, "[I] tell them how I worry about this, worry about that. I'm upset. I'm not happy. And I'm so sick. What should I do?" Tran continues his account, indicating that he tells his doctor his general story, but there are things he does not tell:

> I tell him anything, almost you know. But lies. I have this sickness and it just makes me like, feel dying's better than living you know? I got—suicide. I never told him, you know.

Yet, later in our dialogue, Tran indicates that because his doctor knows him well and takes his personal feelings into account, the doctor tries to tell him good things "to make him feel comfortable." Tran believes that if the doctor knew he had been contemplating suicide, the doctor would say, "Oh, you don't do that. We are in America. We don't do that." Tran believes the doctor communicates with him to help him understand and cope with his condition.

Tran uses the word "understanding" to refer to the ways providers handle the circumstances surrounding his illness. For Tran, those who are not afraid to touch him, understand him and his disease.

> And some nurses, they stay with you, literally. They understand you, you know? And they understand the disease. They're not scared of touching you. That way, you're feeling good. [Others] come down here, and they seem like they're scared; they keep away from you, you know? That's when your feelings go down . . . That's what makes me sometimes say, 'Go away.'

As Tran's accounts reveal, understanding is essential to his sense of self, the lifting of his spirits, and the development of positive relationships with his providers.

Tran's physician, Dr. Gilbert, indicates that his patient has had to deal with his acute and life-threatening illness quite a few times. Dr. Gilbert's accounts of his patient Tran and their interaction focuses on what he describes as Tran's inability to understand and cope with his disease.

> He's a man who has spent a great deal of time—difficulty accepting his problem, has not sought out help, emotionally and psychological-ly for his problems . . . support groups in town. He has not, and per-haps it's cultural because he is not Caucasian, perhaps some of it is just him. He's a very frightened individual. His situation is very diffi-cult—is difficult for everybody, since he's not been able to communi-cate very easily his problems, other than his extreme anxiety and vul-

nerability, emotional vulnerability . . . not even to his family. He has a great deal of difficulty dealing with his family. There have been times when I've had to spend my entire session with him, dealing only with that issue; with trying to get away from the medical opinions, and dealing only with how he's feeling at that time.

Dr. Gilbert, in his account, attempts to explain the reasons why he believes Tran lacks accurate knowledge and an understanding of his disease.

I hate to use the word absurd, but he makes a lot of unknowledgeable assumptions about his disease and what's been happening. We've had to try to deal with that, but even when you deal with that on an—in an informational way, he's incapable, he's incapable of grasping the significance—still clings to his—his—I'm not coming up with the right word—but his beliefs on how he should be reacting with the disease and how other people around him are vulnerable to his disease.

Dr. Gilbert is aware of Tran's anxiety and suggests that as his patient gets sicker, he copes better with his emotions:

I have noticed that the sicker he's gotten, and the more towards his eventual demise, his death, he's taking things a bit easier. . . . There's no question to me that he's depressed, and yet, he's faring up under it better, now that he's sicker, than he was when he was well. When he was well, he was so full of anxiety that he was just overwhelmed with his anxiety. Now that he's much sicker, he knows that it's near the end and that his mortality is near, he's not as depressed. He's not nearly as anxious about it.

Dr. Gilbert's account suggests a relationship between severity of illness and acceptance as a form of understanding that Tran has reached over time. Yet, his account also provides a theory about how Tran's lack of accurate knowledge and his anxiety about his disease often create difficulties in dialoguing with his patient and in gaining his participation.

Tran's nurse, Lorie, provides a contrasting account. In her experience with Tran, he is "one of those rare patients that knows exactly what's going on." In describing what she believes is important for understanding Tran, she states:

That he does have a family. He has a wife and a little boy. He is quite concerned about them. He's a very intelligent man. He knows exactly what's going on. He's one of the rare patients that knows exactly what's going on.

She accounts for his intelligence in a number of ways:

> He knows, of course; this isn't new to him. He's had—you know, he's been diagnosed for a long while now. So, he's had a chance to get used to it all, and, he's not—a lot of this isn't new to him. He knows what's going on . . . I think he's done a little research on his own. And, like I say, he's quite intelligent, and he asks a lot of questions, and he wants to know what you're doing, and why you're doing it, and, so forth.

Lorie sees Tran as the kind of patient that is easy to understand and work with. But she also accounts for their ability to dialogue as being related to the amount of time he and most other patients spend on the Neuropulmonary unit.

> Being on this floor, in particular, we have our patients for a long time; a lot of time. They're here for months, weeks, or whatever; a long period of time. So, if I'm not communicating with them, there's bound to be somebody else here who is. So, there's a good reason for asking questions. And, physicians are pretty good, for the most part, about supplying—if you have a question, they're pretty good about answering. [You need to ask] if you're not sure what facts they know, what they don't know, or how willing they are to talk about—especially, like, somebody with—like an AIDS patient, how willing they are to talk about it, you know, how they got it, or whatever. That doesn't really matter anymore to them—just the fact that they have it, and that's it.

Lorie accounts for her own understanding as developing over time in her relationship with this patient and in her own willingness to ask questions. Her account reveals that she is a keen observer of the degree of understanding that her patients and families develop over time as well.

> Like I say, [Tran] he knows what's happening. So, he has had time to think about what he wants to do. It's been quite some time. He's been in and out of here several times, so he has had some time to think about it. He has come through the home care routine of care at home; you know, self-administered, or, his wife has learned to do all of that at home. So, they're really adapting pretty well, I think, from what I can see. Just him being here. I've never been to his home or anything like that, so I don't know what really goes on. But, his wife is very supportive. They've learned how to—they've taken on the initiative, and learned how to do all this stuff at home. So, that tells me a little bit about them, and, that they're willing to put out some effort to, you know, make life as normal as possible for him, or whatever

that may be. He understands, like I say, what it means to have a low count, or white count, or whatever, and what that implies for him, and what his—he knows that certain things he can and can't do. He's real personable; he doesn't hesitate to share his feelings. His communication is a little hard, sometimes, to understand, because he has such a heavy accent, but he is willing to talk.

So, for Lorie, it is easier to talk with a patient like Tran who knows what is going on than with patients who know nothing. Lorie herself is not afraid to ask questions of Tran, of his wife, of other nurses, or of the doctor. She understands that Tran may need more of her participation and understanding as he gets sicker.

He hasn't had to lean on me, so to speak, for too, too much, other than some emotional support. He makes his needs known, so—but, I think, as he gets sicker, that it's going to be more—me giving and he taking, than an equal type of thing. Well, I think it puts you on an even keel—you know what's going on, he knows what's going on— you know what he's thinking and feeling, and he knows what you're thinking and feeling. It makes a big difference, if you're on the same wavelength.

Clearly, all four accounts—the researcher's, Tran's, Dr. Gilbert's, and Lorie's—provide different versions of different stories. Yet all reveal a great deal about their own and others' understanding and participation in the context of health care delivery. The same is true for understanding in the context of providing short-term care for a young stab-wound victim.

Understanding in the Context of Caring for a Stab-Wound Victim

Rushing to Cofer General from school to interview a patient before he is discharged, I put on my "walking shoes" in order to get to my car and make it to the hospital before the patient's 3:00 p.m. discharge. I take the elevator to floor 11 South, the 39 bed medical-surgery unit. This particular unit deals with numerous life-threatening conditions: heart failure, diabetes, gall bladder surgeries, and cancer. The physicians are described as both "generalists" and "specialists," and their average contact with patients is five minutes or less.

I look for a familiar face—Robin, the clinical coordinator, whom we had met earlier that month to discuss our research project. I see her in the hall and motion hello with my right hand. Robin approaches me and I remind her that I am here to interview Steve. She informs me that she is really busy today and as she begins to talk with me about the interview she pauses, looks down the hallway, and says she has to take care of something. I am left standing in the frenzied hallway of 11 South.

Soon thereafter, Robin introduces me to Mary, Steve's nurse, and I ask her if she would be willing to talk with me about her interaction with Steve. She smiles and says she is willing. Robin and I continue down the hallway to Steve's room, and we find that he is speaking with a local police officer. Robin has to rush off again, so I wait patiently at Steve's door. I wait for approximately 15 minutes as Steve talks with the police officer and then makes a phone call. Finally, Robin leads me into the room and introduces me to Steve: "Steve, this is Jennifer." Suddenly, Steve embraces me in a hug and asks what I am doing at the hospital. I am puzzled and don't yet know how to respond. Robin asks: "Do you two know each other?" At that point, Steve looks at me closely and says: "Oh my god, you look exactly like my ex-girlfriend. I thought you were my ex-girlfriend." I look anxiously at Robin, there is a slight pause, and then the three of us begin to laugh.

As we attempt to let the previous incident pass, Robin explains that I am here to ask Steve some questions about his stay at Cofer General Hospital. Earlier Robin suggested that since Steve is a "high verbal" patient, he should be a good participant for our study. Steve is staying in a room with two other patients, so Robin recommends that we close the drape around his bed for "privacy." However, the televisions and conversations remain readily apparent in the background. I am seated in a chair next to Steve's bedside as I explain the nature of participatory health care and ask Steve what "it would mean to him to have an 'authentic voice' in talking with his physician or nurse about his health care." Steve responds bluntly: "I don't know. I'm lost." I realize that I will have to reframe and reformulate several interview questions.

Through the dialogue that transpired between the researcher and the three participants during the dialogic interview, different stories are revealed. Steve is a 27-year old Hispanic man. His long, wavy hair makes him look more like a teenager than a 27-year-old man. Steve was stabbed in the chest and has been in the hospital for a week. Mary, one of Steve's primary nurses, is of Filipino descent and has been a clinical nurse for 20 years. Steve's physician is Dr. Reid, a young Caucasian man. Dr. Reid has worked in the County Hospital and currently practices at Cofer General Hospital where he treats trauma patients (gunshot victims, stab wound victims, car accident victims, etc.) on a regular basis. In the following accounts, contradictions, similarities, and difficulties in provider-patient communication are illuminated.

As I reframed my first interview question, I asked Steve what he thought "would be important for his physician or nurse to know about him." He responded: "That I'm not very patient." As we both discussed our individual trait of impatience, I asked Steve if he had voiced this to his providers; he responded:

No. I haven't told them. I should have told them that, because every time I want my medicine, it takes them like an hour to get it to me. You know, that just stresses me out. And, I should have told them that, and that I'm not very patient, so, 'Bring me my medicine when I want it.'

Steve continued his story to explain the action he took to relieve his anxiety and to resolve the stress of not getting his medicine:

I even had to go as far as having a different nurse, because she never brings my medicine on time. And, it starts hurting, you know? It would take her too long to bring my medicine; like an hour, an hour and a half sometimes, from the time I called her to the time I got my medicine, and it wasn't because it wasn't time for me to have my medicine, because it was. I keep track; I'm supposed to have it every three hours. One day I was wrong. I was an hour off. So, I was wrong. I looked on the book, and I saw that I was wrong, so I didn't say anything else.

A deeper understanding of Steve's preceding account is illuminated when Mary provides her account of the same situation. Mary was asked to describe a specific case when she had difficulty understanding Steve, or when she felt the patient didn't understand her, or when the interaction was inhibited in some way. As Mary told the beginning of her story, she chuckled at the thought of being described as "mean"

I have a patient that actually said, "I don't want Mary as my nurse." Because I was "mean" [Mary laughing]. And, first of all, you know, "I need a pain medication." I think this is a communication problem, so it was my fault that he wasn't ready for pain medication; it's too early. I just told the nursing assistant, you know, "it's not time." But, that's not right, because the nursing assistant didn't go back to that patient. It's my responsibility; it's my fault, but, that was the miscommunication as it happened. . . . So all the while he thought I ignored him and I wasn't doing it.

Hence, Mary takes responsibility for the "miscommunication" and provides the researcher with a richer understanding of what transpired between her and Steve. Yet, as is described below, Mary and Steve still find their interaction constrained by different interpretations of reality.

In this particular hospital, the roof of the high-rise building symbolizes a special place for patients to visit. When interviewing patients, "the roof" was often mentioned as a place they would like to visit. Our data suggest that patients and providers tell different versions of different stories about the roof. To most patients, it's an escape from the institutional environment. To most providers, it's a place where patients go to smoke cigarettes. The following discourse reveals how contradictory accounts are revealed, explicated, and understood in the dialogic interview process.

I asked Steve if he often "expressed how he was feeling to his providers." He said

> I always ask if I can go for a walk. I want to know if I can get up and go walk, or go up on the roof and walk; I guess that's where everyone goes. They say it's nice up there. And, I've asked that since I've been in here, since the first day, "Am I going to be able to go up on the roof and walk?" She said, "I don't know, I'll check," and I never got the answer. And, that's been six days ago.

Mary's account substantiates Steve's account of his request to visit the roof:

> He wanted to go to the roof to smoke, and I said, "We need a doctor's order," you know, and he thought I was being mean to him, and things like that.

Later in the interview it was revealed that Steve eventually made it up to the roof. When asked if it was nice up there, he replied:

> It was okay. But, I smelled cigarette butts. I smelled a bunch of cigarette butts . . . because that's where they smoke, and I used to smoke before I came in here, and it just, kind of, made me want to smoke. So, I left there. I don't want to smoke after being through this. I don't think it would be a good idea right now, to smoke, anyway.

According to Mary's account, Steve requested to go to the roof so he could smoke. Yet, it is clear from Steve's account that smoking was the last thing on his mind. The juxtapositioning of these accounts creates an understanding of the conflicting meanings of the two respondents.

As described above, understanding is inhibited by contrasting interpretations, unclear meanings, and difficult situations. In the following accounts, understanding is further constrained as Steve's identity is defined by his physician.

As Dr. Reid sits behind his desk in his blue surgical scrubs, I asked him what he felt was necessary to know about Steve, and how he went about soliciting that information. Dr. Reid found it easy to classify Steve:

He falls into a group that's pretty simple, in terms of their history. . . .
You could ask them, "Do you use drugs?" Most of them are pretty—
pretty good about telling you—they don't see any problem with that,
so they'll tell you, "Yeah, I'm using this or that." You can suggest drug
rehab programs; none of them have ever taken me up on that. Most
of—in this kind of group, the typical gang-bangers—they're pretty
good about telling you; you can ask them frank questions and they'll
tell you, most of the time, because they don't fear you, and they feel
comfortable telling you. I don't think it's, so much, that they think
that's going to help in their care, but most of them will tell you.

Initially, I was attempting to discover how a patient's history influences
provider's health care decisions. Yet the foregoing account necessitated
that I inquire about why personal history was not pertinent in this case:
"So you didn't find background information useful in deciding about
Steve's care?" Dr. Reid quickly responded:

No, his is one of the simpler ones. It's just a little stab wound to the
chest, and, dropped his lung, put a tube in, it comes up, and they get
better, and go out. There was nothing funny about it, nothing com-
pounding, or anything like that. He was a very simple one. So, his past
history, aside from having any medical problems that might complicate his cure, really did not have any influence on my decisions in
terms of his treatment.

In this account, Steve is defined as a "simple case" and his identity as a
unique person is not acknowledged. Later in the interview, Dr. Reid
accounted for how he goes about obtaining information from patients in
the health care context:

Sitting down and talking with the patient for a prolonged period of
time, getting to know them a little better, can help sometimes. . . . It
may be five minutes, it may be a half-hour. You sit down at the bedside,
and make yourself comfortable; don't feel like you have to rush away,
because, I think, a lot of the time, they don't want to burden the doctor. If you make a point to sit down, and feel relaxed with them, then I
think they might be more apt to tell you those sort of things.

Dr. Reid's account is telling when juxtapostioned with Steve's account of
his interaction with Dr. Reid. Steve supplied limited information about
his interaction with Dr. Reid, so I asked: "Have you had much interaction
with your doctor?" Steve replied: "No, I just see him in the morning for a
few minutes. I mean, I'm usually asleep." I continued: "Could you
describe a conversation between you and your doctor?"

No. I really don't talk to him at all. I've only really talked to him—
today was really the only time I've really talked to him. I asked him a
question or something. . . . I just asked him if I was going to get my
tube out. I don't think I asked him anything else; that's about it.

Dr. Reid expressed the importance of "sitting down at the bedside" and
talking with patients. However, Steve's account reveals that in his case this
objective was not achieved.

These accounts uncover patients' and providers' attempts to situate themselves and others in the health care context. Clearly, this process
is complicated by inexplicable events, divergent interpretations, and differing beliefs in health care delivery.

INTERPRETING UNDERSTANDING IN THE
CONTEXT OF HEALTH CARE DELIVERY

The accounting process in the health care context reveals coinciding and
contrasting meanings, interpretations, and realities. Providers' and
patients' accounts depict their efforts to situate themselves in this context
and to understand each other in the face of medical uncertainty, threatened identity, problematic situations, unclear meanings, and contextual
constraints. By participating in their context and juxtapositioning their
situated accounts, we have gained an increased understanding of their
multiple and, at times, contradictory selves as they communicate to provide or receive quality medical care.

We make sense of these accounts and the accounting process by
centering our discussion on three central issues. First, we synthesize and
describe the contribution these accounts make to a theory of understanding. Second, we describe dialogic interviews as a multi-faceted and versatile method for initiating dialogues that contribute to an understanding
of the interaction between communication and context. Finally, we document insights about accounts drawn from these data and indicate alternatives for using account analysis in organizations.

A Theory of Understanding

Understanding through a dialogic lens suggests that through communication we create meanings that did not exist before the interaction
(Bahktin, 1986; Baxter, 1991). What this means in the health care context
is that although providers and patients may attempt to categorize each
other previous to their interaction, a great deal takes place in health care

organizations that shapes new interpretations. Characteristics of individuals, relationships, and contexts facilitate and constrain understanding in diverse ways.

By juxtapositioning the accounts of patients Tran and Steve and their providers, we discover particular impressions of individuals are formed that influence the communication process and the degree of understanding. An "information game" takes place between physicians and patients as they seek and give information (Geist & Hardesty, 1990; Goffman, 1959, 1967). In the process of playing this information game, patients and providers locate and process information about the other's identity, and this information in turn shapes expectations about the roles they will play (Goffman, 1959).

Tran's intelligence or knowledge is a patient cue that both his physician and nurse interpreted as influencing his behavior. Dr. Gilbert's accounts refer to the "absurd" and "unknowledgeable" assumptions that Tran makes about his disease. The physician's account implies that this lack of accurate knowledge has created difficulties for providers and Tran's family and in his patient's acceptance and ability to cope with his disease. As a result, the physician has had to spend entire sessions dealing with only this issue. Yet, in accounting for this difficulty, Dr Gilbert reveals how he views patient characteristics, such as lack of knowledge or unrealistic expectations, as something he must work with to create understanding. At one point in the 90-minute interview with Dr. Gilbert, he suggests that there is an "important relationship between the first-hand information, the bonding, the knowledge, and the general communication."

Tran's knowledge is a central issue in Lorie's account of Tran and her relationship with him. Understanding, in Lorie's view, increases when patients want to learn, ask questions, and become knowledgeable about their disease. In her line of work on this particular unit, individual understanding advances because of the length of time the patient spends on the unit. Hospital stays of over a month and frequent return visits assist in developing understanding through the patient's willingness to disclose emotions, the provider's efforts to work with the patient, and the provider's increased knowledge of the patient's family situation.

Impressions of individuals do not exist in isolation from relationships. Often these impressions critically influence the behaviors of providers or patients and the ways they communicate with one another as indicated earlier (Geist & Hardesty, 1990). Similar to Dr. Gilbert and Lorie, Tran raises the issue of providers' knowledge of his disease and the threat to his identity when they do not seem to understand his disease. Tran acknowledges his own sense of feeling open or closed to communication with providers based on the ways they respond to him. He feels understood when providers do not hesitate touching or getting close to him, and as a result he feels more willing to communicate with them. This is clearly the case for both Tran and Lorie being on what she regards as the same "wavelength," as the juxtapositioning of their accounts reveals.

Steve's impatience as a person and as a patient complicated his communication with Mary and influenced his understanding of the situation. In the very beginning of our interview, Steve revealed that he was "not very patient." His account then explicates how this individual characteristic influenced his interaction with Mary. When accounting for this to the interviewer, Steve realizes that "he should have told them" [his providers] that he was impatient because it "stresses him out" when he doesn't receive his medicine on time. Consequently, Steve "had to go as far as having a different nurse" in order to receive his medicine in a timely manner. Interestingly, Mary does not talk of Steve as impatient. Rather, she accounts for her behavior and the situation as "it's my responsibility" and "that was the miscommunication as it happened." Hence, this particular patient characteristic, impatience, had a significant impact on the communication and understanding that did *not* occur between Steve and Mary. In this instance, the researcher gains the greatest understanding by juxtapositioning the two accounts and discovering why the understanding did not occur.

Relationships between patients and providers inevitably are shaped by the health care context. The complexities and uncertainties of medical work must be continually negotiated as patients and providers communicate in ways to meet their needs (Hardesty & Geist, 1990). For example, Steve and Mary negotiate Steve's request to visit the hospital roof. In this particular incident the contextual rules and procedures of the hospital are revealed. Steve asks Mary if he can go to the roof, and Mary explains that she needs a "doctor's order." According to Steve's account, he had been waiting six days for a response from Mary. In Mary's account she does not disclose whether or not she asked Dr. Reid for permission to let Steve visit the roof. She simply explains that Steve "wanted to go to the roof to smoke" and that Steve thought she "was being mean to him" because she needed a doctor's order. Steve's desire and curiosity ("everyone says its nice up there") to visit the roof is complicated by the hospital rules of needing a "doctor's order." Mary's institutional position does not give her the power to grant Steve permission to visit the roof. This institutional constraint critically influenced Steve's and Mary's impressions of themselves and their relationship.

These accounts contribute to a theory of understanding that reveals both multiple selves across accounts and how impressions of individuals influence the communication, action, and thought processes in relationships. Additionally, taking the context into account (rules, procedures, values, society) reveals structural conditions that influence understanding in multiple ways. Hence, understanding is enhanced when one realizes that individual, relational, and contextual features are interrelated and attempts are made to explicate these interrelationships. It is through dialogic interviewing that researchers are most able to capture and explicate this understanding.

Dialogic Interviewing

The asymmetry in discourse between providers and patients has long been a topic of concern (Maynard, 1991; Waitzkin, 1991). The notion of dialogic interviewing challenges interviewers to communicate with interviewees in ways that overcome the asymmetry that often underminds the interviewee's experience and understanding.

Dialogic interviewing's primary goal is to empower respondents by engaging them in dialogue (Mishler, 1986b; Pacanowsky, 1989). Interviewers, through dialogue, must encourage respondents to express their "authentic voice" in the interview process. When respondents speak in their own "voices," they are likely to tell their "stories" (Mishler, 1986b). In this sense, interviewees and researchers gain a richer understanding of the particular phenomenon as illustrated by the respondent.

Clearly, dialogic interviewing reveals that the storied construction of reality has less to do with facts and more to do with meaning created from the context of explanation in which it is situated (Steele, 1986; Wiersma, 1988). Distortions of the "facts" reveal meanings that can be considered "second realities" which are negotiated between interviewer and interviewee (Ricoeur, 1970; Schafer, 1983; Spence, 1982; Wiersma, 1988).

The standard research interview is fragmented, precategorized, and decontextualized (Mishler, 1986b). Dialogic interviewing provides an alternative method of interviewing in which respondents are not cut off by interviewers so that their x are contextually and temporally grounded.

Accounts in Context

The intuitive and compelling connection between accounts and understanding is revealed when we view a successful account of human activity in everyday life as restoring *or* creating understanding (Shotter, 1984). Essentially, successful accounting may be much aligned with metaphoric thinking or behaving. If, in the process of providing an account, we create a symbol, image, or expression that facilitates a new comparison, we may be doing more than restoring a previous understanding. In the process, we discover new ways to talk about and account for ourselves, our relationships, and the contexts within which we manage our identities.

In the end, it is the researcher who gains the most understanding. Thus, it is here where we must continue to explore the responsibilities we as researchers have toward the individuals and the contexts we study.

By juxtapositioning the accounts of patients and providers, the researcher also participates in the "information game" inherent in health care delivery. As exhibited in the account analysis above, the researcher is privy to information often withheld from and by both patients and providers. What should researchers do with such privileged information? Ideally researchers can impart their understanding of the "information game" to patients and providers and contribute further understanding to health care consumers and organizations. A revelation of patients' and providers' accounts would help to illuminate the asymmetry and multiple interpretations found in medical discourse.

Researchers must acknowledge the reality of alternative world views (Wander, 1983). We should treat each account as a separate story that contributes to further understanding (Denzin, 1992). There is no final truth or final telling—"there are only different tellings of different stories" (p. 124). Hopefully, researchers will embrace these dissimilar accounts as separate, yet invaluable, interpretations of the participants' and researchers' understandings.

REFERENCES

Bakhtin, M. M. (1986). *Speech genres and other late essays* (C. Emerson & M. Holquist, Eds.; V. McGee, Trans.). Austin: University of Texas Press.

Baxter, L. A. (1991, November). *Bakhtin's ghost: Dialectical communication in relationships.* Paper presented at the Speech Communication Association, Atlanta, GA.

Berger, P., & Luckmann, T. (1966). *The social construction of reality.* London: Allen Lane.

Burnett, R. (1991). Accounts and narratives. In B. M. Montgomery & S. Duck (Eds.), *Studying interpersonal interaction* (pp. 121-140). New York: Guilford.

Buttny, R. (1985). Accounts as a reconstruction of an event's context. *Communication Monographs, 52,* 57-77.

Buttny, R. (1987). Sequence and practical reasoning in account episodes. *Communication Quarterly, 35,* 67-83.

Cody, M. J., & McLaughlin, M. L. (1990). Interpersonal accounting. In H. Giles & W. P. Robinson (Eds.), *Handbook of language and social psychology* (pp. 227-256). New York: John Wiley.

Dean, J. P., & Whyte, W. F. (1958). How do you know if the informant is telling the truth? *Human Organization, 17,* 34-38.

Denzin, N. K. (1992). Whose Cornerville is it, anyway? *Journal of Contemporary Ethnography, 21,* 120-132.

Garfinkel, H. (1967). *Studies in ethnomethodology.* Englewood Cliffs, NJ: Prentice-Hall.

Geist, P., & Chandler, T. (1984). Account analysis of influence in group decision-making. *Communication Monographs, 51,* 67-78.

Geist, P., & Dreyer, J. (in press). A dialogic critique of the medical encounter: Understanding, ideology, and social context. *Western States Communication Journal, 57* (2).

Geist, P., & Hardesty, M. (1990). Reliable, silent, hysterical, or assured: Physicians assess patient cues in their medical decision making. *Health Communication, 2,* 69-90.

Gilbert, G. N., & Abell, P. (1983). *Accounts and action.* Gower House, England: Gower Publishing Company Limited.

Goffman, E. (1959). *The presentation of self in everyday life.* New York: Doubleday.

Goffman, E. (1967). *Interaction ritual: Essays on face-to-face behavior.* New York: Pantheon.

Hammersley, M., & Atkinson, P. (1983). *Ethnography: Principles in practice.* London: Routledge.

Hardesty, M., & Geist, P. (1990). Physicians' self-referent communication as management of uncertainty along the illness trajectory. In G. L. Albrecht (Ed.), *Advances in medical sociology: A research annual* (Vol. 1, pp. 27-55). Greenwich, CT: JAI Press.

Harré, R., & Secord, P. F. (1972). *The explanation of social behavior.* Oxford: Basil Blackwell.

Harvey, J. H., Weber, A. L., & Orbuch, T. L. (1990). *Interpersonal accounts: A social psychological perspective.* Cambridge, MA: Basil Blackwell.

Kauffman, B.J. (1992). Feminist facts: Interview strategies and political subjects in ethnography. *Communication Theory, 2,* 187-206.

Light, D. (1979). Uncertainty and control in professional training. *Journal of Health and Social Behavior, 20,* 310-322.

Maynard, D. W. (1991). Interaction and asymmetry in clinical discourse. *American Journal of Sociology, 97,* 448-495.

Mills, C. W. (1940). Situated actions and vocabularies of motive. *American Sociological Review, 5,* 904-913.

Mishler, E. G. (1986a). The analysis of interview-narratives. In T. R. Sarbin (Ed.), *Narrative psychology: The storied nature of human conduct* (pp. 233-255). New York: Praeger.

Mishler, E. G. (1986b). *Research interviewing: Context and narrative.* Cambridge, MA: Harvard University Press.

Pacanowsky, M. (1989). Creating and narrating organizational realities. In B. Dervin, L. Grossberg, B. J. O'Keefe, & E. Wartella (Eds.), *Rethinking communication* (Vol. 2, pp. 250-257). Newbury Park, CA: Sage.

Ricoeur, P. (1970). *Freud and philosophy.* New Haven, CT: Yale University Press.

Riessman, C. K. (1990). Strategic use of narrative in the presentation of self and illness: A research note. *Social Science Medicine, 11,* 1195-1200.

Ruben, B. D. (1990). The health caregiver-patient relationship: Pathology, etiology, treatment. In E.B. Ray & L. Donohew (Eds), *Communication and health: Systems and applications* (pp. 51-68). Hillsdale, NJ: Lawrence Erlbaum Associates.

Schafer, R. (1983). *The analytic attitude.* London: Hogarth.

Scott, M. B., & Lyman, S. M. (1968). Accounts. *American Sociological Review, 33,* 46-62.

Semin, G. R., & Manstead, A. S. R. (1983). *The accountability of conduct: A social psychological analysis.* London: Academic Press.

Shotter, J. (1984). *Social accountability and selfhood.* New York: Basil Blackwell.

Shotter, J., & Gergen, K. J. (1990). *Texts of identity.* Newbury Park, CA: Sage.

Silverman, D., & Bloor, M. (1990). Patient-centered medicine: Some sociological obsercations on its constitution, penetration, and cultural assonance. *Advances in Medical Sociology, 1,* 3-25.

Spence, D. P. (1982). *Narrative truth and historical truth: Meaning and interpretation in psychoanalysis.* New York: Norton.

Steele, R. (1986). Deconstructing histories: Toward a systematic criticism of psychological narratives. In T. R. Sarbin (Ed.), *Narrative psychology: The storied nature of human conduct* (pp. 256-275). New York: Praeger.

Stokes, R., & Hewitt, J. P. (1976). Aligning actions. *American Sociological Review, 41,* 838-849.

Strauss, A., Fagerhaugh, S., Suczek, B., & Wiener, C. (1985). *Social organization of medical work.* Chicago: University of Chicago Press.

Sudnow, D. (1967). *Passing on.* Englewood Cliffs, NJ: Prentice-Hall.

Todd, A.D. (1989). *Intimate adversaries: Cultural conflicts between doctors and women patients.* Philadelphia: University of Pennsylvania Press.

Tompkins, P. K., & Cheney, G. (1983). Account analysis of organizations: Decision making and identification. In L. L. Putnam & M. E. Pacanowsky (Eds.), *Communication and organizations* (pp. 123-146). Beverly Hills, CA: Sage.

Waitzkin, H. (1991). *The politics of medical encounters: How patients and doctors deal with social problems.* New Haven, CT: Yale University Press.

Wander, P. (1983). The ideological turn in modern criticism. *Central States Speech Journal, 34,* 1-18.

Webb, B., & Webb, S. (1968). *Methods of social study.* New York: A. M. Kelley. (Original work published 1932).

Wieder, D. (1974). *Language and social reality: The case of telling the convict code.* The Hague: Mouton.

Wiersma, J. (1988). The press release: Symbolic communication in life history interviewing. *Journal of Personality, 56,* 205-238.

Zimmerman, D. H. (1969). Record-keeping and the intake process in a public welfare agency. In S. Wheeler (Ed.), *On record: Files and dossiers in American life*. New York: Russell Sage Foundation.

APPENDIX A
PATIENT INTERVIEW QUESTIONS

Introduction: We are asking you to participate in this study because we are interested in knowing more about patients' views of their communication with their providers, both their doctors and their nurses. In the next 20 to 30 minutes we will be asking you a series of questions which we would like you to answer based on your OWN beliefs and experiences.

1. In general, do you feel comfortable discussing your medical con–dition with your physician?

2. In general, do you feel comfortable telling your physician other information about yourself, besides your medical condition (e.g., circumstances surrounding your condition, meaning of the condition to you, coping behaviors, past treatment, relationships with others, your personality, your family, your work, your self-care)?

    a. What types of information about yourself have you disclosed to your physician? To your nurse?
    b. Do you volunteer this information to your doctor? To your nurse? When? In what way?
    c. Does your doctor ask you for information other than about your physical condition? If so, what has he/she asked you about?
    d. Does your nurse ask you for information other than about your physical condition? If so, what has he/she asked you about?
    e. If your doctor or nurse are from another cultural background, does it influence what or how you communicate?

3. Do you believe it's necessary for your physician to take this per-sonal information into account *when making decisions about your care?* If so, how so? If not, why not?

    a. Do you feel it's important for you to take part in negotiating with your physician decisions about your treatment, or would you prefer to leave it up to him/her?
    b. Does your physician ask you to make decisions or help him or

her decide about your health care?

   c. Do you feel your relationship with your physician is a partner–
ship?

4.   We'd like you to describe one occasion or example of a time
when you felt your physician or your nurse truly understood who
you are and what you needed from them. In other words, you felt
you could communicate easily and that your relationship with
your physician was a partnership.
Try to describe as specifically as possible what was stated in
this interaction.

5.   A lot of what is written about the need for a partnership between
providers and patients suggests that it isn't necessarily easy to
achieve. Does anything stand in the way of communicating openly and creating this type of interaction with your physician (your
personality, the doctors, the hospital context, etc.)?

   a. Do you sometimes find it difficult to follow your doctor's advice?
If so, what do you do?

   b. If your doctor attempts to convince you to open up or change
your behavior, how do you normally respond?

6.   Can you tell us about a time when you felt your physician or
nurse wasn't listening to you and misunderstood your feelings
and needs; in other words, you felt you did not have an authentic
voice and that your relationship with your physician was not a
partnership.
Try to describe as specifically as possible what was stated in
this interaction.

7.   Do you or your doctor communicate in ways to overcome these
obstacles—to develop this partnership?

   a. What strategies do you use to get the kind of treatment you want?
From your doctor? From your nurse?

   b. What strategies does your doctor use to develop this partnership?
What strategies does your nurse use to develop this partnership?

   c. What advice would you give patients today or tomorrow to
improve provider-patient communication in ways that build this
partnership more fully? What advice would you give physicians?
Nurses?

8.   We'd like to conclude this interview by asking if there is

anything else we have not asked you that you think is important
to tell us about communication between providers and patients?

APPENDIX B
HEALTH CARE PROVIDER INTERVIEW QUESTIONS

Introduction: We are asking you to participate in this study because we're
interested in knowing more about providers' view of their communication with their patients. Previous research suggests there are a great many
differences among providers and patients in the ways that they communicate with one another. We are interviewing physicians, nurses, and
patients to gain their views of what facilitates or constrains communication. In the next 20 to 30 minutes we will be asking you a series of questions that we'd like you to answer based on YOUR OWN beliefs and experiences.

1.   When you talk with your patients what do you want to know about
     them in addition to information about their physical condition?

     a.   Many physicians/nurses say that what they want to know about
          the patient varies—that it depends on the patient. Is this true for
          you? If so, upon WHAT does it depend?
     b.   If a patient is from another cultural background, is there addi-
          tional information you want to know? What for example?
     c.   For example, what information of this type have you solicited
          from_____(use patient's name)?

2.   If the patient does not offer this information, what strategies do
     you utilize to elicit personal information?

     a.   Do you communicate with others to find out more about the
          patient? What kinds of information do you generally seek from
          their families? From their nurse? When? Through what strate-
          gies?
     b.   What strategies have you utilized to gain personal information
          from_____(use the patient's name)?

3.   Do you take this personal information about patients into
     account *when making decisions about their care?* If so, how so? If
     not, why not?

a. How do you communicate your advice to your patients? Are
options negotiated? What role does the family play in this
process? The nurse? Others?

b. Has personal information about_____(patient's name) been
taken into account in making decisions about his/her care?

4.   We'd like you to describe one occasion or example of a time
when you felt you truly understood your patient and what they
needed in their medical care. In other words, you found that the
patient willingly communicated with you and that your relationship with your patient was a partnership.
Try to describe as specifically as possible the communication
that occurred in this relationship.

5.   A lot of what is written about the need for a partnership between
providers and patients suggests that it isn't necessarily easy to
achieve. Does anything stand in the way of communicating or creating this type of interaction with your patients? (the personality
of the patient, your own personality, the hospital system, professional constraints, etc?)

6.   Can you tell us about a time when you felt you had difficulty
understanding the patient's feelings and needs? Possibly you
found out something about the patient or your relationship
developed in such a way that made it difficult to communicate
with them about their treatment and care.
Try to describe as specifically as possible what was stated in
this interaction.

7.   Let's turn to strategies that you or your patient may use to overcome these obstacles—to develop this partnership.

a. When you discover, for example, that a patient is not following
your advice, or they are not communicating openly with you, do
you take steps to determine why the patient is behaving in this
way? What steps?

b. If you were to generalize about why patients do not communicate
openly with you, what would you say?

c. And once you learn what information the patient has not communicated to you, how do you go about convincing the patient to
change their behavior—to be more open, or to follow your
advice? In other words, What strategies do you use to develop this
partnership?

d. What advice would you give to professionals today or tomorrow to improve provider-patient communication in ways that build this partnership more fully? What advice would you give to patients?

8. We'd like to conclude this interview by asking if there is anything else we have not asked you that you think is important to tell us about communication between providers and patients?

■ 8

Ethnographic Analysis of Organizational Cultures

Charles R. Bantz
Arizona State University
Tempe, AZ

■ *Positing the inherent relationship between ethnographic methods and the study of organizational culture, Charles Bantz outlines a 10-stage strategy of ethnographic research. He then offers a method by which to interpret organizational communication culture, focusing on messages, symbolic forms, expectations, and meanings.*

If there ever was a logical method-perspective fit, it is between ethnography and organizational culture. As a method, ethnography centers on the understanding and representation of people and their practices—frequently focusing on localized cultures such as communities, organizations, and social groups. The organizational culture perspective focuses on how people collectively construct an organizational culture through their communicative practices. Thus, for both ethnography and organizational culture, understanding people's practices is the central goal.

This chapter does not present a review of the literature on ethnography, organizational culture, or their intersection (a purpose perhaps better suited to a handbook). Rather this chapter seeks to demonstrate the interrelationship of ethnography and organizational culture by outlining the concepts and illustrating an ethnographic approach to organizational culture.

ETHNOGRAPHY

The large and growing literature on ethnography can be explored in Agar (1980), Geertz (1973), Sanjek (1990), Spradley (1979), Van Maanen (1983, 1988), and other sources. Here I emphasize the fundamental characteristics of ethnography prior to discussing doing ethnographic research in organizational cultures.

The literature on ethnography stretches from anthropology to sociology and from the 19th century to the present. Anthropologists such as Margaret Mead, Franz Boaz, and Clifford Geertz as well as sociologists such as William F. White and Gary Alan Fine are mentioned, often to illustrate "important" ethnographers. Contemporary ethnography, both by name and practice, has moved beyond the bounds of anthropology to include scholars in communication, criminology, education, family studies, justice studies, and organizational studies. While there are numerous definitions of ethnography (see Agar, 1980, for his discussion of ethnography as product and process), a good working definition is the study of and representation of people ("ethno" and "graphy"). The working definition may be modified slightly by substituting "culture" for people.

The most agreed-upon character of ethnography is that the ethnographer must spend time in "the field," intensively working to understand the people (see Agar, 1980). Despite that agreement, each of the critical terms (time, field, and intensive) are intentionally vague. The field may be literally a playing field (Fine, 1987, studied little league baseball), a neighborhood (Conquergood, 1990, is studying gangs and their communicative forms), an organization (Kidder, 1981), rock bands and the social world they inhabit (Schiebel, 1991), communicative practices of a culture (Katriel, 1986, analyzed Israeli talk), or the intersection of cultures (my colleague Christina Gonzalez is completing her analysis of the meeting of Mexican-American and Mexican culture). The amount of time spent in the field may vary from a brief period (Krizek, 1992, studied the closing days of Comiskey Park) to years (Conquergood, 1990, is living in the neighborhood he is studying). The amount of time may vary in relationship with the intensity of the fieldwork—Krizek (1992) not only spent the days of the final home series at Comiskey, but also did preliminary visits, and gathered historical data, while Gonzalez spent more than a year in Mexico. In all of these examples, the ethnographer did sufficient fieldwork to gain a rich understanding of the practices of the people. In some contexts, it is very difficult to gain such an understanding; hence, the length of time and the intensity of involvement will be more than others. For example, gang members (Conquergood, 1990) and massage parlor employees (Douglas, 1976) are less likely to openly disclose the character of their lives than a son visiting Comiskey Park on closing day to pay homage to his deceased father who once took him to see the Chicago White Sox.

As these examples suggest, ethnography is interested in all practices of people—how people "relax," how they talk, how they do work, how they build relationships, how they create organizations. Ethnographers of organizations, then, go into the the organization for a significant amount of time to gain an understanding of how organizational members accomplish both the tasks and social aspects of their membership. With such a mission, it is easy to describe how ethnography is a valuable approach to studying organizational life.

ORGANIZATIONAL CULTURE

Organizational culture has often been discussed since the 1970s and has been significant in the study of organizations in the 1980s and 1990s (Bantz, in press; Pacanowsky & O'Donnell-Trujillo, 1982; Putnam & Pacanowsky, 1983; Schein, 1985). Conceiving of organizations as cultures leads to understanding the symbolic as well as physical character of an organization, so the student of organizational culture will seek to understand the rites, rituals, language, symbols, myths, stories, and values of the organization. The interest in organizational culture led to explanations of organizational success through cultural values (Deal & Kennedy, 1982), as well as investigations of organizational practices (Goodall, 1989).

As a communication researcher, my focus on communication leads me to conceptualize organizational cultures as *Organizational Communication Cultures*, which are symbolic realities (cultures) collectively constructed as members communicate (see Bantz, in press, chap. 2). The Organizational Communication Culture (OCC) perspective argues that through the sending and use of messages an organization's culture is mutually constructed, maintained, and transformed. Given that argument, it is not surprising that the avenue to understanding an OCC is through its messages. Thus, the scholar needs to gather and interpret organizational messages in order to understand the organization's cultural practices.

Betty (looking at report) to Alice: Is this variance for yesterday?
Alice to Betty: Yes.
Betty to Alice: Did they have a problem?
(Alice and Betty discuss variance report.)
(Carol comments to Alice and Betty on problem last night
    with spots not aired properly.)
(Alice & Betty discuss what they did last night. Apparently
    both went out to eat. Alice and Betty discuss receipes.)
Alice to Betty: What the hell do I use for (some ingredient
    he doesn't have)?
(Alice and Betty discuss boyfriends/husbands.)

Example 1. Television/radio station scheduling
("traffic") office. (Wilkes, 1985)

The OCC perspective emphasizes that all messages in the organization contribute to the construction of the culture. The presence of significant amounts of social talk, the particular topics of the social talk, the interrelationship of social and task talk, and the context in which task and social talk occur, all contribute to the Organizational Communication Culture. In Example 1, the facility with which communicators move rapidly from task to social talk illustrates not only the complex weave of the members' communication, but also the different "contents" (dinner out, cooking, a scheduling problem) illustrate a different OCC than one in which the only nontask talk is about one topic such as football.

It is the emphasis on all messages people create and consume that directs the organizational culture researcher toward ethnography. In its focus on people and their social constructions, ethnography is ideally suited to assist the scholar seeking to understand organizational culture. The ethnographer's focus on members' practices necessarily includes attention to their communication. The ethnographer's goal of understanding what they do and why they do it is consonant with trying to understand organizational cultures.

RESEARCH PROCEDURE

The procedure suggested here is greatly abbreviated from my book, *Understanding Organizations: Interpreting Organizational Communication Cultures* (in press). While it is risky to bifurcate the researcher role from the interpreter role (since both roles may occur simultaneously) in describing the process of ethnographic research in organizational cultures, the differentiation seems worth the risk.

The researcher's fundamental goal is to generate a rich fieldwork file, including a traditional fieldwork journal, plus any messages available from the organization (e.g., newsletters, annual reports, bulletin board materials, memos) and background information on the organization (e.g., magazine articles). The richer the fieldwork file, the more likely the project will succeed in developing an insightful interpretation of the OCC.

The ethnographer's approach to a project is often critical to its success. In order to understand the people in an organization, to understand their world, it may be helpful to prepare by means of background reading (e.g., trade papers). This preparation can be especially valuable in contexts in which the organization studied is far beyond the researcher's world. The specific procedure for developing the database for an ethnographic study of an organization is a 10-stage strategy beginning with selecting an organization and closing with exiting the organization or repeating an earlier stage to improve the quality of the work. A brief description of these stages follows.

Beginning. The first stage in gathering data is, of course, selecting an organization. This selection may be directed by conceptual interests (e.g., I am interested in information- processing organizations), your abilities (e.g., as a machinist you can study machine shops), convenience, and accessibility (i.e., you believe you may get permission for the study). In conjunction with selecting an organization, the second stage is deciding whether you will work alone or with others. While many ethnographers work alone, in studying a complex organization with many different types of people, occupations, and locations, multiple observers may be helpful (see Douglas, 1976).

Getting started. The third stage is gaining entrance to the organization. This stage may be extremely simple, as you pick up a phone and your first call leads to approval, or extremely involved and frustrating, as you spend weeks finding who to ask permission and then get turned down. By this point, you need to have consulted with experts on the ethics of doing organizational ethnography to make sure you are proceeding appropriately. (For example, on university campuses there are Human Subjects Committees that can provide guidance.) Once you have gained entrance, you begin spending time in the organization and building rapport with the members. In order to understand organizational cultural practices and gain access to a rich pool of organizational messages, you need to build balanced relationships with a variety of organizational members. This means building trust, yet maintaining perspective, for early in a study you will not know what complex alliances and conflicts you might be "stepping into."

Getting the data. The bulk of the ethnographer's effort comes in stages five through eight: Identifying Messages, Creating a Journal, "Writing Through" the Journal, and Coordinating Data Gathering. In order to understand an Organizational Communication Culture, it is essential that the researcher identify and gather a rich pool of messages. This includes observing informal and formal talk, noting bulletin boards, memos, letters, architectural design, and other available messages. During virtually every moment spent in the field, the OCC ethnographer will be identifying messages. In order to record the messages identified, an ethnographer creates a fieldwork journal filled with notes, examples of messages, floorplans, sketches, and any other information that will contribute to understanding the OCC. Once "created," the journal becomes an ongoing process as the ethnographer reviews previous entries, makes additional comments, clarifies, and even adds material overlooked previously. This "writing through" process is significantly easier with computers, since additional comments are easily added. As one "writes through," it may be apparent that additional information is needed, that insufficient background has been gathered, or that more analysis is needed. Then the ethnographer may coordinate additional data gathering with the rest of the team or seek additional information on his or her own.

Wrapping up. At some point in a project, the ethnographer may begin to grasp an understanding of the OCC and feel it is time to begin to leave the field. In other projects, the press of other obligations may force the issue of exit. In either case, in studying an OCC, I recommend a "phased" exit, where the researcher slowly cuts down the amount of participation, essentially "backing out" of involvement. This phased exit strategy permits one to shift one's perspective slowly from a participant observer to an observer, facilitating the interpretation of the data which permits reversing the exit and returning for data if necessary. The final stage in this approach is the opportunity to repeat earlier stages if necessary, since it is clear that additional "writing through" the journal or even gathering additional messages may be necessary.

Having worked through the multistage approach described above, the OCC ethnographer should have acquired a rich data set that will enable a detailed analysis and interpretation of the messages. Through analysis and interpretation, the researcher is then able to enlarge his or her understanding of the Organizational Communication Culture.

INTERPRETING

The researcher will, of course, begin interpreting the OCC as the data are being gathered. When the ethnographer's attention turns primarily to interpretation, then he or she can select a variety of strategies for interpreting the data. Most often, ethnographers are encouraged to develop their interpretation based on an approach suggested by the data (see Bantz, 1983; Pacanowsky & O'Donnell-Trujillo, 1982). It is also possible to develop an interpretation guided by the OCC Method.

Table 1. The Organizational Communication Culture Method.

Sources of Messages	Analysis of Messages	Symb. Forms	Inference of Organizational Expectations	Meanings
Communicative	Vocabulary	Metaphors	Norms	Constructs
Interactions	Themes	Stories	Roles	
	Temporality	Fantasy Themes	Motives	Relations
Documents	Architecture		Agenda	Among
			Style	Constructs

In the OCC Method (see Table 1), the interpreter who has gathered messages begins interpreting by first analyzing the messages for vocabulary, themes, architecture, and temporality. This means identifying the distinctive vocabulary evidenced in the messages and noting the relationship among different vocabulary words. As Haugen's data from a medical products firm illustrate (Example 2), the vocabulary of an organization can be difficult for the ethnographer to learn.

(Jenny leaves and Sandee enters, again in a hurry.)
Sandee: Do we have three sixty tens on those two fortys now?
Dave: Yes, and we ship them Federal
Sandee: So how do I record them?
Dave: Use the old code under the sixty ten mode number
Sandee: Thanks

Example 2. Technical vocabulary in medical
products firm. (Haugen, 1985)

Once the ethnographer has some grasp of the vocabulary, the additional analyses follow. Thematic analysis focuses on repetitive topics in conversations and written material (e.g., budgets, layoffs). Architectural analysis examines the structure of conversations, memos, letters, annual reports, and even buildings to identify patterns of architecture or structure. So as not to overlook the temporal dimension of the OCC, the frequency, speed, and duration of messages are analyzed.

As one analyzes the messages, it may become apparent that certain symbolic forms are significant contributors to the communicative life of the organization. Symbolic forms include metaphors ("the boss is a killer"), fantasy themes ("back in 1990, we kicked butt and beat the competition to market"), or stories ("remember when..."). The ethnographer is likely to have heard numerous stories by the time the data are gathered, thus stories are often valuable avenues to pursue in interpreting the organizational culture. For example, in our study of television news (Bantz, McCorkle, & Baade, 1980), stories of success (getting the story) over difficulties (weather, equipment, management) were vividly told. These stories helped direct our attention to the cultural importance of getting the story as well as those things seen as obstacles to the workers.

In analyzing the messages and the symbolic forms, the organizational interpreter comes to form some understanding of the meanings of the OCC. To facilitate that understanding, the OCC Method involves the interpretation of organizational expectations and organizational meanings.

The interpretation of organizational expectations is accomplished by inferring the norms, roles, agenda, and motives expressed in messages and their symbolic forms. Organizations develop expectations of appropriate behavior (norms) that are available to all members (even though they may not all understand or agree with the expectations). These expectations range from the seemingly obvious—unless it is a nudist organization, U.S. organizations expect members to wear some clothes—to the extremely subtle—one does not refer to oneself as "I."

Organizational roles are clearly built on norms, for roles refer to differential rights and responsibilities and thus the appropriate behaviors for each role. Interpreters easily identify some roles through vocabulary by noting titles (e.g., "CEO," "Sales Associate"); however, some roles are carefully concealed (e.g., an assassin). As Example 3 illustrates, conversation among people often highlights differential rights and illustrates the hierarchy of organizational life. Further, beyond labeling roles, the interpreter of an OCC is interested in characterizing the role. Thus, careful attention to symbolic forms may help, as stories often highlight differences among organizational members as some stories are of "winners" and others are of "losers."

Nurse in hallway: Mr. Jones—why are you in the hallway?
Mr. Jones: I'm tired of sitting in that room. This place
  makes me feel like an invalid.
Nurse: You really shouldn't be walking round just yet,
  especially here in the hall
Mr. Jones: The way you people act you would think
  I was dying or something
Nurse: Mr. Jones, that's enough. Don't talk like that.
  We just want the best for you. OK?
Mr. Jones: ok. I'll go back to my room now.

Example 3. A nursing station in a major hospital. (Jackson, 1982)

Organizational motives refer not to the psychological reason that someone behaves in a particular manner, but to the expressed reasons for the behavior of self and other. Thus, in analyzing the messages and symbolic forms, the interpreter attends to what members articulate as the motives for their behavior and that of others. Whether the motives presented are self-interested or selfless, directed toward long-term goals or short-term goals, or group or individually oriented, would contribute significantly to understanding the OCC.

In order to infer the organization's agenda (expectations about the structuring of time), the researcher must interpret the temporality of messages with care and attend to other suggestions of how time is structured. For example, if an organization hands each employee a daily schedule with 15-minute assignments, and members tell stories of the firing of someone who lost their schedule, the interpreter has important data for identifying the expectations for time structuring and the character of the structuring.

After extensive fieldwork observation, detailed recording of communicative interactions, the collection of numerous written messages, and careful message analysis, it will be easy for the interpreter to focus on the expectations for *how* members communicate in the organization (style). Organizational Communication Cultures develop patterns of expectations for whether members yell at each other (or in what circumstances they do), whether superiors ignore subordinates' greetings, whether rapid, cryptic phrases are exchanged or long, detailed memos are exchanged.

As is apparent by now, the various expectations are interrelated (e.g., style builds upon norms, roles, and agenda). Example 4 provides a common but clear illustration of the shifting communicative style as one's role shifts between providing customer service and complaining about the customer to peers. Exploring the interrelationships among organizational expectations helps the interpreter begin to see the rich, complex, and potentially contradictory character of an OCC. For there is nothing to prevent organizational cultures from expressing inconsistent and contradictory expectations (and I suspect many readers share my belief that there is every reason to believe organizations do express such inconsistency).

Clerk 2 on phone: Hello? Yes, I need to find out about
an invoice. No that wouldn't be a problem. I will just back it
out of the system. Ok. Goodbye.
(She is very professional on the phone.)
Clerk 2 to Clerk 1: That guy is so stupid! I can't believe
they can run a business like that!

Example 4. Two clerks in a developer's office. (Springer, 1988)

Further, the complexity of expectations directs the interpreter toward the complexity of organizational meanings. While there are numerous approaches to meaning (e.g., Ogden & Richards, 1923) in the OCC Method, the focus is on *constructs* and *relations among constructs*. That is, meanings are seen as collectively created constructions and the relations among those constructions that are available to members.

The interpretation of organizational constructs proceeds throughout a project. The interpretation often begins as the ethnographer notes a central construct necessary for understanding the setting early in the project (or else the ethnographer can't understand the fieldwork). The interpretation of constructs builds upon all the work of the project, as, for example, when vocabulary and metaphors suggest norms, which together imply a construct such as "success." Further, constructs are related to other constructs, as when vocabulary, stories, and roles contribute to interpreting "work," which is related to "success," helping to define successful work in the organization.

REPRESENTING THE ORGANIZATIONAL CULTURE

As the researcher gathers data and the interpreter interprets the data, the process of representing the culture begins. The representation is often exclusively or primarily written (Conquergood's video representations of the Hmong and gang cultures are exceptions; see 1985, 1990). There is no fixed point in writing an ethnography; certainly, it cannot be marked by the completion of the data gathering or the interpretation, for the writing of field notes is an important part of the writing of the report.

Van Maanen (1988) provides a creative view for telling the tale of an ethnography by outlining and illustrating three different voices for the ethnographer (realistic, confessional, impressionistic). While most ethnographic writing in organizational cultures has been realistic (see Kidder, 1981), Goodall's (1989) collection illustrates the confessional style, as does Krizek's (1992) report of the closing of Comisky Park in Chicago. By moving beyond the realistic tale, the confessional and impressionistic tales more clearly locate the ethnographer in the organization (making clear the role of the researcher in the construction of the data) and typically provide a more vivid description of the organizational culture.

APPLYING CULTURAL DATA TO
ORGANIZATIONAL DEVELOPMENT

Knowledge about organizational culture can be of great utility to modern organizations. When knowledge about the nature of a particular culture is coupled with recognition of the role of communication as a primary channel for disseminating cultural information, several directions for promoting cultural development in organizations become apparent. The Organizational Communication Culture (OCC) method described in this chapter can generate descriptive data about the primary cultural themes and logics that influence the ways organization members interpret and respond to organizational phenomena. Kreps (1990) suggests that cultural themes vary in terms of strength (how well integrated they are within the organization) and impact (whether they have productive or destructive influences on the organization), with strong productive cultural themes enhancing organizational effectiveness by encouraging solidarity and cohesiveness among organization members, by promoting members' pride in the organization and in their organizationally designated roles, and by facilitating cooperation and coordination. By using the OCC method to identify and evaluate the strength and impact of cultural themes, leaders can utilize formal and informal channels of communication to reinforce strong productive cultural themes, promote weak positive themes, and minimize the destructive influences of negative themes.

Analysis of organizational culture is an important component of organizational development efforts. For example, Brown and Kreps describe in an earlier chapter how analysis of organizational stories can provide relevant information about organizational culture for directing organization development efforts. Similarly, data gathered with the OCC method about organizational culture can help the organizational development researcher evaluate the status of organizational health by identifying culturally based performance gaps (cultural themes that undermine the organizing process and cause problems in organizational life). Cultural analysis can also help the organizational development researcher develop intervention strategies to address the cultural problems identified, as well as increase the effectiveness of intervention implementation by directing the development of intervention strategies that are sensitive to and complementary with cultural themes and values.

CLOSING

Understanding organizational meanings and organizational expectations can be accomplished through an ethnographic exploration of organizations. The Organizational Communication Culture Method is only one such approach for achieving understanding. Whether or not you utilize the OCC Method, I hope this description has sensitized you to the possibilities of ethnographic research for gaining an understanding of organizational cultures. All of us spend much of our lives involved with organizational life. Attending to the communicative constitution of organizations can bring us an understanding that may make that involvement more rewarding.

REFERENCES

Agar, M. H. (1980). *The professional stranger: An informal introduction toethnography.* New York: Academic Press.

Bantz, C. R. (1983). Naturalistic research traditions. In L. L. Putnam & M. E. Pacanowsky (Eds.), *Communication and organization: An interpretive approach* (pp. 55-71). Beverly Hills, CA: Sage.

Bantz, C. R. (in press). *Understanding organizations: Interpreting organizational communication cultures.* Columbia: University of South Carolina Press.

Bantz, C. R., McCorkle, S., & Baade, R. (1980). The news factory. *Communication Research, 7,* 45-68.

Conquergood, D. (1985). *Between two worlds: The Hmong shaman in America.* Chicago: Siegel Productions.

Conquergood, D. (1990). *The heart broken in half.* Chicago: Siegel Productions.

Deal, T. E., & Kennedy, A. A. (1982). *Corporate cultures: The rites and rituals of corporate life.* Reading, MA: Addison-Wesley.

Douglas, J. D. (1976). *Investigative social research: Individual and team field research.* Beverly Hills, CA: Sage.

Fine, G. A. (1987). *With the boys: Little league baseball and preadolescent culture.* Chicago: University of Chicago Press.

Geertz, C. (1973). *The interpretation of cultures.* New York: Basic Books.

Goodall, H. L. (1989). *Casing the promised land: The autobiography of an organizational detective as cultural ethnographer.* Carbondale: Southern Illinois University Press.

Haugen, T. (1985). *Medical products firm.* Field notes, University of Minnesota, Minneapolis.

Jackson, T. (1982). *Nursing station in a major hospital.* Field notes, University of Minnesota, Minneapolis.

Katriel, T. (1986). *Talking straight: "Dugri" speech in Israeli Sabra culture.* Cambridge: Cambridge University Press.

Kidder, T. (1981). *The soul of a new machine.* Boston: Atlantic-Little, Brown.

Kreps, G. L. (1990). *Organizational communication: Theory and practice* (2nd ed). White Plains, NY: Longman

Krizek, B. (1992). Remembrances and expectations: The investment of identity in the changing of Comiskey. *Elysian Fields Quarterly, 11,* 30-51.

Ogden, C. K., & Richards, I. A. (1923). *The meaning of meaning: A study of the influence of language upon thought and the science of symbolism.* New York: Harcourt, Brace & World.

Pacanowsky, M. E., & O'Donnell-Trujillo, N. (1982). Communication and organizational cultures. *Western Journal of Speech Communication, 46,* 115-130.

Putnam, L. L., & Pacanowsky, M. E. (1983). *Communication and organizations: An interpretive approach.* Beverly Hills, CA: Sage.

Sanjek, R. (Ed.). (1990). *Fieldnotes: The makings of anthropology.* Ithaca, NY: Cornell University Press.

Scheibel, D. F. (1991). *Organizational communication culture and the social worlds of rock music.* Unpublished doctoral dissertation, Arizona State University, Tempe.

Schein, E. H. (1985). *Organizational culture and leadership: A dynamic view.* San Francisco: Jossey-Bass.

Spradley, J. P. (1979). *The ethnographic interview.* New York: Holt, Rinehart, and Winston.

Springer, T. (1988). *Two clerks in a developer's office.* Field notes, Arizona State University, Tempe.

Van Maanen, J. (Ed.). (1983). *Qualitative methodology.* Beverly Hills, CA: Sage.

Van Maanen, J. (1988). *Tales of the field: On writing ethnography.* Chicago: University of Chicago Press.

Wilkes, R. (1985). *Television radio station scheduling ("traffic") office.* Field notes, University ofMinnesota, Minneapolis.

■ 9

The Dialectical Nature of Ethnography: Liminality, Reflexivity, and Understanding

Lynette Seccombe Eastland
Lewis & Clark College
Portland, OR

■ *How does the ethnographer comprehend experience, occupying at once both participant and observer roles, yet existing "betwixt and between?" Lynette Eastland explores the dialectical nature of ethnography and its liminality, arguing that experiencing insider/outsider, self/other tensions is inherent in the process of ethnographic work. Illustrating her essay with four instances of her own research, she challenges the reader to confront the interdependence of knowledge about other and knowledge of self.*

The method of ethnography reflects "a bedrock assumption held historically by fieldworkers that experience underlies all understanding of social life" (Van Maanan, 1988, p. 3). It is the nature of that experience that is the subject of great speculation and discussion, and it is something that most ethnographers wonder about both as they are engaging their subjects in the field and as they struggle at home with how to get them onto paper. In this chapter, I add to the dialogue by suggesting that the strength of ethnography is to be found in the working-out of the contradictions and dilemmas, so often addressed as problematic, which ethnographers face. I further suggest that this has to do with the emotional, intuitive, liminal nature of the ethnographic process, and I address, within the variously liminal nature of my own work, how that process works. I begin by exploring those ideas that can contribute to this discussion: the dialectical nature of ethnography, liminality, the self/other relationship, and reflexivity. I suggest that the insider/outsider issue has been reframed into a self/other issue, and I address how it is that "getting comfortable" and "keeping one's distance" are not necessarily something with which one struggles, but a natural by-product of what it means to negotiate a stance and do the research. Furthermore, I suggest that it is the "emotionality" of that negotiated space that provides the understanding necessary for ethnographic analysis.

THE NATURE OF ETHNOGRAPHY

The doing of ethnography is fraught with contradictions and dilemmas, and much has been written of late about those predicaments in which ethnographers find themselves. Many of these discussions call for a radical rethinking of the political, ethical, and personal aspects of what it means to be "in culture, while looking at culture" (Clifford, 1988, p. 93). The focus may vary considerably, but all address the relationships inherent in the dialectical nature of the ethnographic process. The foci of some of these discussions include the relationship between the ethnographic process and the ethnographic product (Agar, 1990), between the self that "participates" and the self that "observes" (Jackson, 1990), between being in the field and being at home (Geertz, 1988), between being an owner of one's field notes and a guardian of other's thoughts and expressions (Jackson, 1990), between the intimacy of bodily experience and the detached nature of academic discourse (Conguergood, 1991), between experience and representation (Jackson, 1990), between being self-reflexive and being emotionally detached (Geertz, 1988), between feeling and intellectualizing (Conguergood, 1991), between "becoming" the experience and simply observing it (Adler & Adler, 1990), and between presenting the written product as an objective analysis or a persuasive text (Conguergood, 1991). Ironically, while we often address these dilemmas as the problematics of ethnographic experience, it is precisely the dialectical nature of the experience that allows it to work so well. The key to understanding this rests in the "liminality" of the experience.

LIMINALITY

Jackson (1990), in discussing the "liminal" nature of field notes, defines "liminality" as a state possessing the characteristics of being "betwixt and between." It is, she says, a state of tension, accompanied by a heightening of the sensibilities that is a feature of human beings coping with ambiguity. It is highlighted in ritual and symbol and often accompanied by high affect. "Twilight," she maintains, "is a temporal liminality, swamps a geo-graphical one, lungfish a zoological example, hermaphrodites a sexual liminality" (p. 9).

For Turner (1974), liminality represents "the midpoint of transi-tion in a status-sequence between two positions" (p. 231). In the study of ritual forms, a "limen" is a "threshold." Liminality is the central phase in the tripartite process, referred to by ethnologist and folklorist von Gennap as "rites of passage" (Turner, 1974, p. 232). Ritual, von Gennap maintains,

> *separates* specified members of a group from everyday life, *places them in a limbo* that was not any place they were before and not yet any place they would be in, then *returned* them, changed in some way, to mundane life. (Turner, 1974, p. 232, emphasis added)

The second phase, the liminal phase, he says, constitutes a threshold between the secular and the sacred.

Jackson (1990) equates field notetaking with ritual liminality and provides an example for the purposes of her argument:

> Let's imagine me watching a ritual during my field research in the Northwest Amazon. The ritual itself, a male initiation rite, has all the features associated with ritual liminality: ambiquity, a dissolution of most or all categories and classifications, role reversals, a suspension of numerous rules, periods of seclusion, and a stress on the absolute authority of the elders. . . The other ritual I am engaged in, fieldwork and fieldnote-taking, involves similar liminalities. To begin with, I am only marginally participating in the Tukanoan ritual; for one thing, I am not a native, and furthermore, the work I am engaged in requires that I not participate fully. My continual movement back and forth between participant and observer roles, between incorporation into the community and dissociation from it is a quintessentially betwixt and between status. My behavior, especially my fieldnote-taking, serves to remind me, and them, that I am in the field, but not of it. (pp. 9-10)

In surveying 70 fieldworkers, Jackson (1990) found that virtually all the respondents expressed "strong and ambivalent feelings" about their field notes. She posits that a clue to the strong feelings lies in the striking limi-nality of fieldwork. The claim of liminality can be made for many aspects of the ethnographic experience. I suggest that it is fruitful to extend the notion to the relationship between the ethnographer and the "other" (subjects/setting). Furthermore, I contend that variously liminal positions emerge from the contradictory aspects of individual projects and that the struggle involved in negotiating a stance enables the ethnographer in "getting into" the experience of the other.

SELF/OTHER

The ethnographic enterprise consists of a negotiation with the subject/setting to achieve a balance which "feels good" to the ethnographer—a bodily criteria for an academic pursuit. "Your measure of success," says one of Jackson's respondents, "is how comfortable you feel . . . and to what degree you become socialized to the culture" (Jackson, 1990, p. 14). The ethnographer strives to achieve a "precarious, liminal balance between being an insider and an outsider" (Jackson, 1990, p. 14). Dissolving the tension, getting too comfortable, is referred to in frantic whispers as "going native." Not ever being comfortable, never reaching a state of rapport with your subjects, means a failure to experience what is needed for you to understand the other. Many ethnographers are not, and have never been, very comfortable with this liminal state. We tend to see it as a state of high frustration, a dilemma to be "gotten around," or a problem to be solved (Van Maanan, 1988, p. 78), but ironically, it is the liminal nature of the process that makes it work so well. Within liminality, the researcher works at negotiating a stance, formulating a relationship with the respondents, and finding a way "to be" in the setting. In the subtle interplay between researcher and setting, the predicament is not only managed, but the magic of ethnography occurs. The ethnographer is able to not only engage, but simultaneously to disengage, and thereby observe experience while also living it.

REFLEXIVITY IN ETHNOGRAPHY

Geertz (1988) observes that reflection on methods in ethnography has long been taboo. The myth, he maintains, that ethnography has something to do with sorting "strange and irregular facts into familiar and orderly categories—this is magic, that is technology" (p. 3) has been exploded. What ethnography is, he says, is less clear. "That it might be a kind of writing, putting things to paper, has now and then occurred to those engaged in producing it, consuming it, or both" (p. 3). However, he continues, examination of ethnography as such has been impeded by several considerations, none of them reasonable from Geertz's perspective. One of these objections focuses on the unpopularity of reflexivity. "Excessive concern," Geertz contends, "which in practice usually means any concern at all, with how ethnographic texts are constructed seems like an unhealthy self-absorption, time wasting at best, hypocondrical at worst" (p. 1). Fortunately, he continues, the number of confessional and analytical accounts is growing, providing more insight into the ethnographic process. A second obstacle exists in the opinion that paying attention to how knowledge claims are advanced undermines our capacity to take them seriously. "Attention," he says, "to such matters…is supposed to lead to a corrosive relativism in which everything is but a more or less clever expression of opinion" (p. 2). Perhaps it is that ethnographers are victims of their own ethnographobia and fear finding out that a process they see as scholarly, and maybe even "magical," can more aptly be described simply as "biased" or "emotional."

Liminality clearly speaks to the emotionality of fieldwork and to the writing practices that follow it. The shape of the ethnography takes place within the experience of the ethnographer, and ironically, it is just that which we have tried to screen out of many of our more traditional methods of inquiry. Conguergood (1991) refers to ethnography as an *embodied practice*, "an intensely sensuous way of knowing" (p. 180), and he calls for an acknowledgment of that—a return to the body. "Participant observation," he says, "privileges the body as a site of knowing," while in sharp contrast, most academic disciplines regard mental abstractions and rational thought as "both epistemologically and morally superior to sensual experience, bodily sensations, and the passions" (p. 180). In spite of this, Conguergood claims, "published ethnographies typically have repressed bodily experience in favor of abstracted theory and analysis" (p. 181). The bodily aspects of ethnography have always been there, it has been the acknowledging of them that we find problematic.

How the emotionality of the relationship between the observed and observer works in the experience of individual researchers has been addressed, therefore, primarily on the ethical or theoretical level or in the experience of ethnographers who are removed by the safe distance of history, and certainly more often in anthropology, where it is the primary method, than in communication. Clifford (1988), for instance, examines the processes of Conrad, Griavli, and Malinowski; and Geertz (1988) uses Levi-Straus, Evans-Pritchard, and Benedict to illustrate his points. Aside from some confessional fieldwork accounts, the intent of which is often to reveal how it was that the researcher "overcame" the dilemmas of ethnography (Van Maanan, 1988), reflexivity and critical examination have taken place largely apart from recent ongoing field research. Furthermore, the advice to "detach oneself" from the setting denies both the emotionality of the process and the notion that the writing is a further "construction" of the experience.

REFRAMING THE INSIDER/OUTSIDER ISSUE

When we initially began to explore the possibilities of using ethnographic methods in studying organizations, we were concerned with what we considered the basic issues raised by the violation of the scientific norm of objectivity. One issue that captured our attention and was much explored during the 1970s was the issue of insider vs. outsider; the crux of that concern being "which stance is more likely to enable researchers to understand the setting, but also enable them to distance themselves from it (objectivity) to be able to clearly analyze and assess it?" The insider/outsider issue became much less relevant when (a) we began to see stance as a process rather than a static point; and (b) when we began to accept the assumption that there are many organizational realities, rather than one objective one. We began to ask the really difficult questions about ethnography, focusing on the *nature* of the inherent dilemmas, rather than on ways to avoid them, or on the either/or choices based on them.

The issue of the relationship between ethnographer and subject/setting has shifted from the insider/outsider distinction to a self/other distinction; its nature is no longer clearly defined. This represents a move that will enable us more clearly to explicate the processes in which we are engaged and to understand more fully the explanatory power of ethnographic research. In the following sections, I discuss the increasingly liminal nature of my own fieldwork experiences, making explicit the emotionality of the space I negotiated in "getting comfortable" in the setting. In addition, I address how that process enabled me to construct understandings of the experience of the "other."

PROJECT ONE: THE DILEMMA OF DRIVING BUS

Each setting and each set of relationships make different demands on the ethnographer, and the ways in which the relationships are constructed is often linked to access. Access determines what you see and how you see it. A study I did in graduate school taught me much about the negotiation between the ethnographer and the subjects/setting.

I had made a decision to study a local transit company. My initial desire was to conduct a rather traditional study, gaining access through company management, constructing and administering questionnaires, and conducting interviews. Instead, I found myself hanging out with bus drivers, riding buses, and recording passenger-driver interaction. Several factors in my negotiation with the subjects/setting led me to make an alteration in the way I approached the project. The reception I received from management was less than enthusiastic. Actually, it could more accurately be described as hostile. I tried repeatedly to make an appointment to speak with them about gaining access to the driver's lounge and conducting interviews that would include both management and drivers, but they bluntly informed me I should keep off the property. I was disappointed, but still determined, and I became more and more interested in the face of their insistence. I had met several drivers and was intrigued by the way they talked about their relationships with the company and with the passengers. I decided to spend the summer riding buses and hanging out with bus drivers. I spent a considerable amount of time writing field notes, taping conversations, and listening to after-shift talk in a local bar, and I began to understand the dilemmas of driving bus and the difficulties of the boundary-spanning organizational role they were playing out in their day-to-day experience. This aspect of *their* experience interested me because of *my own* experience. I saw in *their* frustrations and in *their* use of humor as a means of coping, my own frustrations and my own methods of coping. The kind of access I was able to gain determined what I saw, and my own experience influenced how I saw it. I couldn't become a bus driver and spend the summer driving around in the heat. I could listen to their experience and I could find in their experience aspects of my own.

Danforth (1982) in the introduction entitled "Self and Other" to his book, *The Death Rituals of Rural Greece,* addresses the point in the ethnographic experience when the experiences of self and other intersect:

> As I sat by the body of a man who had died several hours earlier, and listened to his wife, his sisters, and his daughters lament his death, I imagined these rites being performed and these laments being sung at the death of my relatives, at my own death...When the brother of the deceased entered the room, the women...began to sing a lament about two brothers who were violently separated as they sat clinging to each other in the branches of a tree that was being swept away by a raging torrent. I thought of my own brother and cried. The distance between Self and Other had grown small indeed. (p. 7)

Riccoeur (1977) posits that the aim of ethnography is to reach an understanding of the self via an understanding of the other. "To understand a text," he claims, "is at the same time to light up our own situation, or, if you will, to interpolate among the predicates of our own situation all the significances which make a 'welt' of our 'umwelt'" (p. 321).

It is at the intersection of my experience/their experience that the liminal nature of the relationship becomes evident. In sensing their dilemma, I sense my own. I am neither fully in their experience, nor fully in mine. I am, as Jackson (1990) says, in a state that is betwixt and between.

PROJECT TWO: BECOMING A COLLECTIVE MEMBER

In the early 1980s, I began three years of fieldwork (Eastland, 1988a) with a collective of 13 women who owned and operated a feminist bookstore and coffeehouse in a western city. Twenty Rue Jacob was a place where women (particularly feminists—primarily students and faculty from the local university) came to spend time. Some brought school work, others sat and talked, read the feminist literature, and drank coffee or herb teas. As a graduate student and a feminist, I easily fit the role of customer. I spent hours each day sitting, visiting, and working, and could easily watch the interaction between customers and collective members. I was also privy to much of the interaction that went on between collective members, since informal business meetings were frequently held in the coffeehouse.

It quickly became clear to me, however, that the collective consisted of a group of friends who spent time together outside the business. I was 'betwixt and between' in that while I was becoming an accepted part of the setting, I was not a collective member. It became apparent, too, that many important discussions were taking place and major decisions were being made outside the setting— over dinner or lunch, or while socializing. My position was not really "comfortable" as a researcher, because I was missing a significant amount of organizational information, or as a feminist, because I frankly wanted to experience "being a collective member." It was also somewhat uncomfortable because the work load was often heavy and most collective members were managing jobs or graduate school on the side. For as much time as I spent in the setting, I felt I wasn't making much of a contribution. Often in the afternoons there would be one woman working and eight or nine customers needing food or browsing in the bookstore. I was clearly a part of the setting, both to myself and to others who sometimes would ask me for help, but I was not a collective member, not a decision maker, and not really a "friend." My desire was to "experience" collective membership in order to fully understand it.[1] My involvement was falling short of my conception of what it should be. I was an observer, but clearly not a participant.

A shift took place as the tension between "watching" and "doing" accelerated. I became enough a part of the setting that it was no longer comfortable to watch one person juggle several duties. I began to answer the phone, to refill coffee cups, and to help people open the shop or

---

[1]There are diverse positions along an objective/subjective continuum from which ethnographers approach their work. This particular stance is most clearly representative of a radical hermeneutical position which suggests that in order to attain the true members' perspective, researchers must "become the phenomenon" they are studying and then reflect on their own experiences. This is only one of a variety of subjectivist stances from which ethnographers proceed.

close up for the night. I found that I had much in common with several of the collective members by virtue of my graduate student status, and my feminist perspective and friendships began to grow. At the same time that I was trying to find a way to be with them, they were finding a way to be with me. It was clearly a reciprocal process that took place in the interaction between us.

Jackson (1989) wants to reestablish "the intimate connection between our bodily experience in the everyday world and our conceptual life" (p. 18). His project, "radical empiricism:"

> stresses the ethnographer's *interactions* with those he or she lives with and studies, while urging us to clarify the ways in which our knowledge is grounded in our practical, personal, and participatory experience in the field as much as our detached observations. (p. 3)

This is a shift, Conguergood (1991) maintains, from Other-as-theme to Other-as-interlocuter, or from monologue to dialogue (p. 182).

I found myself invited to join in on many social occasions and was then able to access both the decision making and the discussions of ideology, which were the focus of my study on contradiction and belief systems. I became an honorary collective member and soon was helping make and serve sandwiches and sell books and jewelry to customers. I worked on special projects, such as coordinating a book signing party during a Women's Conference or planning Friday night 'womyn only' events. The point here, of course, is not the extent of my involvement. It is the *nature* of the process I went through in defining it *in conjunction with* others. Another ethnographer, or a different project, calls for a 'different' process. Nor is the ultimate point of involvement, the tenuous place at which me/not me becomes blurred (the "comfortable" place), the end of the ethnographic effort. The living out of the liminal phase not only takes the ethnographer to the threshold of the sacred, but it also returns him or her to mundane life, changed by the experience.

In addressing the ethnographer as author, Geertz (1988) distinguishes between "being there" (researcher) and "being here" (writer), yet another dichotomous relationship within the ethnographic enterprise. That return to mundane life is the place where the ethnographer interprets and presents in some written or spoken form his/her experience of the 'other,' the being here of Geertz's distinction. Field experience is captured in field notebooks and sometimes on audio or videotape and most surely in the memory of the ethnographer, to be reexperienced by others in diverse ways. The process of disengaging from the field, returning to one's other existence, is as liminal as the process of engaging. In disengaging from the bookstore, I was again betwixt and between. I was no longer a part of that setting, and not quite a fully functioning graduate student, but still very much friends with the people who were still at the bookstore. But clearly, the *way in which I participated* determined the kinds of access I was able to achieve and enabled the understandings which I constructed.

PROJECT THREE: MANAGING A MARGINAL POSITION

In sharp contrast, a field project which I conducted during the summer of 1987 yielded a very different kind of process. The setting was a women's publishing company in a western city. The group was very open to my involvement and welcomed my interest as an indication of the galloping success of their firm. Growth, however, was bringing with it a crisis, a serious split between the employees and the manager/owner, which was a result of the transition from a small, feminist, cause-oriented publishing company to a money-making business enterprise. During my time there, I took on an ambiguous/marginal role which, while initially difficult to navigate, ultimately enabled me in understanding the dynamics. Rather than a gradual integration into the setting—a single movement toward some threshold—the process in this organization involved continually locating and relocating myself in relation to two groups of 'others.' I existed in a continual state of tension.

Initially, I was introduced to the staff by the owner/manager and was located physically at a vantage point in the main room from which I could observe the comings and goings of the staff. The offices were small, staff meetings were held at the table where I was situated, but much interaction took place in the hallways and in and out of the cubicles. I was, without a doubt, able to feel clearly the tension in the office, but unable to access the source or understand the perspectives of those on either side of the conflict. Although it was a feminist workplace with an emphasis on egalitarian work relationships, the serious split that was developing between the manager/owner and the employees led to an atmosphere of suspicion, and initially the rest of the staff were unsure of what to do with me. I sensed that the focus of greatest interest for me in the workplace was in the conflict that was emerging, but how to gain access to that conflict was unclear.

It was not difficult to obtain the perspective of the owner/manager. Aside from the board members, she was alone in her perspective and saw me as a potential ally. She invited me to lunch and was very open about the changes and the problems the organization was experiencing, but expressed a great deal of frustration and anger. Initially, this made my status in terms of the other employees even more difficult; but what turned the situation in my favor was the fact that the staff's frustration level was great also, and they began to see me as a potential link to her. In addition, I was, as an ethnographer, a good listener. They did not feel they had her ear, but saw me as a possible ally through which to plead their case. Although I had made it explicit that I was not there to study "organizational effectiveness," they had no other category in which to place me and so saw me as an organizational "specialist."

The point at which I began to take on a "comfortable" role with the staff came in the second week of my observations, when I began making out-of-work appointments for interviews. Before long, staff members began inviting me to their group lunches and I became the "listener" for both sides. It was a role with which I felt both comfortable and uncomfortable. While neither side really expected me to "plead their case," I was emotionally very betwixt and between. There were ways in which I related to the perspective of both groups. Both groups, in very many ways, were part and parcel of my own life experiences. Both perspectives represented me and not me. I could understand the desire on the part of the manager/owner to experience growth and success, and at the same time I could relate to the feelings of exploitation which staff members were experiencing. It was in managing the ambiguity, in experiencing the liminality, that I was able to gain insight into the change that the organization was going through.

Jackson (1989) positions radical empiricism within and against traditional empiricism. What traditional empiricism attempts to suspend, control, or bracket out—"the empirical reality of our personal engagement with and attitude to those others"—radical empiricism privileges as "the intersubjective grounds on which our understanding is constituted" (p. 34). In this situation, my understandings were constituted in the complex set of relationships I negotiated with these two struggling groups of individuals. I had a unique position in the situation; I was part of both groups and yet not a part of either. I could stand between them and watch the struggle, and yet I could move easily in and out of each group in a way that no one else could. Again, I was "betwixt and between" in a very real sense.

PROJECT FOUR: THE ETHNOGRAPHER
AND SELF-TRANSFORMATION

The next project I wish to discuss (Eastland, 1989b) took place during two periods of involvement, the first lasting several years (1983—1987) and the second lasting about one year (1989). During the first time period, I was exclusively a participant. It was during the second period that I experienced the process I wish to discuss.

This project is particularly suited to a discussion of the predicaments inherent in participant-observation ethnography because of the nature of my initial involvement and my reintegration into the setting. The organizational focus of this study was 12-step recovery programs (Alcoholics Anonymous, Narcotics Anonymous, and Adult Children of Alcoholics). My initial involvement had been with Adult Children of Alcoholics. As the popularity of these programs increased, I became interested in exploring them from a different perspective—that of researcher. My motivation was threefold. First, I was intrigued by the success of 12-step programs and wanted to explore the communicative aspects of the process of recovery that such groups facilitated. Second, I was interested in understanding the nature of my own previous experience in the setting, and third, it provided an excellent opportunity for me to explore my relationship to my work. Interestingly, these motivations represented three important and oft-discussed components of the ethnographic process in general—self, other, and text—and all three were "writ large" in this project. In the three previously discussed projects, the focus was primarily on the second of these aspects, the relationship between the ethnographer (self) and the other. In discussing this project, I will expand my comments to include more directly the relationship of the ethnographer to his or her own experience (self to self) and the predicaments inherent in it.

As a previous participant in 12-step programs, I found myself living out Malinowski's "I was not only there, I was one of them, I speak with their voice" tradition of ethnographic experience (Geertz, 1988, p. 22). Geertz contends that Malinowski "made of ethnography an oddly inward matter, a question of self-testing, self-transformation; and of its writing, a form of self-revelation" (p. 22). In this experience, the self-transforming, self-revealing possibilities of ethnography became very clear for me. In engaging the other, I was also engaging parts of myself—both the part of me that had experienced this process earlier (the recovering self), and the part of me that was looking back from where I was now (the recovered self).

Self/Other: A Dilemma of Access

Several factors influenced the way in which I approached the setting. First, while I had not attended meetings for some time, I still considered myself an insider and therefore subject to the rules of the setting. One of these rules was particularly problematic, not only because of my "insider" stance, but because of the usual ethical considerations with which all ethnographers struggle. The rules regarding anonymity in the setting would ultimately determine for me what counted as what kind of data. In 12-step programs, the tradition of anonymity is so strong that it is included in the ritual readings at the beginning of every meeting. Twelve-step meetings provided a perfect place to collect the kind of data in which I was interested—personal stories of change and talk about the ways in which individuals made sense of them—but anonymity demanded that "what gets said here, stays here."

One option would have been to construct composite stories that were made up of fragments of several contributions, but this seemed like a poor choice given my focus on personal processes and sense-making. Another option would have been to approach individual contributors after meetings and solicit their personal stories for inclusion in my data. Again, this seemed a poor option. My own experience in the setting told me that such a procedure would cast me in a suspicious light and make it very difficult to gather informants. Actually, I found that these constraints functioned to facilitate the research. The fluid structure of meetings allowed me to remain detached from my researcher self while attending meetings. I posted notices on announcement boards in several meeting settings, and few people made the connection between the notice and my presence at meetings.

In most cities, there are several 12-step meetings at several sites every day; and since many individuals may be involved in more than one recovery program at a time, participants chose meetings and sites that are convenient for them at the moment. Hence, meetings usually have a fairly fluid attendance, and there are few regulars at most meetings. This worked to my advantage in negotiating my relationships with respondents. I was dealing in this study with two kinds of relationships: the relationships I had with my secondary informants, those individuals who attended meetings I attended; and my relationships with my primary informants, those individuals who responded to my need for interviewees. In a sense, these two kinds of relationships differed considerably and provided a built-in means of managing my stance. When attending meetings, I did not make an effort to distance myself from what was going on, nor did I attempt to form specific research relationships. At meetings I was another recovering individual, looking for support and providing it for others. It was in this relationship that I was able to understand the emotional aspects of recovery. It provided the means for me to "become the informant" in the here and now, as well as to revisit places I had once been. The ethnomethodological dictum to "become the phenomenon" allows the ethnographer to experience the setting and then to reflect on his or her own experience (Garfinkel, 1977). I had done this in two ways. I called forth a previous part of my own experience and reexperienced it in the here and now, and I participated as a person who was still recovering. My stance reflected the radical hermeneutical belief in expanding the ethnographic focus to encompass the ethnographer's own feelings and experiences in the field, as well as his or her relationship with informants (Rabinow, 1977).

My interactions with others during and after meetings were constrained by my membership status. The stories I heard, the struggles I empathized with, were not a part of my data, but added a dimension of understanding to my analysis. In my relationships with my primary informants, I became a researcher, but clearly a researcher with an insider's perspective. My interviews with the 23 informants in my first study were unstructured conversations that ranged from one hour to six hours. They took place either in my home or in theirs and differed radically from my casual interactions with individuals in meetings. Prior to the interviews, I had not met most of my informants. They contacted me through notices I had posted and they were, like many recovering individuals, eager to talk about their own experiences. Occasionally, I shared some aspect of my own experience with them in order to direct the taped conversations, but for the most part they held the floor and I listened. In both settings, I was well aware of my liminal status. I "was" but "was not" a researcher when I attended the meetings; and I "was not" but "was" an adult child of an alcoholic when I interviewed respondents. The shift, in both settings, provided me with a device to move in and out of my own experience.

The difficulty of transforming human life into academic discourse has moved ethnographers to an appreciation of process, boundaries, multiple identities, and the embodied nature of fieldwork. Conguergood (1991) notes that many have turned to a performance-inflected vocabulary (p. 187). Geertz (1983) observes that "in the social sciences, the analogies are coming more and more from the contrivances of cultural performance than from those of physical manipulation" (p. 22). Turner has contributed much to this trend by defining humankind as homo performans, "humanity as performer, a culture-inventing, social-performing, self-making and self-transforming creature . . . inspired by the struggle for meaning" (Conquergood, 1990, p. 81). He suggests, Conquergood notes, that the ethnographer learns ritual processes "on their pulses," in coactivity with their enactors. The image conveyed here is one of emotional learning—a far cry from the detached kind of ethnography we often practice.

In this particular project, I moved in and out of my own experience. As Danforth (1982) had, I often saw myself in the experience of the other, and they sometimes saw themselves in me. The liminality of my position was always somewhat uncomfortable, but I was also clearly on a "threshold," and it was from that vantage point that the experiences of both myself and of others became understandable.

CONCLUSION

A couple of years ago a colleague invited me to participate in a panel discussion on qualitative methodology at a regional conference. I enthusiastically accepted and announced that my topic would revolve around the question, "Where do I leave off, and where do my data begin?" Later, it occurred to me that my colleague had punctuated that question very differently than I had intended. She heard me asking the question: "At what point in time does the researcher cease observing and begin writing?" What I had in mind was the notion of boundaries: "How much of my data is me and how much of me is my data?"

Much about ethnography causes one to wonder; there are more questions than there are answers. "Our appreciation and understanding of ethnography," Van Maanan (1988) says, "comes like a mist that creeps over us while in the library and lingers with us while in the field" (p.xii). One reason the process is so difficult to pin down is because it is so individual. It varies for each ethnographer in each project that he or she undertakes. In the projects discussed here, I found myself in variously and increasingly liminal positions. While what I have addressed is the liminal nature of the relationship between self and other, other aspects of the ethnographic process are also curiously liminal.

An assumption that has been around for a long time is that "if the relationship (rapport) between the observor [my experience] and the observed [their experience] can be managed, the relationship between author [being there] and text [being here] will follow" (Van Maanan, 1988, p. 5). It was in thinking through this chapter that I realized how very closely related these two seemingly disparate relationships are.

The writing of ethnography also demands of the ethnographer a negotiation of sorts and is also liminal in nature. Just as the ethnographer is "betwixt and between" in the field, he or she is "betwixt and between" at home. He or she is not fully there, but not fully here either. The writing process, Van Maanan (1988) contends, "is anything but a straightforward, unproblematic description or interpretive task based on an assumed Doctrine of Immaculate Perception." It is rather, he continues, "a complex matter, dependent on an unaccountable number of strategic choices and active constructions" (p. 73). In constructing his or her text, the writer again engages and disengages the subjects in order to present their experience in the text he or she is constructing. The successful account relies on bridging the gap between "engaging others where they are and representing them where they aren't" (Geertz, 1988, p. 130).

Whether it is in the field or in front of the computer, the relationship between self and other in ethnography has been largely unexplored in the discipline of communication. In an ethnography published in the early 1980s by Katriel and Philipson (1981), the authors observe:

Our study of American "communication" has led us to think of
ethnography less as a journey into a foreign land or culture, and
more as a journey into no-man's land, which is neither the territory of
the self nor of the other. As every Israeli child who was taken on the
mandatory field trip to the border knows, one cannot risk more than
a few steps into unsettled territory. In doing so, however, one
becomes aware not only of the existence of the other's territory, but
of one's own, the concept of territory in general. The ethnographer,
like the careful tourist, pays his or her tribute to the border at designated spots, but the border stretches and winds between these spots
as well, and it is in this unmarked territory that the "person" searches
for a sense of personal meaning. (p. 316)

Goodall (1990), in a recent essay to commemorate the 75th anniversary
of the Speech Communication Association, uses the border metaphor to
suggest that a new frontier of communication research is available for
scholarly exploration. At this border lie the relationships between and
among researcher, subject, and setting. Goodall contends that communication research practices are indeed a "no-man's land," in which there is
an absence of context and a negation of self and other. "To be meaningful," he says, "experience must include three sources of potential information: knowledge of and about self, knowledge of and about others, and
knowledge of and about the context in which meaning can be attributed
to the experience" (p. 266). What was once a simple designation of insider or outsider has evolved into a complex set of relationships out of which
the ethnographic product emerges through many twists and turns of
interpretation. "This view of self," Goodall continues, "as an actor within
webs of relationships reveals that knowledge about the self is always interdependent with knowledge about others" (p. 267).

This chapter has been an attempt to begin the exploration of that
no-man's land to which Katriel and Philipson (1981) and Goodall (1990)
refer. It suggests that it is in the managing of these relationships, in the
dialectical play between self and other, that understanding emerges.
Further, it suggests that it is those very aspects of the experience that we
prefer to ignore—the emotional, the intuitive, the liminal aspects—that
enable that understanding of both self and other. Communication is central to self/other/setting relationships. It is, Goodall suggests, "a bridge
between or among selves, and it places at the forefront of communication
theory the issue of linguistic representation of human experience" (p.
267). In this chapter I explored the liminal nature of ethnographic experience within the context of the predicaments I have encountered in my
own research. I showed how the dilemmas in ethnography, rather than
problems that need to be solved, or obstacles that need to be circumvent-

ed, are the essence of the ethnographer's experience and are integral to the dialectical process which enables ethnographic understanding. It is in unraveling these relationships within our own experiences that we will discover the ways in which ethnography works.

REFERENCES

Adler, P., & Adler, P. (1990). The past and future of ethnography. *Journal of Contemporary Ethnography, 16* (1),4-24.

Agar, M. (1990). Text and fieldwork: Exploring the excluded middle. *Journal of Contemporary Ethnography, 19* (1),73-88.

Clifford, J. (1988). *The predicament of culture.* Cambridge: Harvard University Press.

Conquergood, D. (1991). Rethinking ethnography: Towards a critical cultural politics. *Communication Monographs, 58,* 179-187.

Danforth, L. (1982). *The death rituals of rural Greece.* Princeton, NJ: Harvard University Press.

Eastland, L. (1988a). Ideology and contradiction in a feminist organization. In A. Taylor & B. Bate (Eds), *Women communicating* (pp. 251-273). Norwood, NJ: Ablex Publishing.

Eastland, L. (1988b). *Recovery as an interactive process: Explanation and empowerment in personal transformation.* Paper presented at the Alta Conference on Interpretive Approaches to Organization, Alta, UT.

Garfinkel, H. (1977). What is ethnomethodology? In F. Dallmayr & T. McCarthy (Eds.), *Understanding and social inquiry* (pp. 240-261). Notre Dame: University of Notre Dame Press.

Geertz, C. (1983). *Local Knowledge: Further essays in Intrepretive anthropology.* New York Basic Books.

Geertz, C. (1988). *Works and lives: The anthropologist as author.* Stanford: Stanford University Press.

Goodall, H. L. (1990). A critical inquiry concerning the ontological and epistemic dimensions of self, other, and context in communication scholarship. In G. Phillips & J. Wood (Eds.), *Speech communication: Essays to commemorate the 75th anniversay of the Speech Communication Association* (pp. 264-292). Carbondale: Southern Illinois University Press.

Jackson, J. (1990). Deja entendu: The liminal qualities of anthropological fieldnotes. *Journal of Contemporary Ethnography, 19* (1), 8-43.

Jackson, M. (1989). *Paths toward a clearing: Radical empiricism and ethnographic inquiry.* Bloomington: Indiana University Press.

Katriel, T., & Philipsen, G. (1981). "What we need is communication": Communication as a cultural category in some American speech.

Communication Monographs, 48, 301-317.

Rabinow, P (1977). *Reflections of fieldwork in Morocco.* Chicago: Univeristy of Chicago Press.

Ricoeur, P. (1977). The model of the text: Meaningful action considered as text. In F. Dallmayr & T. McCarthy (Eds.), *Understanding and social inquiry* (pp. 316-334). Notre Dame: University of Notre Dame Press.

Turner, V. (1974). *Dramas, fields, & Metaphores: Symbolic action in human society.* Ithaca: Cornell University Press.

Van Maanen, J. (1988). *Tales of the field: On writing ethnography.* Chicago: The University of Chicago Press.

■ *10*

Compatible Theory and Applied Research: Systems Theory and Triangulation

Mark Hickson, III
University of Alabama at Birmingham
Birmingham, AL

Russell W. Jennings
CMR Consortium
Phoenix, AZ

■ *Mark Hickson and Russell Jennings advance the position that research methods must be consistent with theoretical orientation. Arguing for triangulation of methods, they show how systems theory is compatible with the complexity inherent in organizational communication and the varied methods required to study the phenomena. They offer two illustrations: an organization that failed to adapt to larger systemic demands, and an organization that successfully addressed the multiple levels of a problem which could have been debilitating.*

Research in communication has been ongoing for more than 2,500 years. Yet it has received extensive attention over the past 30 years. In large measure this is because variable testers have been attempting to create models by laboriously assembling tested variables with the hope of creating a distinguishing theoretical base. Unfortunately, the models more accurately reflect a behavioral science paradigm than the functional relations of people engaging in communication. In the case of communication research, the parts—variables—do not equal the whole—people communicating. While one would naturally presume that these variable testers are operating from a philosophical base in positivism, many claim that their philosophical base is in pragmatism. They claim their theory (to the extent that there is one) works. Although the research works under controlled conditions, the communication it purports to define is a much grander affair, subject to the vicissitudes of an uncontrolled world. The overriding question seems to be, "Proves what?"

Many quantitative studies simply correlate one variable with another. Such studies omit intervening variables, as in the case of the high positive correlation between the height of elementary school children and their reading ability. Such a study omits the fact that the older children are generally taller and have taken more reading courses.

Qualitative researchers, however, are not exempt from their own criticism. Many, including but not limited to Ellis (1991), have shown that applied researchers often lack an apparent desire to build models from which theory can be built. Others tend to recyle their favorite methodology regardless of the research question. To answer organizational research questions, it would appear that the first question that needs to be asked is,"What is the organization?"

To answer such a question many go to organizational charts as an actual reflection of relationships and communication flow. However, in the everyday lives of members of organizations, these charts are rarely of concern. Such organizational charts are used only when a member of the unit violates a norm regarding the use of formalized channels. For example, when staff person A goes above the authority of line person B to line person C, and when B finds out about it, B is irritated and often explains to A that A has used an inappropriate means of communication. A goes on to explain that all of this took place as a casual conversation in the elevator. Such behavior is normative in the informal chart—the influence-based grapevine.

In a sense, for a limited time, the informal chart overrides the formal chart. B, however, is not satisfied because of the content of the conversation. That is, casual conversation is supposed to be about casual topics such as, "How is your family? What did you think of the Redskins yesterday? Boy, this elevator certainly is slow, isn't it?" The more the conversation gets to the work environment and the work situation, the more it becomes formal—at least from B's perspective.

There is a rule in someone's head. Was the rule always there? Or was the rule generated from the fact that A violated a nonpreexisting rule which turned into a rule the moment it was violated? Or did it become a rule when C called B into his office to discuss what A had said?

How much confidentiality is there for C to maintain in order to protect A, who was ignorant of the rule? Another question involves the extent to which B was punished for A's comments. That is, was the nature of the conversation between A and C strictly informative or was it rhetorical? Is A simply giving information to C, trying to get B to change policies or procedures, or trying to get B fired?

Most of these questions cannot be answered with a survey asking to whom did you talk last week and what was said. Intent, channels, degree of formality, topic of conversation, and the like are difficult to uncover using traditional investigative approaches to method. Even if a participant observer were there, chances are he or she would miss the conversation as well as the useful meaning each participant has assigned to the event.

Obviously there are several different methods that researchers use to try to determine what really goes on in the organization. In this chapter, we present one option for a theoretical base and one option for a methodological base. Each has been chosen because the authors believe the theory and the method should be compatible with and mutually supportive of one another. Finally, we will provide two examples from our research to support our contention. We begin with a general discussion of the organization.

THE ORGANIZATION

Organizations are collectives of individuals established to pursue specified multiple objectives on a more or less continuous basis. There are as many different types of organizations as there are objectives: industrial corporations, bridge clubs, government agencies, and religious groups to name just a few. Central to the specified objectives of the organization is the perpetual objective of maintaining the organization's existence. Therefore, dual clusters of purposes of organizations arise: (a) to produce a product/service, and (b) to "keep on keeping on."

For maintenance, the organization must adapt to the needs and desires of its environment—both internal and external. For example, when a religious organization discovers that attendance is low, some adjustment is needed for the organization to maintain its existence. There may be a change in the type of service, the time of the service, or even personnel. The organization, then, must participate in information collection.

Consider a radio station that receives the results of a professional survey indicating that it has the city's lowest audience appeal. The management must process that information. It may be that the station is getting a slightly lower audience than its next competitor; or it may be that the station is attempting to reach a specialized audience without regard to the masses. It may be, however, that the station is doing something "wrong." In the latter case, the management will need to make adjustments based on processed information.

A mail order house receives a letter from a customer stating that he ordered an item and enclosed a check for the purchase amount. He claims that he received his cancelled check from the bank, but never received the item. The company must check its records, and if there is an error it must be corrected. Accurate records of communications must be maintained. The organization must have an accurate and complete system of information storage and retrieval. From a business perspective, formal organizations exist in reality only by virtue of their communication records—their so-called "paper trail."

Decisions and adjustments are made on the basis of available information. Certain information must be transmitted to various segments of the organization's environment. Internally, the employee wants to know where all of her pay goes: social security, income tax, insurance, and the like. Externally, the public gains information about a company through mass media, and the clientele receives information in the form of goods and services offered by the organization. All of this is part of organizational communication. Just as formal channels are never discussed unless there is a violation, so too is the case with communication. The organization is aware of its own peculiar communication only when it does not work.

Communication, then, may be the most important feature in organizations. Some researchers have stated that the communication system may be synonymous with the organization itself. This is especially the case when the organization's function is information processing, but it is noteworthy that all organizations have an information-processing function.

A SYSTEMS VIEW

Organizations are open systems; they are in habitual interaction with their environment. They receive inputs through complaints, requests for goods/services, requests for explanations, and so on. They distribute output in the form of products/services/information. They also adapt their internal function and structure to meet environmental needs. If a product's demand is reduced, internal changes will follow. If demand increases, internal adjustments are made.

Bennis (1966) described an open system as "an adaptive structure actively encountering many different environments, both internal and external, in its productive efforts" (p. 45). Katz and Kahn (1966) applied open systems theory to the study of social organizations. They listed nine characteristics of such systems: (a) the importation of inputs, (b) the throughput, (c) the output, (d) the system as a cycle of events, (e) negative entropy, (f) information input and the coding process, (g) homeostasis, (h) differentiation, and (i) equifinality.

Of the five subsystems needed to achieve these nine characteristics, two are of particular interest to this study: maintenance/adaptation and production. Production is concerned with the input/output ratio of the goods/services offered by the organization. The maintenance/adaptive component is a homeostatic component in that there are perimeters drawn within which the system maintains a dynamic equilibrium. This is by no means indicative of the status quo; it is dynamic. Dynamic refers to a high energy availability with only a limited range of stability. Examples of production dynamics might include widely ranging production performance, or information that has a range of meanings. It is, then, the adaptive component that keeps the organization functioning in a steady state.

It is through communication that most adaptation occurs. Since the context is dynamic, the next available source of control resides in stable, reliably interpretable communication which can be managed intentionally. For this reason, a systems model and a communication model are depicted to indicate ideal functioning of the organization.

THE SYSTEMS MODEL

The adaptive component may be defined as "one which adjusts to changes in the environment to maintain a high or at least acceptable level of performance" (Black, 1968, pp. 32-33). When the adaptive function supersedes the productive function in importance, interdependence among components is of prime importance. Particularly in organizations that are highly political, there is a need for a strong adaptive component because the system must respond to various incoming messages from diverse segments of the environment. As such, the adaptive component focuses on external events, and generally includes marketing research, customer, public, community, and government relations, health, safety, security, EEO, and contracts, while its internalized equivalent focuses on employee and labor relations, training and development, career development, staff development, auditing, and so on. These are adaptive subsystems because each either signals the supersystem of activated dynamic tensions that need to be addressed, or are adaptive mechanisms in their own right that immediately confront or modify impending conditions of change or adjustment. In most cases, larger organizations operate from the presumption that "it is easier to make the world adjust than it is to adjust to the world" (Katz & Kahn, 1966, p. 89). Of course, this choice between internal and external change depends upon the degree of openness enjoyed by the organization and the degree of responsiveness manifest in the targeted populations. Since the adaptive system must endure a level of ongoing vulnerability, its focus is long term as opposed to short term, and its methods are indirect as opposed to direct. This is the stuff of ambiguity.

Several factors must be considered to facilitate successful adaptation. First, internal change must reflect the environment's norms. Second, existing institutions or individuals should be used to activate the adaptive process. New institutions often are subject to mistrust because of their short histories. Third, internal adaptation is more efficient when induced by a high-status member of the organization; third-party (consultative) induction adds external objectivity which also may be needed. Such third-party interventions also can produce an increase in resistance. Since such interventions either come from unknown sources or seem to work from unknown presumptions and assumptions, the messages they transmit must, to some degree, be self-validating—meaning to provide some degree of apparent relationship with experienced reality. The acceptance of the change or adaptation messages requires differing levels of validation. Those messages that pose a limited threat or create a limited level of tension require less stringent forms of validation than those posing greater degrees of threat or tension. There seems to be a critical mass juncture at which the level of threat or tension is sufficiently intense to preclude any message being valid. No matter how compelling the information (data or evidence), any conclusions drawn or actions taken are considered risky, unacceptable, or unbelievable.

Finally, adaptation is easiest during a period of crisis. As indicated in social psychology, individual beliefs and perspectives are most vulnerable to influence when they experience a high state of anxiety or a higher level of confusion and threat (Cialdini, 1984, p. 21).

Within the adaptive component, there is the adaptive subcomponent which is responsible for the adaptive functioning of the component itself (meta-adaptation). It is composed of coding and information disposition procedures. The coding processes are in effect "tagging" or labeling functions, as might be associated with proprietary information, while the information disposition function determines what information goes where for what purposes and to be used by whom.

In the beginning stages, there is a need for interpreting information input in terms of type: positive or negative. The adaptive component, however, may not be able to classify the input as positive or negative. This may be caused by the ambiguity of a message or by a lack of knowledge about the intentions of the transmitter. If the information input is considered negative, the next evaluation step begins. (A similar process may occur with positive information input; however, for the sake of brevity, the process of negative input is explained here.)

The source (transmitter) is then evaluated for power potential. Many times the source is only generically known, such as a memo from the executive staff, which is frequently written by someone who is not part of the executive staff. Information coming from a particular organizational function, such as, finance, operations, human resources, and so on, is truly unknown except for the power inherent in the function. Unfortunately, most ordinary receivers have learned to harbor suspicion about some sources and message forms. This suspicion provides a major means of understanding and forming agreement with the message. Part of our cultural determinism is to maintain traditional sources and message forms in a non grata status. We are taught to *disbelieve* politicians and lawyers, to *believe* medical doctors and police officers, to *disbelieve* bosses and professionals, and to *believe* "blue collar workers" and clergy. If the source is considered powerful, it is reevaluated for degree of power. At this point the subcomponent determines the degree and type of adaptation needed for the counteraction of the threat and the maintenance of the system.

This adaptation may be considered with any of the following. First, there may be a necessity to adapt the job roles and job descriptions of the organization's members. For example, there may be a need for some position that does not exist or the termination of an unnecessary position. Second, there may be a need for adaptations in the interrelationships among members of the system. There may be a need to adapt the individual's attitudes, knowledge, or skills levels. There also may be a need to increase or decrease the formality between members. Third, there may be a need for changes in policies and procedures. These include such matters as hiring and firing, job attendance and time schedules, public relations, and planning cycles. There also may be a need to redesign the work being done. Determinations for the need to adapt are brought about by the various segments of the environment: an atypical event, the board of directors, the target population with its own needs, and the general public with other needs as well as self-generated perceptions of the need for adaptation and change. Such determinations are frequently in the form of a system "flag"—a drop in profits, excess overtime, a rise in numbers and types of grievances, and so on. Similarly, these adaptational "flags" signal some overperformance of the system—exceeding profit projections, too many people "banking" vacation time, plans moving faster than scheduled, and so on.

Although the adaptive component is an interesting theoretical concept, it is only through production that the acute manager can visualize progress. Three types of information are important, therefore, to the production component: (a) information about the needs of the target population, (b) information about environmental resources to answer these needs, and (c) information about the operation capability of the production system, for example, system operation capacity.

The transformation process is one of matching these three kinds of information so that the information becomes meaningful to the environment in terms of problem solving. The coordinated information is then transmitted to the environment through varied information channels (mass media, person-to-person, etc.). The environment uses the output and eventually submits a new problem to the organization. Thus, the system must be sensitive and responsive to the new problems and to the changing environment. Frequently, the systems are sensitive to environmental signals and information, but not because of the form of their organization or the capabilities of individuals in the system. These factors make responsiveness either not possible or at least conditional. In large measure, this systems approach explains somewhat what happens between a research and development unit and its relationship to a marketing/sales unit.

Simultaneously, the environment sends information to the adaptive component. Information inputs are those data transmitted by the environment to the system; their content is concerned with the system's immediate or latent functioning. Production input is information about the environment and its problems. Information input is information about the functioning of the organization. Both are transmitted by the environment, but they go to different destinations within the organization and have a different kind of content—production input exists in the form of specific, technical detail, while organizational input exists in the form of more generic social information.

In summary, the organization is operationally defined as an adaptive system with the general function of adapting to the needs of the environment as regards the identification and resolution of problems of the target population. The system is considered open both internally and externally; it is open to information input from outside and inside the system. There are two communication functions occurring simultaneously within the system. The energy is transformed through a coordinating process, and eventually there is a production output (for example, air bags become standard equipment on new cars). At the same time, there is a continual flow of information regulating the system and precipitating the system's adaptation to environmental change.

There are two principal sources of information input: (a) the environment, and (b) the system itself. The sources for the two are the system's productive output and internal non-alignment within the organization, which is manifested through statements indicating insecurity as well as job absence and negligence by system members. Information input is based on the homeostasis of the system as well as the coherence and integrity of its members.

Regarding information input from the environment, those messages considered to be from "authorities" or authoritative in form are of primary concern. Authorities are individuals outside the organization who are evaluated by those inside the organization as having enough power to terminate the organization. Similarly, authoritative information can be in the form of alarms, system rejection of an action, or historically relevant information.

Information input is the aspect of the adaptive process of primary concern in this investigation because it is through information input that the adaptive process is triggered. Information input is readily recognizable and essential to the operation of the system. Such input can be either positive or negative depending on how it affects the homeostasis of the system. There are six alternative responses to information input. It is possible to (a) adapt the system, (b) adapt the environment, (c) make conditional or partial adaptation, (d) make no adaptation and maintain operations according to existing methods, (e) do "jeri-rigging" or maladaptation, or (f) make no response. If the system's output is congruent with the needs of the environment, there is little or no negative input. However, when the environment's needs are not met by the system, negative information input does occur. Negative input typically produces an automatic response or reaction. The communication model is, then, a microcosm of the system model.

THE COMMUNICATION MODEL

Communication is defined as the transmission of information from one source and the reception of and response to the information by another. The various stages of this process can be defined in the following manner: (a) the initiation (including the generation and organization of data into an informational form) and transmission is the distribution of output by the environment in the forms of production input and information input for the system (for example, providing raw materials—production; and surveys about quality of product—information); (b) the retrieval and selection of information is the process of receiving that information (by the system); and (c) the interpretation and response is the method by which the system determines how to return information to the environment.

In this model, information input is emphasized. Information input that is negative is defined as non-reinforcing, nonexpanding, restricting, and possibly, even terminal. This input is opposed (or somehow reacted to) by the system's current methods of operation. Positive input is reinforcing, possibly expanding input. This input is categorized by the system as data used to sustain the status quo (or to move directly to adaptation). While there is a need for response, the need is minimal.

There are four types of information that enter the system. Problem intake data are gathered from sectors of the environment with which the system is primarily concerned. These data indicate existing problem areas in the environment for which the system seeks solutions. Solution intake data are received from the environment to solve the problems posed by the problem intake. Third is information input. Finally, there is personal information which is not critical to the transformational process. These are data about personnel that most often are not concerned with the system in their content.

There should be a self-activating mechanism in the system to deal with information input. If this input is positive, it may readily be accepted for internal reinforcement, or it may go through a similar process as negative input. If it is negative, several determinations are made. After seeing it as negative, the source of the message is evaluated for its power. If the source does not have enough power to force adaptation, the messages are acknowledged, but no adaptive action is taken. If the source does have power, further action is necessary.

If the system determines that the power of the source is high, adaptive action is taken with a relatively short time lapse between the message reception and the system response. In the case of low power, the system may or may not take adaptive action; often any adaptation made in such cases will be minimal and/or temporary. The information input systems make note of the low power sources and store it in preparation for further attempts by the source. Of course, a major question relates to whether the source has actual power—demonstrable, or merely attributed power—power assigned to the source but not necessarily demonstrable. The greater the source of power, the more immediate and complete is the adaptive process. When some change is indicated by positive input, the responsibility may be overtaken by the supportive and maintenance components of the system instead of the adaptive component. When the input is unclassifiable (one cannot tell whether it is positive or negative), it may go through the same process as negative input; it may be accepted, or it may be dismissed from the system. If the input is ambiguous—lacks consensually interpretable meaning—it is treated as negative input or defined as a "worst case" situation and immediately resisted.

This communication model may be used as the criterion for the effectiveness of organizational communication. This model can then be compared and contrasted with another model drawn from empirical data of how the organization actually functions. If there are discrepancies, they should be noted. The organization's awareness of these discrepancies can contribute to improving its communication at all levels and with various segments of the environment (Hickson, 1973). It also can reflect the existent state of communication, which is maintained to counteract the effects of a dysfunctional organization. It creates an illusion of stability by permitting unvalidated information to operate as if it were valid.

METHOD FOR COLLECTING EMPIRICAL DATA

Given the ideal type model of Max Weber (Freund, 1968, pp. 32-86) presented above, it now becomes necessary for the researcher to gather data for the empirical model (Glaser & Strauss, 1967). The method suggested here is that of triangulation (Campbell & Fiske, 1959; Denzin, 1988; Hickson, 1992; Hickson, Roebuck, & Murty, 1990; Lincoln & Guba, 1985; Webb, Campbell, Schwartz, & Sechrest, 1970). The term "triangulation" is derived from the surveying profession and was tagged for social science research by Campbell and Fiske (1959). "If a proposition can survive the onslaught of a series of imperfect measures, with all of their irrelevant error, confidence should be placed in it" (Webb, et al., 1970, p. 3). Two pertinent questions are; How many constitutes an onslaught, and what kind of information is used to perform the measurement—not the yardstick itself, but the "yard-of-something" being measured?

Denzin (1988) has indicated that there are several different approaches that a researcher can take to achieve greater reliability and validity using qualitative methods. They include data triangulation (using different times, different places, different subjects), investigator triangulation (more than one researcher, Douglas, 1976), theory triangulation (using competing theories), and methodological triangulation (using different data collection techniques, possibly including some that are quantitative, Fielding & Fielding, 1986).

Data triangulation and investigator triangulation are most common in organizational communication, as has been undertaken by the International Communication Association's organizational communication audit. However, when funding is more limited, an individual investigator might triangulate either theory or method to ensure greater accuracy. Generally speaking, qualitative researchers are more "wed" to a theoretical approach; thus, methods are often triangulated (Hickson, 1977, 1983; Lincoln & Guba, 1985; Stacks & Hickson,1991).

It is important to note that the triangulation procedure may not begin until the research has been undertaken. Such an approach provides flexibility in a qualitative approach that is not inherent in a quantitative undertaking. Such flexibility is especially important in attempting to measure a model in which adaptability is the most important characteristic.

CASE ONE: AN ANTI-POVERTY AGENCY

While the bureaucratic model is most utilized in federal governmental agencies, such has not necessarily been the case with anti-poverty groups (Hickson, 1971). The primary reason for this is that Lyndon Johnson's program involved utilizing indigent workers in such organizations. To some degree, these workers (from the poverty population) were even used in an administrative capacity.

Such organizations were locally supervised by a board of directors, who were also bureaucratically overseen by regional and national offices of the Office of Economic Opportunity. In large measure, regional and national supervision was conducted by formal, written communication.

In the senior author's initial stages of a 6-month participant-observation study, the researcher worked in a local office as a volunteer for at least four hours a day during the period. In the first few weeks, he simply tried to create rapport with members of the organization, indicating that he was going to try to gain as much information about their communication as possible, but would not intervene in any decision making.

During the remainder of the time, the researcher collected information from local newspapers, attended meetings of the administrators and the board, undertook extended unstructured interviews with all members of the organization, photocopied letters, answered the telephone, and kept a log of the various messages that entered the organization.

The rapport created in the first two weeks allowed the researcher to discover very precise data. Personal as well as organizational data were obtained. It became obvious (after about four months) that there were a number of conflict situations present. Administrators were uncertain as to their duties, some deciding to try to do everything, others deciding to do nothing. These were relatively untrained administrators. They were basically unaware of the actions of field workers, and the administrators and field workers rarely had any interaction.

The board was comprised of local politicians and representatives from the poverty population, all of whom had an "axe to grind." While the board would occasionally make a decision, in many cases, the administrators paid no attention to the decision. The local media found the agency to be a governmental waste.

With only about two months to go, the researcher determined that critical incidents would ultimately decide the fate of the organization. It was here that a decision was made to determine what these communication critical incidents were and how they were utilized by the organization.

Four cases finally were found to be critical. The first was a report written by a consultant for the regional office. One of the recommendations read: "It is felt that only by the above structural changes (as graphed in Appendix I) can the information flow and planning functions for community development and goal achievement be obtained." The report was sent to the local organization and the regional office. Administrators apparently did not view the consultant as a power source. At the next board meeting, one member indicated that he had talked with someone at the regional office and it was his understanding that "both county boards must work together [and] there will be no more [agency] if no work program is planned between the two counties." The board was not viewed as a power source.

The agency continued to do the same things in the same way. While members were frightened, they probably had no knowledge of how to create better information channels or planning procedures. Board members were part time and unpaid.

The third case was a poorly written letter to the agency, by a mother complaining about discrimination in the Head Start (preschool) program. The agency made no response to the letter.

Finally, the division chief of the regional office sent a letter to the director of the local office, outlining specific changes that needed to be made. By this time, it was too late. The agency did not know where to get help, and its members lacked the expertise to answer queries and demands on its own. Only through the triangulation of participant observation, open-ended interviews, quantitative content analysis, and critical incident analysis could such a determination have been made.

The local organization was terminated by the regional office six and one-half months after the first critical incident. While the study was only a case study, Hickson (1971) characterized such organizations in the following manner: "The agency was established for two reasons: (1) to continue functioning to maintain itself as a 'limb' of federal bureaucracy, and (2) to fail" (pp. 106-107). It succeeded in both. It performed its first function until it performed its second function. Incompetent personnel were hired. Incompetent trainers trained the incompetent workers. The workers became more incompetent. These incompetent workers were given impossible demands. The workers tried to satisfy the impossible demands. But, alas, the agency failed.

CASE TWO: A NUCLEAR POWER PLANT

While employed as a senior manager at a nuclear production facility, the junior author was assigned to investigate a unique case in which racial discrimination was charged. In this particular case, an order was issued by a regulatory agency specifying the psychological testing of all reactor operators. The order was issued to the company operating the reactor, and a particular testing agency was specified to do the testing. Although reactor operators were tested at the time of their employment, the psychological standards had been revised and upgraded, and all operators had to be tested under the new guidelines.

Although the company had a reactor operator psychological testing policy, no policy existed to cover retesting. Additionally, the operators were members of a union that had an existing contract with the company and any revision of testing standards would open the entire testing issue to renegotiation with the union.

As a practical matter, the union was informed of the testing order, and they agreed to proceed with the testing while taking the issue under advisement. This meant that the testing could begin, but the union was reserving the right to curtail their members' participation in the testing or the use of the testing data until the union was fully aware of the meaning—the possible actions that could be taken as a result of the testing, or the implications of that meaning—and what recourse of action would be available to them if they disagreed with the company's actions in response to the testing results.

The testing process occurred in two phases: Phase One involved a paper-and-pencil test, and Phase Two involved an interview with a staff psychologist. The paper-and-pencil testing was to develop a current profile of each operator. The interview was to provide additional levels of information to that derived from the testing. Taken together, the presumption was that these detailed profiles would provide clear indication of any behavioral tendencies in each operator that might compromise their ability to perform their jobs safely and effectively in the reactor control room.

A group of 30 reactor operators were to be tested. After the first eight operators had been tested, the company and the regulatory agency were given a preliminary report by the examining agency indicating that 5 out of the 8 should be withdrawn from duty for further interviews. No reason was given, but because of the significance of their jobs, the five were assigned other duties until additional interviewing could be completed and the results interpreted. The second interviews would be conducted by different psychologists to neutralize any interviewer biases in data collection or interpretation. Quite naturally, the employees put on reassignment were resentful and vocal about this situation. As one indicated, "This is all politics. I was fit enough to run this g__d___n reactor for the past ten years. So what's changed now?" The resentment and operator resistance to the psychological testing became focused when a number of the affected operators complained to their union representative that they were being rejected by the psychologist because of racial bias—the primary psychological interviewer was a black woman. Based on these complaints, the union filed grievances for each of the five operators placed on reassignment. This meant that a grievance procedure would automatically go into effect—an adaptive procedure used by the company and the union to stabilize emerging and potentially disruptive internal forces.

The grievance procedure involved three steps or levels of information intensity. In step one, the basics of the case would be discussed, and a finding would be made whether there were sufficient grounds to investigate further. The discussion would be based on "preliminary fact," which involved readily verifiable data that would indicate whether or not labor contract and company policies had been negatively impacted. If basic impact was found or if "reasonable doubt" could be asserted, the second step would go into effect. "Reasonable doubt" is based on the prudent action theory. The second step involved greater depth of the investigation including "hard data," testimony, and discussion of the information's meaning. If the finding at the second step indicated an impact of sufficient magnitude to negatively affect operating rules, policies, or union contract conditions, a final step would be recommended in which proposed resultant actions would be discussed and negotiated with expectation that an agreement would be reached by all parties. The entire procedure depended upon providing sufficient valid and reliable detail about the situation to allow an acceptable conclusion and negotiation. This is particularly demanding since some of the data were tangible—as in the case of the pencil-and-paper data, some were testimony to actual events—as in the interview responses, some was interpretive—as in the meaning assigned to the pencil-and-paper and testimonial data, and some was speculative—as in the projections and potentialities for behavioral reactions. Investigation of the specifics of each situation had be conducted by both the company and the union so that all parties were assured of valid, reliable information. Based on this information, a hearing would take place before company and union representatives, and a determination would have to be made regarding whether or not the psychological evaluations were indeed appropriate and valid, and what actions would be taken, depending upon the finding. The junior author was assigned to conduct the company's investigation. The company investigator had to be of the senior manager level with authority to move across organizational boundaries and to access the needed information. The same principle applied to the union representative. More important, if the issue went to arbitration, the investigators needed status equal to the arbitrator to ensure a "fair hearing."

Since this situation emerged from a regulatory directive, the investigation had to begin there. In fact, what did the directive actually specify? The directive specified the need for retesting within a specified time period and alluded to a subsidiary document that specified the psychological factors being examined. This document was reviewed. Both documents had to be treated as primary sources—essentially as empirical facts, valid and requiring direct action. The investigation began with the directive and the testing criterion specifications because the issuing agencies were the supersystem under which all the other systems in this case were operating. The subsystems in this situation were the company, the union, the testing organization, the reactor operators as a job classification group, and the professional psychologists who operated as experts—even though, in some ways, the union and the testing organization had more power and authority in the situation. None of these subsystems had the capacity to overrule the supersystem.

The second step in the scenario was to review two other sources of information—the company's policies covering reactor operators and employee psychological testing and the union agreement. These also had to be treated as primary sources of information since they were the basic rules and specifications for making decisions about reactor operator testing. These two sources were of equal importance to the regulatory directive because they were the existing definition of reality from which both the company and the unions had agreed to work. Additionally, since this was a grievance investigation, specified forms of information and data had to be observed, for example, corroboration of testimony was necessary, tangible data had to be validated, and so on. In the hierarchy of subsystems, the company's policies, procedures, and practices were important because they were the operational ground rules under which the reactor operators actually functioned. Thus, the ground rules provided authority and control over the actions of the operators, but did not represent an expert system that carried significant credibility in its interpretation of events to the operators or the union.

A third step was followed: deriving information from the expert sources—the nonaffiliated psychologists and psychometricists regarding the validity and reliability of the paper-and-pencil test—and verifying about the objectivity of the interviewing procedure and the information derived from that process. This information was treated as expert testimony; however, the fundamental themes of each commentary were cross-validated with the other "experts" in order to determine the reliability. Similarly, some research studies were consulted to determine the validity of the expert opinions. This group was also a subsystem that could provide expert information but had no authority or control over any other subsystem, unless one might consider the implication of professional control over the examining psychologists.

A fourth step involved the review of the preliminary reports from the testing organization. These reports identified the operators and the recommendation for further interviews; however, no explanatory information was provided.

Finally, a fifth step involved interviewing each of the reactor operators who had undergone testing. During these interviews two themes were prominent. First, each person indicated high concern about what the testing would mean for them as individuals and for their continuation as reactor operators. Second, each had heard information prior to the testing that the interviewing psychologist was confrontational, unfriendly, and generally biased against the reactors—all of whom were white and male. One persistent fact dominated almost all the testimony of the operators—they had been forewarned by the same individual, the first operator to be tested. Although this persistent report hinted at "a rumor gone wild," the investigation needed to continue to ensure that the rumor could be clearly identified as the source of the grievance, and the conclusions could be focused on the production problem—the psychologically specified features of the reactor operators.

At this juncture, then, the five sources of information were examined: The paper-and-pencil testing, the directive, company policies and procedures, and the union contract were treated as valid and reliable; expert testimony was treated as informed opinion that carried significant authority because a number of psychologists were consulted and their responses thematically cross-validated against the other opinions; the interview information derived from the reactor operators, which was cross-validated against each other and the interviewing psychologist's own version of the event; and the psychological interview results, which were cross-validated among themselves and with the accounts given by the reactor operators. Vertical validation was achieved by comparing the data with each higher level of information obtained.

A final issue had to be investigated. In fact, did the upgrade in psychological standards create an unnecessary job jeopardy, or did these new standards ensure a level of behavioral predictability needed to ensure safe operation of the reactor? This issue was investigated in two ways. First, ergonomic specialists were consulted regarding the actual requirements needed to safely operate the reactor given the control room configuration and the functional procedures used in operating the reactor. This expert testimony demonstrated that an extremely low probability existed for actual misconduct and error to occur if procedures were followed and adequate supervision was present. Second, case histories of reactor operators with similar psychological profiles were reviewed to determine what kinds of behavioral responses had occurred under a variety of circumstances. The review revealed that no behavioral or functional difficulties had occurred over a wide range of other circumstances. Thus, the issue of operating safety was denied.

The step-one grievance meeting was held with the company representatives, union representatives, and reactor operators attending. The results of the investigation were presented and discussed. The company and union representatives determined that the charge of racial bias was unfounded because it came from a sole source and the multiple interviews produced highly similar findings. With this finding they thereby dismissed the grievance application. However, the panel went on to find that the upgrade in psychological standards did create unnecessary job jeopardy for the reactor operators and that the application of the standards needed to be renegotiated by the company with the issuing agency. The company agreed to work with the testing agency in developing testing guidelines that would alleviate unnecessary anxiety and reaction among employees undergoing psychological testing, for whatever reasons. Finally, the union and company representatives found that testing and retesting procedures and standards needed to be included in the union contract, and this would be a significant issue in new contract negotiations.

The capacity of these proceedings to produce valid conclusions and to propose viable action was based on being able (a) to use a wide variety of data, some of which was in a state of flux; (b) to cross-validate tangible, testimonial, expert, and projective data in a manner that each would support or resist the other; (c) to develop emerging strategies for interrelating the differing types of data into a clear, meaningful scenario; (d) to draw multileveled conclusions from the data—conclusions about the initiating allegation, conclusions about the actual events, conclusions about the processes involved, and conclusions about potential events; and (e) to provide a stable database for subsequent actions.

As a result of this event, the psychological standards were reviewed and modified, and the company and union did establish an agreement on testing and retesting procedures. The company's policy was modified to include retesting and the activity procedures connected with the testing/retesting of the reactor operators. Additionally, the testing agency developed an interview procedure and protocol that reduced the possibility of bias and charges of impropriety. Finally, the reactor operators were all tested, and those not meeting the standards were reassigned to other duties or opted for retirement. Most important, the adaptive function was reinforced further by its capacity to use a wider range of data both to monitor the company and the environment and to create appropriate responses when needed.

REFERENCES

Bennis, W. G. (1966). *Changing organizations.* New York: McGraw-Hill.

Black, G. (1968). *The application of systems analysis to government operations.* New York: Praeger.

Campbell, D. T., & Fiske, D. W. (1959). Convergent and discriminant validation by the multitrait-multimethod matrix. *Psychological Bulletin, 56,* 81-105.

Cialdini, R. B. (1984). *Influence.* New York: William Morrow.

Denzin, N. K. (1988). *The research act: A theoretical introduction to sociological methods* (3rd ed). Englewood Cliffs, NJ: Prentice-Hall.

Douglas, J. D. (1976). *Investigative social research: Individual and team field research.* Beverly Hills, CA: Sage.

Ellis, D. (1991). The oneness of opposites: Applied communication and theory. *Journal of Applied Communication Research, 19,* 116-122.

Fielding, N. G., & Fielding, J. L. (1986). *Linking data.* Beverly Hills, CA: Sage.

Freund, J. (1968). *The sociology of Max Weber.* New York: Pantheon Books.

Glaser, B. G., & Strauss, A. L. (1967). *The discovery of grounded theory: Strategies for qualitative research.* Chicago: Aldine/Atherton.

Hickson, M. L., III. (1971). *A systems analysis of the communication adaptation of a community action agency.* Unpublished doctoral dissertation, Southern Illinois University, Carbondale, IL.

Hickson, M. L., III. (1973). The open systems model: Auditing the effectiveness of organizational communication. *Journal of Business Communication, 10,* 7-14.

Hickson, M. L., III. (1974). Participant-observation technique in organizational communication research. *Journal of Business Communication, 11*(1), 37-42 54.

Hickson, M. L., III. (1977). Communication in natural settings: Research tool for undergraduates. *Communication Quarterly, 25* (1), 23-28.

Hickson, M. L., III. (1983). Ethnomethodology: The promise of applied communication research? *Southern Speech Communication Journal, 48* (3), 182-195.

Hickson, M. L., III. (1992). Qualitative/descriptive (participant- observation) methodology. In D. W. Stacks & J. E. Hocking (Eds.), *Essentials of communication research* (pp. 147-172). New York: Harper Collins.

Hickson, M. L., III, Roebuck, J. B., & Murty, K. (1990). Creative triangulation: Toward a methodology for studying social types. In N. K. Denzin (Ed.), *Studies in symbolic interaction* (Vol. 11, pp. 103-126). Greenwich, CT: JAI Press.

Katz, D., & Kahn, R. L. (1966). *The social psychology of organizations.* New York: Wiley.

Lincoln, Y. S., & Guba, E. G. (1985). *Naturalistic inquiry.* Beverly Hills, Sage.

Stacks, D. W., & Hickson, M. L., III. (1991). The communication investigator: Teaching research methods to undergraduates. *Communication Quarterly, 39* (4), 351-357.

Webb, E. J., Campbell, D. T., Schwartz, R. D., & Sechrest, L. (1970). *Unobtrusive measures: Nonreactive research in the social sciences.* Chicago: Rand McNally.

■ *11*

Situating Three Contemporary Qualitative Methods in Applied Organizational Communication Research: Historical Documentation Techniques, the Case Study Method, and the Critical Approach to Organizational Analysis

Pat Arneson

University of Northern Colorado
Greeley, CO

■ *In this chapter Pat Arneson outlines research procedures and strengths of three qualitative methods. Historical documentation provides a longitudinal evolutionary view of the organization, case studies describe an understanding of dynamics operating within dramatic organizational situations, and critical analysis seeks to facilitate social change by revealing the hidden ways communication oppresses and dominates organizational actors.*

IINTRODUCTION

Scholars conceptualize organizations to be systems of shared meanings where members act in coordination with each other. Coordinated behaviors result from members' sharing common interpretations of their joint experience (Louis, 1983; Pfeffer, 1981; Smircich, 1983). Dynamic activities which integrate "role coordination, interdependence, and interlocked behaviors" comprise organizations (Putnam & Cheney, 1985, p.

131). Consensus among organizational participants produces organized action.

Organizational communication involves "the processing and interpreting of messages, information, meaning, and symbolic activity within and between organizations" (Putnam, 1983, p. 1). Organizational communication research examines process inherent to interaction. Krippendorf (1970) stated, "communication research requires data that are rich enough to contain explicit evidence about *processes of communication*" (p. 241, emphasis in original). Process emphasizes *how* something occurs rather than the outcome or results obtained.

Patton (1990) recommended employing qualitative research methods to study process for several reasons. First, process suggests a fluid and dynamic phenomena. Describing and understanding process dynamics enables researchers to isolate critical elements that contribute to program successes and failures. Second, consider that individuals typically experience process differently. An inductive, naturalistic approach reveals the variety of perspectives available regarding organizational processes. Third, depicting process requires detailed description. Qualitative evaluation enables the researcher to become intimately acquainted with the details of the organization. Qualitative research methods offer insight beneficial to applied organizational communication researchers.

Interpretive methods respect the composition of meaning and activities under study by recognizing that people creatively adapt their behavior to all situations. Interpretive research methods recognize the continual cycles of the creation, interpretation, and re-creation of meaning fundamental to social awareness. Communication researchers examine how social actors interpret their experience and construct reality. The value of information gleaned from a situation is best gauged by its usefulness or the merit it holds in explaining the way humans communicate.

This chapter examines three interpretive research methods not discussed in earlier chapters: the use of historical documents, case study research, and the critical approach to understanding organizations. It should be noted that qualitative methodological procedures do not occur in a strict linear fashion; phases proceed and retrograde through various levels during the research process. Following an examination of each method, the potential it holds for applied organizational communication research is noted.

FROM HISTORICAL DOCUMENTATION
TO HISTORICAL PERSPECTIVE

A researcher who understands the history of an organization may better assist organizational decision makers in solving problems. If a researcher ignores the historical data of an organization, the present situation could be misinterpreted. Researchers should not undervalue historical documents when seeking to resolve current organizational concerns.

Historiography refers to the body of techniques, theories, and principles associated with historical research, "a way of addressing data and sources, asking questions, and building theories based on evidence" (Goodman & Kruger, 1988, p. 316). Historical research entails the use of documents and artifacts to study the organization. The evolution of an organization exhibited in historical documents frames an historical perspective. Historical documents lend perspective by relying on historical information about the organization to explain the current situation. Documents provide a perspective on institutional processes and offer participants' accounts of organizational life. They provide information about tacit themes, social roles, commonalities among people, and enable the understanding of an organization's culture (Burgess, 1982). Historical accounts assist researchers in examining the social process of an organization. An historical perspective offers an understanding of the present, which emerges from historical documents (Lawrence, 1984).

The search for resources and an analysis of evidence characterizes historiographical research. Researchers must not be satisfied simply to record facts. An historian makes judgments and attempts to establish relationships between facts. Therefore, facts must be placed in some significant pattern, rather than simply reported (Goodman & Kruger, 1988).

Researchers progress through several phases in conducting historical research. Initially, the researcher formulates a general research question(s) so data may be channeled in some way for it to be useful. A particular dimension of the organization becomes the focal point. The focus may be a chronological progression, aspects of a person's life, principal turnings or changes in a person's life, or an individual's style of adaptation (Burgess, 1982). Focusing on a dimension of the organization provides insight into the communication process which may not be readily apparent or available in present-day observations, including occurrences prior to the research, private interchanges which would not be otherwise revealed, or goals and decisions unknown to the researcher. Organizational records reveal information about program decisions, background, activities, or processes.

Sources must be secured and examined which answer the research question. A researcher may use primary or secondary, public or private, solicited or unsolicited documents (Burgess, 1984). Primary sources are gathered firsthand; they directly relate to the organization, people, or events studied (e.g., minutes, contracts, letters, memoranda, reports). Secondary sources describe events. They are derived from and based on primary sources. These sources may include transcripts or summaries of primary source materials (Burgess, 1984; Handlin, Schlesinger, Morison, Merk, Schlesinger, Jr., & Buck, 1970). The general public may view public documents (e.g., actuarial records on the population, political and judicial records, mass media outputs), whereas personal information is contained in private documents. Unsolicited documents or artifacts originate for personal use or for the use of the organization (e.g., annual reports, 10-Ks), rather than for the purpose of research. Researchers may solicit the assistance of organizational members to produce documents which present a contemporary view of organizational life (e.g., diary, record of specific activities). Researchers frequently use solicited documents in conjunction with interviews to understand organizational experiences. Such documents present an historical view of the organizational problem.

Each source should be critically examined by the researcher. Burgess (1984) suggested researchers learn about the preparation of each document. Researchers should authenticate each document to determine the presence of forgery or misrepresentation. An individual's motives for writing a document should be determined to reveal possible distortion and deception. In addition, consider the meaning of the availability (or absence) of documents, possible bias, and inaccuracies in documents.

The researcher may face ethical dilemmas associated with the use of historical documents (Bailey, 1978; Burgess, 1982; Jones, 1985). The primary way to overcome ethical dilemmas is to account for documents, informants, and the context in which data gathering occurs. Respecting each of these elements in any research situation will enhance the strength of the study.

Researchers must analyze the content of each document for its ability to support or refute an interpretation. Continue the search for documentation until all resources have been examined and clear patterns of the insight available in documents emerge. Even though organizational decisions involve constraints on time and resources, do not ignore historical data relevant to answering the research question. Determine if available sources frame an argument for answering the question at hand. If so, present conclusions, using evidence available in the document to support these conclusions, along with a justification of the position offered (Goodman & Pryluck, 1974).

This brief overview offers a consideration of issues involved in historical research. Historical research is of great value to organizational communication research. Goodman and Kruger (1988) outlined the potential of historiography for management research; however, their ideas may be adapted to other aspects of organizational research. Three strengths of historiography involve framing the research project, theory construction, and hypothesis generation.

Historical understanding may aid in focusing the research and identifying and evaluating data sources. The historical method requires researchers to confirm the authenticity, informational value, and importance of data (Barzun & Graff, 1977). Goodman and Kruger (1988) echoed other researchers' assertions, noting "historians are the most attuned of any researchers to the danger of bias, inaccuracy, and distortion in documentary sources" (p. 320).

Historiography offers a foundation from which to assemble and analyze data and to build theory. Again drawing from other researchers, Goodman and Kruger (1988) suggest that (nonquantitative) historians, "instead of being less theoretical should see themselves as the true pioneers of theory. They are pressing at the frontiers of our present theoretical knowledge, intuitively combining and exploring models from all of the social sciences" (p. 321). The process of document analysis includes "question formulation, data analysis and criticism, and inductive reasoning" to generate theories and hypotheses (p. 321).

Historiography also holds potential for hypothesis generation. Carefully reconstructing situations to identify relationships between events may result in theory construction. Historical research emphasizes multiple causes which enables the researcher to view the project within the larger context of theory.

Historical documentation may be used in conjunction with additional research methods to assist organizational information users. Documents may suggest ideas about questions to pursue through the use of other research methods (Patton, 1990). Documentary materials provide an historical setting for contemporary fieldwork. "Historiography should be considered a supplement to more traditional research techniques, especially those areas in which methods are required to assess multiple causes from multiple perspectives" (Goodman & Kruger, 1988, p. 323). Historical documentation offers a contextual foundation for identifying and understanding organizational problems. Invaluable historical perspective becomes available through the use of documents.

THE CASE STUDY METHOD OF
ORGANIZATIONAL ANALYSIS

The literature presents a variety of interpretations regarding case studies. Division exists between methodologists who choose not to discuss the case study as a unique method of inquiry, researchers who equate case studies with ethnography or participant observation (Babbie, 1992; Burgess, 1984), individuals who employ exploratory case studies prior to employing an alternate research strategy (see Yin, 1989, p. 23), and scholars who specifically identify procedures for case study research (Patton, 1990; Yin, 1989). Rather than delineate issues of debate regarding the status of case study research, this section outlines procedures for using a qualitative orientation to case studies and discusses the value of this technique for applied organizational communication research.

The case study approach offers a specific technique for collecting, organizing, and analyzing data. Researchers using this method gather systematic, in-depth information about each case under examination. A case study comprehensively describes and explains the variety of components in a given social situation. Case study inquiry "investigates a contemporary phenomenon within its real-life context; when the boundaries between phenomenon and context are not clearly evident; and in which multiple sources of evidence are used" (Yin, 1989, p. 23). Case study research proposes to chronicle events, depict occurrences, offer instruction, and contextually illuminate the phenomenon of interest (Guba & Lincoln, 1981).

The case study method may be appropriate if the unusual success or failure of a particular case puzzles organizational leaders, or if the critical nature of one or a few cases concerns policymakers. Qualitative case studies most appropriately address programs directed toward *individualized* outcomes. Standardized quantitative measures are most appropriate when common outcomes for all participants is the goal (Patton, 1990, p. 54). To enhance outcomes, the case study design can be derived from and matched to a program or organizational philosophy. Several steps mark the implementation of the case study method.

Initially, researchers focus the project by defining a research question(s). Scholars may wish to review literature pertaining to constructs under study to provide better grounding for the research (Eisenhardt, 1989), or they may select to use a grounded theory approach. Each of these orientations to case study research will provide valuable insight about the organization.

Researchers select a case(s) for examination from the specified population. A case may be identified as a person, event, time period, critical incident, decision or set of decisions, organization, process, program, or institution (Patton, 1990; Yin, 1989). The case sampling technique will greatly influence data analysis. Patton (1990) carefully discussed research purposes associated with critical, extreme, typical, and varied case sampling techniques. A qualitative case study seeks to describe the unit of analysis "in depth and detail, in context, and holistically" (Patton, 1990, p. 54).

A case study protocol should be designed and used to guide the investigation (Yin, 1989, pp. 72-80). The protocol provides an overview of the case study project, identifies research methods, and outlines specific procedures to be used in the field. The protocol should include researcher credentials, site access information, general sources of information about the topic, and procedural reminders. In addition, the protocol identifies case study questions to consider when collecting data, potential sources of information for answering each question, and "table shells" for documenting data. The protocol also includes a guide for writing the case study report, including a report outline, narrative format, specific bibliographical information, and other forms of documentation.

Raw case data consist of all information collected about the case under study that relates to the research question. Yin (1989) suggested using multiple sources of evidence that converge on the same set of facts or findings to create a case study database. Researchers may draw policy-relevant conclusions from evidence offered in documents, archival records, interviews, physical artifacts, participant-observation, and direct observations (Patton, 1990; Yin, 1989). Investigators should seek to construct a chain of evidence, making explicit links between the questions asked, the data collected, and the conclusions drawn.

Patton (1990) identified an optional step involving the construction of a case record. During this phase, "information is edited, redundancies are sorted out, parts are fitted together, and the case record is organized for ready access either chronologically and/or topically" (p. 387). Investigators should consider constructing a case record when a great deal of unedited raw data exist that must be edited and organized before writing the final case study. However, researchers may choose to work directly from the raw case file data to write the final report.

Data analysis involves writing the case study narrative. The case study provides a descriptive account of the person or program under investigation. It offers all the information necessary to understand that case. Each case study narrative should allow the reader to clearly understand the case as a unique, holistic entity. Depending on the purpose of the research, it may be appropriate to compare and contrast individual cases. However, prior to cross-case analysis, researchers must present an individual interpretation of the phenomenon of interest in each case. Following within-case analysis, cross-case patterns may be investigated.

Finally, the researcher offers a report to decision makers. Case study reports may be either written or oral. Yin (1989) identified three procedures for constructing the case study report, regardless of the form it takes. First, identify the audience for the report. Second, develop the compositional structure. Yin (1989) suggested six different structures: linear-analytic, comparative, chronological, theory building, "suspense," and unsequenced structures. Third, follow verification procedures (e.g., ask subjects or informed persons to review the report). Writing the report is the most difficult step in the case study method. The researcher may wish to compose some sections early, while continually rewriting other aspects of the report (e.g., methodology section). This final step completes the case study process. This method offers valuable insight for applied organizational communication researchers.

Case studies enable researchers to understand special people, a particular problem, or a unique situation in great depth. Given the availability of information rich cases of the phenomenon under investigation, the case study method may be a viable approach for researchers to use. Most current organizational topics are appropriate for case study research. In fact, strategic management and business policy is most often taught using the case and simulation method (Glueck & Willis, 1979).

Case study research focuses on understanding the dynamics present within single settings. Case studies may involve single or multiple cases, numerous levels of analysis, or an embedded design which employs multiple levels of analysis within a single study. Researchers may gain valuable insight about the organization when they seek to understand individual differences, variations from one setting to another, or variations between program experiences. "Attempts to reconcile evidence across cases, types of data, and different investigators, and between cases and literature increase the likelihood of creative reframing into a new theoretical vision" (Eisenhardt, 1989, p. 546).

Eisenhardt (1989) identified several situations in which case studies are suitable, including:

> when little is known about a phenomenon, current perspectives seem inadequate because they have little empirical substantiation, or they conflict with each other or common sense. Or, sometimes, serendipitous findings in a theory-testing study suggest the need for a new perspective. (p. 548)

In these situations, theory building from case study research is appropriate because case studies do not rely on previous literature or prior empirical evidence.

Case studies offer a comprehensive description of organizational events. The case study method contributes an inside look at communication within the organization which shapes members' behaviors. Such an orientation may be helpful when constructing a theory of organizational communication.

CONSTRUCTING A CRITICAL THEORY OF
ORGANIZATIONAL COMMUNICATION

Over the past decade, the critical tradition has greatly contributed to our understanding of organizational communication. In addition to seminal works (e.g., Giddens, 1979, 1982; Habermas, 1972, 1975, 1979), several excellent pieces discuss the history and development of critical research in organizations (Deetz, 1982, 1985; Deetz & Kersten, 1983; Frost, 1980). This section briefly discusses issues of critical theory and the use of research methods to accomplish the critical task.

Critical theory directly examines communication, a system central to understanding organizations. Critical researchers examine meaning structures, seek to uncover hidden elements of domination, and suggest appropriate action to overcome systematically distorted communication. Organizations are structured to alienate individuals. "Political, economic, and community forces and individual interests are inscribed in organizational arrangements, social relations, and in every perception" (Deetz, 1982, p. 139). These interests result in blockages, repressions, and distorted communication within the organization. Critical theory engages dialectical analysis to reveal elements of domination and the foundation which supports them.

Pryor (1981) explained "critical theory is 'critical' by the very fact of its being dialectical" (p. 26). Dialectical analysis presupposes objective reality to be different than it appears. On the surface, objective reality appears orderly, coherent, and stable. Underneath the surface, dialectical analysis reveals a struggle of opposing forces which produces objective reality. These contradictory forces (diversity) constitute the surface appearance of the phenomenon (unity). Critical theorists recognize that events and objects comprising the social world may be viewed as contradictory albeit mutually dependent structures. Critical research discloses societal contradictions.

Systems of meaning that shape knowledge may be distorted. Systematically distorted communication in organizations leads to a false consensus. Marcuse (1964, p. 84) noted the contribution of technical vocabularies and technical knowledge toward closing "the universe of discourse." Critical research seeks to reopen organizational reality to discourse by exposing repressions and blockages associated with power distribution, while also providing action to overcome them.

Deetz (1982) identified rhetorical action as central to this move. Traditionally, rhetoric has been associated with the exercise of power and recognized in opposition to dialectic and the discovery of truth. However, Valesio (1980) supported rhetoric "as on the side of truth and as opposed to ideology and the forces which sustain false consensus" (Deetz, 1982, p. 140). Rhetorical expression overcomes predominant definition. From this perspective, rhetoric is in service of dialectic. Suppression is the absence of dialectic; rhetoric reopens the discussion suppressed by the dominant discourse (see Apel, 1979; Cheney & McMillan, 1990; Conrad, 1983; Deetz, 1983, 1992; Simons, 1990; Valesio, 1980).

Critical theorists seek to identify domination as a precursor to enabling rhetorical voice. Pryor (1981) identified several considerations for developing a critical theory of communication. Elements significant to theoretical development include interpretation, praxis, language, influence of ideology, historical and developmental emergence of phenomena, contextual understanding of actors' communication, domination, and reproduction of interests.

Critical theory demands a dialectical understanding of the interpretive process, through which organizational members share meaning. Pryor (1981) identified two major dialectical relationships operating in the interpretive process. First, a dialectic exists between praxis and interpretation. Individual behavior is a continuous stream of action, and interpretations emerge from action. Therefore, praxis determines interpretation, *and* interpretation determines future action in the social and physical world. Praxis acknowledges that people can in effect change the world which "renders emancipation possible." Second, a dialectic exists between socially shared meanings and individual creativity. Interpretation is a creative act *and* the creation of new meanings implies the destruction of previous meanings. "Interpretation is dialectical; a tension exists between permanence as manifested in shared social understandings, institutions, and structures *and* change, as implicit in individual creativity" (Pryor, 1981, p. 31).

Communication emerges from and temporarily resolves the tension between permanence and change. The tension, however, will never be entirely resolved. Deetz and Mumby (1990) identified a risk associated with any emancipatory position—the risk of replacing one privileged form of discourse with another. They argued for a perpetual critique to continually overcome the arbitrary structure of interests which ground every discourse. Symbolic interaction or linguistic interpretation as a form of praxis enables other forms of activity (Habermas, 1970). Therefore, interpretation is a central concern for a critical theory of communication. Language influences, directs, and controls our everyday lives. Critical theory must examine organizational (public) constraints on language in addition to the development and transcendence of those constraints.

Ideology also influences the process of communication. People express ideology through communicative behaviors. Ideology provides the foundation for theories, attitudes, and values. People identify their interests and evaluate how to best accomplish goals indicative of their ideological orientation within the social context (Deetz & Mumby, 1990). "The process of ideology-critique should not attempt to discover the 'truth' that ideology distorts, but should rather be concerned with unpacking the ways in which social reality is constructed" (Mumby, 1988, p. 47). This process enables critical theorists to conceive new ways of thinking about organizational reality.

A critical analysis of communication must be related to the social context in which communication occurs. A critical analysis offers a critique of both the individual (subjectivity) and the social (objectivity). "Critique is always critique of the subject and object in dialectical tension. Thus, a critical analysis of communication would be both a critique of the individual creation of communication, and the social context in which that creation occurs" (Pryor, 1981, p. 28).

Critical theorists view social facts as historically situated. Analysis of these "facts" reveals a human potential denied under the current system. Organizational structures provide the framework for communicative interpretations. A critical analysis of communication must consider the historical development (movement) of communication forms. A critical analysis reveals the underlying relationships which yield meaning structures. Critical theorists should focus on the formation and deterioration of communicative phenomena which determine the interpretation of objects/events. Self-interests develop from historically determined structures. A critical analysis of communication reveals how certain interests dominate. Further, it reveals the reproduction of domination in social fact (Deetz & Mumby, 1990).

Society mediates social facts. For critical theorists, this mediation calls "facts" into question. Critical researchers do not blindly accept dominant social interpretations; they question and reframe interpretations of reality. This reflection allows the researcher to examine "what it means to do social research, to reconsider what communication theory could be, and to re-evaluate what interests or purposes such a theory might serve" (Pryor, 1981, p. 35). Researchers must consider the communication event in the light of possible forms the event may take if contextual circumstances were different. The researcher continually asks, "Is the observed phenomenon necessary? Could it exist in any other form?" (Pryor, 1981, p. 29). In this way, a critical theory of communication emancipates individuals from alienation.

Dialectic directs researchers to engage in critical examination. Pryor (1981) identified three important methodological considerations in critical research. First, critical theorists focus on contradictions in the social world. Second, researchers engage in historical developmental analysis. This means they focus on emergent rather than persistent structures and relate changing people to changing circumstances. Third, critical analysis is directed toward the future. Researchers seek out possibilities available in social facts and look for potentialities within the event.

Dachler and Wilpert (1978) identified four interdependent dimensions of participation in organizations to which a critical researcher should attend:

(1) the values, assumptions, and goals of the implementers—why the project is introduced; (2) the properties of participation—the form it takes, who is involved, and what range of issues it covers; (3) the contextual boundaries of the project—the nature of society, the organization itself, and groups and individuals within the organization; and (4) the outcomes of the project for individuals, groups, the organization, and society as a whole. (Deetz & Kersten, 1983, p. 170)

These conditions allow the researcher to identify sources of domination in projects and recognize the potential available in a communicative event.

Further, the critical researcher must select a research method(s) which best reveals dialectic in the organization being investigated. The context determines the appropriate method to use: Ignoring context will distort the reality of communication. The method must be consistent with "the larger social theory and with the demands of a particular organizational analysis" (Deetz, 1982, p. 142).

Critical researchers tend to reinterpret existing research rather than begin new projects; this makes it difficult to isolate methods best suited for critical research. However, it is clear that no specific method is appropriate for all critical analyses. "In the reciprocal moves between understanding and explaining, a number of different procedures and analyses are necessary, including quantitative analyses and empirical methods developed in hermeneutics, semiotics, and structuralist writings" (Deetz & Kersten, 1983, p. 170). Most important, researchers should not emphasize the research procedure over the phenomenon being researched. The communication phenomenon must remain primary.

In addition to relying upon accepted research techniques, methodological alternatives for use in applied research continue to emerge. The development of participatory action research (emerging from participatory research which followed action research) emphasizes pragmatic organizational change and development. In participatory action research, some organizational members actively participate with the researcher throughout the research process from initial design through action implications (Whyte, 1989, 1991). Such alternatives respond to the most persuasive claim for attending to critical research in organizations: the inevitability that "the more detailed and empirical the studies become . . . the more resistant existing structures of power and control will be" (Deetz, 1985, p. 121).

Deetz and Kersten (1983) clarified the value of critical research: Critical research seeks to accomplish social change. Social change occurs through identifying and removing constraints which distort communication by serving the interests of one group over another. Critical research contributes "to the establishment of free and open communication situations in which societal, organizational, and individual interests can be mutually accomplished" (p. 148). Organizational members must understand why organizational decision making represents certain interests more fully than others, recognize why they may be unable to act in relation to their interests, conceptualize where and how interest misrepresentation occurs, and exhibit the desire and ability to represent their own interests (Deetz, 1985). Organizational leaders need to recognize that creating new social forms will actualize human interests and develop human potential through greater participation in the workplace. This process may be consistent with principles or goals currently desired by the organization (Deetz & Kersten, 1983). Critical examination can benefit all organizational participants.

This section overviewed aspects relevant to constructing a critical theory of organizational communication. This truncated discussion cannot serve to fully explicate issues involved in this form of applied research. Rather, it acknowledges the growing importance of critical research in organizations.

CONCLUSION

In accomplishing applied research, investigators must emphasize the *process* of communication. Additionally, consideration should be given to how a review of relevant literature contributes to understanding the research problem. The research method best suited to respond to an organizational situation must be selected. This chapter outlined procedures for three research methods which may be used in applied organizational research. Historical documentation provides an historical perspective of the organization and assists researchers in framing the research project, constructing theories, and generating hypotheses. Case studies offer an understanding of the dynamics present within an organizational setting. A critical theory of the organization strives to accomplish social change by overcoming dominant organizational discourse. Each method holds value for examining the process of communication in organizations.

The chapters in this text carefully discuss the significance of qualitative methods for applied organizational communication research. Interpretive researchers should not overlook additional qualitative methods and contemporary data analysis techniques which may be useful, including forms of structuralist, metaphor, and semiotic analysis. Enhancing our use of applied communication research will pragmatically benefit organizational leaders, offer an opportunity for theoretical advancement in our field, and encourage public recognition of the value of our work (Kreps, Frey, & O'Hair, 1991).

REFERENCES

Apel, K. O. (1979). *Towards a transformation of philosophy* (G. Adey & D. Frisby, Trans.). London: Routledge & Kegan Paul.

Babbie, E. (1992). *The practice of social research* (6th ed.). Belmont: Wadsworth.

Bailey, K. D. (1978). *Methods of social research.* New York: Free Press.

Barzun, J., & Graff, H. F. (1977). *The modern researcher* (3rd ed.). New York: Harcourt Brace Jovanovich.

Burgess, R. G. (1982). *Field research: A sourcebook and field manual.* Boston: George Allen & Unwin.

Burgess, R. G. (1984). *In the field: An introduction to field research.* Boston: Allen & Unwin.

Cheney, G., & McMillan, J. J. (1990). Organizational rhetoric and the practice of criticism. *Journal of Applied Communication Research, 18*, 93-114.

Conrad, C. (1983). Organizational power: Faces and symbolic forms. In L. L. Putnam & M. E. Pacanowsky (Eds.), *Communication and organizations: An interpretive approach* (pp. 173-194). Newbury Park: Sage.

Dachler, H. P., & Wilpert, B. (1978). Conceptual dimensions and boundaries of participation in organizations: A critical evaluation. *Administrative Science Quarterly, 23*, 1-39.

Deetz, S. (1982). Critical interpretive research in organizational communication. *Western Journal of Speech Communication, 46*, 131-149.

Deetz, S. (1983). Negation and the political function of rhetoric. *Quarterly Journal of Speech, 69*, 434-441.

Deetz, S. (1985). Critical-cultural research: New sensibilities and old realities. *Journal of Management, 11*, 121-136.

Deetz, S. (1992). *Democracy in an age of corporate colonization: Developments in communication and the politics of everyday life.* Albany: State University of New York Press.

Deetz, S., & Kersten, A. (1983). Critical models of interpretive research. In L. L. Putnam & M. E. Pacanowsky (Eds.), *Communication and organizations: An interpretive approach* (pp. 147-171). Newbury Park: Sage.

Deetz, S., & Mumby, D. K. (1990). Power, discourse, and the workplace: Reclaiming the critical tradition. In J. A. Anderson (Ed.), *Communication yearbook 13* (pp. 18-47). Newbury Park: Sage.

Eisenhardt, K. M. (1989). Building theories from case study research. *Academy of Management Review, 14*, 532-550.

Frost, P. J. (1980). Toward a radical framework for practicing organizational science. *Academy of Management Review, 5*, 501-508.

Giddens, A. (1979). *Central problems in social theory.* Berkeley: University of California Press.

Giddens, A. (1982). *Profiles and critiques in social theory.* London:

Macmillan.

Glueck, W. P., & Willis, R. (1979). Documentary sources and strategic management research. *Academy of Management Review, 4,* 95-102.

Goodman, R. S., & Kruger, E. J. (1988). Data dredging or legitimate research method? Historiography and its potential for management research. *Academy of Management Review, 13,* 315-325.

Goodman, R. S., & Pryluck, C. (1974). The tape recorder interview as data in film history. *Speech Monographs, 39,* 306-311.

Guba, E., & Lincoln, Y. (1981). *Effective evaluation.* San Francisco: Jossey-Bass.

Habermas, J. (1970). Toward a theory of communicative competency. *Inquiry, 13,* 360-375.

Habermas, J. (1972). *Knowledge and human interests* (J. Shapiro, Trans.). Boston: Beacon Press.

Habermas, J. (1975). *Legitimation crises* (T. McCarthy, Trans.). Boston: Beacon Press.

Habermas, J. (1979). *Communication and the evolution of society* (T. McCarthy, Trans.). Boston: Beacon Press.

Handlin, O., Schlesinger, A. M., Morison, S. E., Merk, F., Schlesinger, A. M., Jr., & Buck, P. H. (1970). *Harvard guide to American history.* New York: Atheneum.

Jones, R. A. (1985). *Research methods in the social and behavioral sciences.* Sunderland: Sinauer Associates.

Kreps, G. L., Frey, L. R., & O'Hair, D. (1991). Applied communication research: Scholarship that can make a difference. *Journal of Applied Communication Research, 19,* 71-87.

Krippendorf, K. (1970). On generating data in communication research. *Journal of Communication, 20,* 241-269.

Lawrence, B. S. (1984). Historical perspective: Using the past to study the present. *Academy of Management Review, 9,* 307-312.

Louis, M. R. (1983). Organizations as culture-bearing milieux. In L. R. Pondy, P. J. Frost, G. Morgan, & T. C. Dandridge (Eds.), *Organizational symbolism* (pp. 39-54). Greenwich, CT: JAI Press.

Marcuse, H. (1964). *One-dimensional man.* Boston: Beacon Press.

Mumby, D. K. (1988). *Communication and power in organizations: Discourse, ideology and domination.* Norwood: Ablex Publishing.

Patton, M. Q. (1990). *Qualitative evaluation and research methods* (2nd ed.). Newbury Park: Sage.

Pfeffer, J. (1981). Management as symbolic action: The creation and maintenance of organizational paradigms. In L. L. Cummings & B. M. Staw (Eds.), *Research in organizational behavior* (pp. 31-52). Greenwich, CT: JAI Press.

Pryor, R. (1981). On the method of critical theory and its implications for a critical theory of communication. In S. Deetz (Ed.), *Phenomenology in rhetoric and communication* (pp. 25-35). Washington, DC: Center for Advanced Research in Phenomenology & University Press of America.

Putnam, L. L. (1983). Organizational communication amendment. *Spectra, 19*, 1-2.

Putnam, L. L., & Cheney, G. (1985). Organizational communication: Historical development and future directions. In T. Benson (Ed.), *Speech communication in the twentieth century* (pp. 130-156). Carbondale: Southern Illinois University Press.

Simons, H. (1990). *The rhetorical turn: Invention and persuasion in the conduct of inquiry.* Chicago: University of Chicago Press.

Smircich, L. (1983). Organizations as shared meanings. In L. R. Pondy, P. J. Frost, G. Morgan, & T. C. Dandridge (Eds.), *Organizational symbolism* (pp. 55-65). Greenwich, CT: JAI Press.

Valesio, P. (1980). *Novantiqua: Rhetorics as a contemporary theory.* Bloomington: Indiana University Press.

Whyte, W. F. (Ed.). (1989). Special issue: Action research for the twenty-first century: Participation, reflection, and practice. *American Behavioral Scientist, 32* (5).

Whyte, W. F. (Ed.). (1991). *Participatory action research.* Newbury Park: Sage.

Yin, R. K. (1989). *Case study research: Design and methods.* Newbury Park: Sage.

■ 12

Self-Consciousness and the Qualitative Researcher: Understanding Qualitative Methods and Organizational Ecology

Paula Michal-Johnson
Villanova University
Villanova, PA

■ *In explicating a definition of qualitative organizational research, Paula Michal-Johnson explores the ramifications of various aspects of a definition and encourages the reader to reevaluate taken-for-granted research categories. She then brings into sharp focus the issues of social and ethical responsibility inherent in the use of qualitative research methods in organizations by applying the principles embodied in the National Research Act to field research and analyzing possible consequences. Michal-Johnson compares the ecology of organizations to that of their biological counterparts and issues a strong ethical challenge to organizational researchers.*

Several years ago an idealistic consultant conducted a needs assessment study for an up-and-coming high technology consortium. The well-funded group was in the throes of a management power struggle between an often absent, hustling and debonair chief operating officer, and a vice-president with good technical skills but underdeveloped social skills. Depth interviews with all key staffers revealed deteriorating faith in management, benign neglect of many key responsibilities, and a lean staff that was stretched beyond its limits. Staff meetings were an endurance contest, but unproductive. All participants in the interviews were grateful for the opportunity to share their assessments with a third party they had grown to trust. Some were hopeful that the results of the needs assessment would function as a wake-up call to the executives. Great care was taken to describe those themes which came out of the interview narratives without revealing the identity of the contributors.

The final report was presented to the chief operating officer and was placed in a file with promises that things were going to change. Many things did change dramatically in the six months that followed; none, however, were linked to the problem areas cited in the report. Almost half of the staff interviewed found other jobs because nothing had happened as a result of the intervention. The simple act of bringing in an outsider to review the organizational processes and member relationships heightened expectations that change was possible. When change stagnated, the disappointed reactions were focused on the unfulfilled promises inherent in the needs assessment.

Does this needs assessment count as qualitative, organizational research? It involved depth interviews of all members of the organization. The consultant studied the interview transcripts, interpreted them by searching for those common concerns and themes across the body of the interviews, and synthesized the concerns and issues to allow the meaning of the concerns to be raised without compromising the anonymity of the respondents. The reports were not generalizable to other organizations and were hence unique to this organization, and they produced detailed description. In the next few paragraphs we will try to determine the answer to this question.

WHAT COUNTS AS QUALITATIVE ORGANIZATIONAL RESEARCH?

At this point it is useful to focus attention on the criteria we use to frame qualitative organizational research. Examining a standard definition of qualitative methods as it applies to organizations may prove fruitful in answering the question. According to Van Maanen (1983, p.9), "Qualitative methods refer to an array of interpretive techniques which seek to describe, decode, translate and otherwise come to terms with the meaning, not the frequency of certain more or less naturally occurring phenomena." The methods most often used in organizational communication research (see Bantz, 1983, p. 64) include participant observation, interviews, and reviewing organizational outputs, organizational documents, memoirs, and training/instructional manuals.

Whether the techniques are grounded in phenomenological, ethnomethodological, or other narrative/interpretive frameworks, the following statements may serve to unify qualitative or interpretive methods: (a) The underlying assumptions of qualitative research are different from those of quantitative research; (b) qualitative methods are more closely aligned with language as a tool for constructing meaning than are quantitative investigations; (c) qualitative research is bound inextricably to a specific time and place and thus yields an idiosyncratic snapshot of the organization that is peculiar to its members and their milieu; (d) there is more emphasis on revealing how people interact and their means for doing so than in questions of organizational task or structure thus research questions are often framed from the "how" perspective; (e) qualitative researchers are also interested in data that are seen as nonrational or intuitive, or sometimes coincidental; (f) the interaction of the researcher and the organization is an important element to be studied; and (g) the lived experience of organizational members in the organization results in detailed narrative descriptions.

Some of the methods illustrated in this volume fall purely in the qualitative realm. For instance, depth interviewing in the field setting within an ethnomethodological framework clearly functions as a descriptive process for gathering participants' own perceptions, as Mason's chapter exemplifies. On the other hand, the critical incident technique as illustrated in the chapter by Query and Kreps, may function as a bridge between strictly qualitative and quantitative research. While the incidents themselves function as narratives, they are then systematically counted, and the strength of a category is determined by the number of cases or incidents in a particular category. The more content-analytic studies using Bulmer's (1979) analytic induction process may be referred to as quasi/qualitative, depending on the assumptive base of the researcher. If we use these criteria and Van Maanen's (1983) definition as the vehicle for determining what counts as qualitative organizational research, we may find it simpler to discuss the relevant issues in the preceding chapters.

There are, however, issues that can be raised about whether an investigation counts as qualitative organizational research that does not naturally fall into the parameters set forth above. The following question-laden section is intended to spur reconsideration of those conditions we continuously weigh when we engage in applied research in organizations. Is it simply the use of particular qualitative methods that helps us ascertain whether research meets our own internal definitions of what counts as qualitative organizational research? For example, do taking ethnographic field notes; conducting focus groups, critical incident, or depth interviews; or analyzing narratives or accounts justify the investigation as a qualitative organizational research effort? If the methods conform to the rigor and standards of fine qualitative research, elicit information, and offer insight into the organizational communication process, then it might be safe to say that it does count. Still there may be other factors to consider. Is it reasonable to talk about reliability and validity in qualitative research as do Kirk and Miller (1986)? Does the form or style of the research report help us determine whether work is seen as qualitative organizational research?

Several ancillary questions also may play into the picture as we assess what counts as qualitative organizational research. First, given that research funding is an important enabler for much organizational research, does the source of funding impact whether we characterize a piece of work as research or as consultation? Some may feel that payment for such investigations changes the dynamics of the process such that the consultant becomes a "gun for hire." I would argue that the commitment of the investigator to retain professional distance and provide information about the organization to the organization can create an environment in which completed studies meet the primary requirements of qualitative research. Second, if the research is initiated at the behest of an organization or at the insistence of an investigator, does it affect whether work is considered research? It can be argued that questions of loyalty may muddy the waters for the researcher. Third, does the intended audience for the research report determine whether qualitative data gathering in an organization is described as research? If it is reported to a representative of the organization only or to a conference or appears in a journal, does this differentially "authorize" the work as duly constituted and sanctioned qualitative organizational research? The consultant/researcher may negotiate with organizational members for permission to publish findings provided that anonymity is insured. In organizational research, which is almost by nature applied, are there ways to resolve the tensions that exist in defining the subject of this book? As a reader, please continue the inevitable discussion about what counts as qualitative organizational research and evaluate your own experiences in light of these queries.

This chapter argues that organizational communication has experienced a virtual explosion in the use of qualitative research methods; that there are particular elements inherent in the use of qualitative methods that challenge researchers to function ethically; and furthermore, that protecting the human members of the organization and the delicate balance that is the organization is as important as the research itself. Just as ecosystems in the earth fall prey to external factors, so too the research enterprise may impact the organizational ecosystem favorably or unfavorably. The next segment of this chapter accounts for the growing presence of qualitative organizational research and defines the parameters of it in the context of current thought regarding protection of human subjects and organizations.

THE MAINSTREAMING OF QUALITATIVE
RESEARCH IN ORGANIZATIONS

As communication researchers attempt to better understand the quality of organizational life, we are inevitably drawn into the tensions between quantitative and qualitative approaches to describing phenomena based on our own experiences and preferences. Spirited debates on the philosophy of science more than a decade ago spawned by the reading of Kuhn's (1970) and others' critiques of positivism often divided graduate schools into camps of radical quantitative and radical qualitative researchers. Positivists enjoyed their capacities to measure constructs and accused the other side of simply being phobic of multivariate analysis. Phenomenologists seemed convinced that they were gifted with insights which heathen positivists could never achieve. Luckily for all, the righteous indignation between the two schools has somewhat subsided. Many of us are no longer convinced that we are intrinsically better human beings because of our respective world views. Pragmatically, research on organizations is often best managed through the use of multiple perspectives and tools because different methods challenge different sets of assumptions about how organizational life is conducted. As Hickson and Jennings suggest, triangulating across approaches may offer the most powerful observations.

The resurgence of interest in qualitative methods of doing organizational/institutional research in the late 1970s and early 1980s (see Putnam & Pacanowsky, 1983; Reason & Rowan, 1981; Schwartz & Jacobs, 1979; Van Maanen, 1983) is undeniable. Simply by perusing the bibliographies of the articles in this volume, we can see how the emerging body of literature on qualitative organizational research methods has grown. With this growth also comes a greater degree of sophistication by the users of these methods. It is not difficult to make the argument that qualitative investigation in organizations has arrived as a research orientation. As with most activities involving the human enterprise, intense use of these methods forces a sense of social and ethical responsibility into sharper focus.

BROAD ETHICAL ISSUES IN QUALITATIVE
RESEARCH IN ORGANIZATIONS

The qualitative organizational researcher must be cognizant of the many organizational situations that pressure research professionals to compromise their methods. Researchers may unwittingly become pawns of the organization's agenda or system, or may produce information that, if unfavorable, may be dismissed as biased, not disseminated to research participants, or thrown away. The following aspects of the research climate/environment complicate the research enterprise and challenge researchers to remain vigilant. For instance, how does the qualitative researcher handle power plays? Often qualitative organizational researchers/consultants may feel their data are being held ransom if they are asked to trade explicit description of organizational processes for access to the organization's members. Whether money changes hands or not, the power relationships may seem immutable. In addition, if researchers report their investigations to scholars at conferences or in journals, to what extent must they camouflage organizational processes to respect the confidentiality of the organization, rather than report the thick description that is the primary contribution of the method? Can the experience of the intervention or research project ever truly be conveyed to a reader or audience member?

Pressures of time also constrain qualitative researchers. The length of time it takes a qualitative researcher to understand the context of the organization so that interpretations and analyses can be accurately constructed varies from organization to organization. Comprehending the flow of the organizational process often takes months, even years. In addition, it is difficult to assess to what extent organizational members perform new or different vocabularies because of the presence of the researcher or because the time is viewed as "special time." To what extent are research participants performing for the researcher, or recreating for the researcher who interviews (reactive effects)? Also, when those who control entree expect full reports quickly after data are collected, they may unduly rush the analysis. At times, it may seem easier to resort to more economical means of reporting that compromise the method. Any one or all of these pressures may exist for qualitative researchers in organizations; some may succumb to them while others may consider that forewarned is forearmed.

PERSONAL AND ORGANIZATIONAL ECOLOGY: THE IMPACT OF QUALITATIVE METHODS ON QUALITY OF LIFE IN THE ORGANIZATION

As the dutiful graduate student working on a dissertation in the early 1980s, I walked in and out of the offices of more than 50 managers and supervisors, asking them to describe the most and least difficult dismissals they had conducted over the past three years. My goal was short term: to get into the organizations, collect my data, and get on with my critical incident study of manager's perceptions of dismissal interviews. I was struck by the willingness of the managers to talk about these sensitive interviews, thinking that for many it may have been the first time anyone had asked them to think about the interview process. Some of their stories were wrenching tales of inexperience and mistaken causes for dismissal. Admittedly in 1980 and 1981, there was little concern expressed by my committee about the confidentiality of the interviews or the anonymity of the managers whose incidents I examined. Now, as chair of an

Institutional Review Board, I shudder at my own naiveté in entering the lives of organizational members with nothing remotely resembling a consent form to assure research participants that the tape recordings used in the interviews would be handled with the utmost care and concern for confidentiality.

In this next section I argue that (a) qualitative organizational researchers interested in communication ought to consider the spirit of federal regulations for human subjects, rather than merely the letter of the law when monitoring the impact of their research on the organization as well as organizational members and further, (b) the criteria established to protect human subjects has important implications for the ways qualitative researchers design and implement qualitative research in organizations.

Federal regulations protecting human subjects did not go into effect until 1974 with the National Research Act. The laws proscribing those strategies researchers must use to protect human subjects are often interpreted narrowly by researchers and institutions as affecting only research receiving federal funding. In reviewing the excerpts below from 46.102 of the updated regulations (see Federal Policy, 1991), assess how the definitions may be applied to the sorts of research methods presented in this volume. Explicating how these regulations are important to qualitative researchers of organizations may help to ground our work in the context of ethical research behaviors.

First, "*human subject* means a living individual about whom an investigator conducting research obtains . . . data through intervention or interaction with the individual or identifiable private information" (Federal Policy, 1991, p. 28013, emphasis added). Research participants in organizational inquiry function as human subjects as they are interviewed and observed, especially in qualitative studies.

"The term *intervention* includes both physical procedures and manipulations of the subject or the subject's environment that are performed for research purposes. Interaction includes *communication or interpersonal contact between the investigator and the subject*" (Federal Policy, 1991, p. 28013; second emphasis mine). It is difficult to deny that most of the qualitative research methods reported in this book engage the researcher and the subject in some form of intervention or interaction. "Private information is that information about behavior that occurs in a context in which an individual can reasonably expect will not be made public. It is individually identifiable" (p. 28013). In participant observation, in which individuals may be unaware that private information is being observed, the issue of unaware disclosure comes into play. As we review the sorts of issues qualitative researchers may explore, such as sexual harassment, diversity, performance criteria, termination processes, and decision making, it becomes easier to see how comments made by research participants might be perceived as bearing some risk.

Minimal risk means that the probability and magnitude of harm or discomfort anticipated in the research are not greater in and of themselves than those ordinarily encountered in daily life or during the performance of routine physical or psychological examinations or tests. The federal regulations apply particularly to research such as surveys, interviews or observation of public behavior if any of the following issues are involved. If human subjects are identified and if disclosure of the human subjects responses outside the research could reasonably place the subjects at risk of criminal or civil liability or be *damaging to the subjects' financial standing, employability or reputation* (Federal Policy, 1991, p. 28013; second emphasis mine)

While the researcher's own skill in muting comments of specific individuals in reports to organizational members, granting agencies, or publications is expected, we can easily imagine the potential for harm if "confidential" candid information from depth interviews about supervision, for instance, were ever linked to a specific individual in the mind of a decision maker in the organization as reported in casual conversation or banter. Focus groups are particularly vulnerable to this charge in that they often bring together individuals who know one another in the organization, as Herndon's chapter suggests. While focus group facilitators ask that everyone regard the information in the session as confidential, there is a potential risk. Researchers may not be able to truly guarantee confidentiality.

Researchers, paid or otherwise, entering an organization affect the ecology of the organization. Call them participant observers, ethnographers, narrative scholars, or evaluation specialists, these researchers inevitably rub up against the fabric of the organization in a host of ways as they utilize their developed or developing skills to elicit information through interaction or observation.

In looking at the regulations and definitions listed above, it is clear that qualitative studies generate data that are at once more definitive and identifiable; questions of confidentiality and/or anonymity challenge the researcher to fairly frame the critical issues in the data without compromising the continuing organizational life of its members. Some methods may be more invasive than others. Depth interviews, for instance, are more likely to reveal identity via content specific situations or duties that are performed by only a few individuals, particularly in a small organization. The topic of study may also introduce a need for concern as it might relate to someone's continuing employment, as Muto's chapter illustrates. I worked on a grant project evaluating a health care organization and discovered quickly that upper-level managers in the organization considered information collected as "theirs"; consequently, data storage was moved to a site off the premises of the organization to insure that managers were not tempted with the data on site. Thus, security of thick description, accounts, and observations is an inherent part of insuring the protection of organizational members.

One of the cornerstones of protecting human subjects is grounded in the research subject's ability to withdraw from the study. To this end qualitative organizational researchers should employ informed consent as they elicit accounts or cultural narrative through oral interviews or written reports, discussion from focus groups, or content analysis of documents. Research participants must recognize that participation is voluntary *and* can be withdrawn without affecting their status in the organization. Withdrawal may become a thorny issue in research in organizations. If, for example, the organization has contracted with evaluation researchers for an evaluation of particular programs, can a program director realistically "refuse" to participate? Are there implicit pressures to comply that make the event indirectly coercive?

In short, as qualitative organizational researchers, it is incumbent upon us to acknowledge the demands our methods make of the researcher and the research process, the individual and the organization. It may be useful from time to time to function as devil's advocates in our use of the methods we see explicated in this book. First, we need to understand the limits of our research perspectives and tools. Whether we use ethnography, participant observation, focus groups, cultural narratives, or other qualitative tools, we must examine how they interact with the organization to produce data or information. Second, most researchers in organizations do not meet an institutional review board in their research of organizations. Hence, the relevant concerns in protecting human subjects and organizations rest with the researcher, not with the organization. As students of organizational communication processes, we must recognize that the ecology of the entities we explore are surely as delicate as their biological counterparts. In reading each of the chapters in this book, it is certainly instructive to examine how each method intrudes upon people and their organizations.

REFERENCES

Bantz, C. (1983). Naturalistic research traditions. In L. Putnam & M. Pacanowsky (Eds.), *Communication and organizations: An interpretive approach* (pp. 55-71). Beverly Hills, CA: Sage.

Bulmer, M. (1979). Concepts in the analysis of qualitative data. *Sociological Review, 27*, 851-877.

Federal Policy for the Protection of Human Subjects (1991, June 18). *The Federal Register*, 56(117), 46CFR, Part II, 28012-28018.

Kirk, J., & Miller, M. M. (1986). *Reliability and validity in qualitative research.*

Beverly Hills, CA: Sage.

Kuhn, T. (1970). *The structure of scientific revolution.* Chicago: Phoenix Press.

Putnam, L., & Pacanowsky M. (Eds.). (1983). *Communication and organizations: An interpretive approach.* Beverly Hills, CA: Sage.

Reason, P., & Rowan, J. (Eds.). (1981). *Human inquiry: A sourcebook of new paradigm research.* New York: Wiley.

Schwartz, H., & Jacobs, J. (1979). *Qualitative sociology: A method to the madness.* New York: The Free Press.

Van Maanen, J. (Ed.). (1983). *Qualitative methodology.* Beverly Hills, CA: Sage.

Author Index

Subject Index